Pilgrim's Wilderness

Pilgrim's Wilderness

Tom Kizzia

 CROWN PUBLISHERS / New York

A True Story of

Faith and Madness on

the Alaska Frontier

All rights reserved.
Published in the United States by Crown Publishers, an imprint of the
Crown Publishing Group, a division of Random House, Inc., New York.
www.crownpublishing.com

CROWN and the Crown colophon are registered trademarks of
Random House, Inc.

Grateful acknowledgment is made to HarperCollins publishers and Hodder and
Stoughton Limited for permission to reprint excerpts from *The Road to McCarthy*
by Pete McCarthy. Copyright © 2002, 2004 by Pete McCarthy. Reprinted by
permission of HarperCollins Publishers and Hodder and Stoughton Limited.

Library of Congress Cataloging-in-Publication Data
Kizzia, Tom.
    Pilgrim's wilderness: a true story of faith and madness on the Alaska
frontier/by Tom Kizzia.—1st ed.
        p. cm.
    Includes bibliographical references.
    1. Hale, Robert (Robert Allen), 1941–2008. 2. Hale, Robert (Robert Allen),
1941–2008—Family. 3. Pioneers—Alaska—McCarthy—Biography.
4. Fundamentalists—Alaska—McCarthy—Biography. 5. Criminals—Alaska—
McCarthy—Biography. 6. Abusive men—Alaska—McCarthy—Biography.
7. McCarthy (Alaska—Biography). 8. Dysfunctional families—Alaska—
McCarthy. 9. Incest—Alaska—McCarthy. 10. Cults—Alaska—McCarthy.
I. Title.
        F914.M33K59   2013
        979.8'05092—dc23   2012016502

ISBN 978-0-307-58782-4
eISBN 978-0-307-58784-8

Printed in the United States of America

Book design by Barbara Sturman
Map illustrations by Jeffrey L. Ward
Jacket design: Eric White
Jacket photograph: Marc Lester/Anchorage Daily News/MCT/Landov

10 9 8 7 6 5 4 3

First Edition

For Emily and Ethan

As I walk'd through the wilderness of this world,
I lighted on a certain place, where was a Denn; And I
laid me down in that place to sleep: And as I slept
I dreamed a Dream. I dreamed, and behold I saw a
Man cloathed with Raggs, standing in a certain
place, with his face from his own House, a Book in his
hand, and a great burden upon his back.

—John Bunyan, *The Pilgrim's Progress,* 1678

Contents

Author's Note   xi

Map   xiv

Prologue: Third Month   xvii

Part One: Pilgrim's Trail   1

1   The Road to McCarthy   3

2   History's Shadow   27

3   The Bollard Wars   33

4   Sunlight and Firefly   58

5   Motorheads   67

6   The Rainbow Cross   80

7   Hostile Territory   94

8   Holy Bob and the Wild West   109

9   God vs. the Park Service   116

10   The Pilgrim's Progress   136

Part Two: The Farthest-Out Place   153

11   Hillbilly Heaven   155

12   Flight of the Angels   177

13   The Pilgrim Family Minstrels   194

Part Three: Out of the Wilderness   215

14   A Quiet Year   217

15   The Wanigan   220

16   Exodus   242

17   Pilgrim's Last Stand   251

18   The Man in the Iron Cage   271

Epilogue: Peaceful Harbor   283

Sources   293

Acknowledgments   307

Photography Credits   311

Author's Note

I N THE winter of 2002, a man with the wild gray beard of a biblical prophet showed up in the remote Alaska ghost town of
McCarthy with his wife and fourteen children. He called himself Papa
Pilgrim. His family found a deserted mining camp in the mountains
nearby, deep inside North America's largest national park, and set
about building a homestead life straight out of the country's pioneer
past—packhorses, goat milk, bear meat. Fiddles and guitars. And a
Caterpillar D5 bulldozer. By the Seventh Month—the Pilgrim Family
did not use the pagan names of the calendar—they were at war with
the National Park Service.

I was a reporter for Alaska's biggest newspaper. Pilgrim was wary
of reporters, bureaucrats, police officers, and park rangers. He said he
would let me ride on horseback to the homestead to hear his story, in
the company of his adult children, because my wife and I had a cabin
of our own near McCarthy.

The cabin had actually been my wife's idea. She had old ties to the
small Wrangell Mountain community. For me those mountains had

mainly been a place to go camping, but Sally used to play the fiddle at dances in McCarthy's tinder-dry Hardware Store and knew all the local characters and feuds. We were both East Coast refugees and had professional interests in the area as well—Sally, a Sierra Club lobbyist working to protect Alaska's still-wild federal lands, and me, a former American Studies major scribbling down stories of manifest destiny for the paper. After we met and married, we built a small cabin on her dream spot, a river bluff inside Wrangell–St. Elias National Park and Preserve. Pilgrim seemed to believe this pioneering impulse would make me sympathetic to his struggles. He called me "Neighbor Tom."

Pilgrim's battle with the park appealed to Alaska's romantic notion of itself. His renunciation of modern life and fight against the advancing forces of government made him a hero to some. Pilgrim had the scapegrace appeal of a Western outlaw, but he presented himself above all as devoted to family and Scripture—traits that squared him in the public eye and gave consequence both to his defiance of authority and to his pious engagement with his Lord's creation. His secrets were cloaked, as a state prosecutor later put it, "under the guise of pursuing the Alaskan dream, of carving out a piece of the Alaska frontier, where a man pits his strength and that of his family against the wild." Such anachronistic strangeness might have been a red flag anywhere else, but it elicited great sympathy in McCarthy, where the arrival of federal agents in Park Service uniforms had only recently unsettled old habits of mind about independent self-sufficiency and dominion over nature.

Papa Pilgrim said it seemed like God's plan that a McCarthy "neighbor" would arrive to tell his tale. It may be that, in an empty wilderness, the individual stands out more, making it easier to believe an intervening deity would go to such trouble. Certainly Pilgrim liked to tell his own story as a God-wrought tale of redemption. His turning points involved scenes of credulous wonder and signs from above. Let me propose, then, before passing to Pilgrim's story, such an opening scene in the pioneer life of Neighbor Tom: a late-summer evening in the year we built our cabin in the Wrangells. I'm sitting with my bride on an open promontory above the canyon—Inspiration Point, Sally called it, in mock-solemn national park style. We listen to the river, and she rests her head on my shoulder as the moon comes up in a lazy northern trajectory, its yellow light peeking through a notch in the mountains, then vanishing behind the next summit, half-appearing a second time and setting again, and finally floating free—a magical triple moonrise.

Or so it seemed, from where we sat. I realize now it was nothing more than the turning of the indifferent heavens.

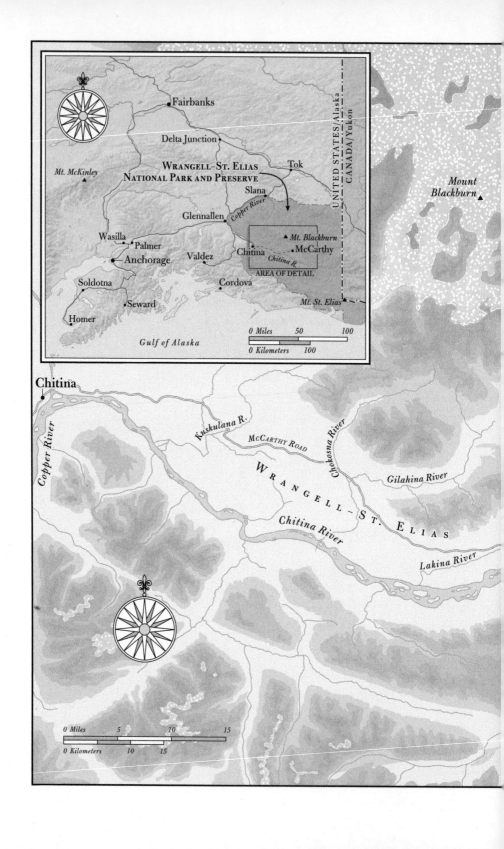

Fairbanks

Delta Junction

Wrangell–St. Elias National Park and Preserve

Tok

Mt. McKinley

Slana

Copper River

Glennallen

Mt. Blackburn

Wasilla

Palmer

Valdez

Chitina

McCarthy

Anchorage

Chitina R.

AREA OF DETAIL

Soldotna

Cordova

Seward

Mt. St. Elias

Homer

Gulf of Alaska

UNITED STATES/Alaska
CANADA/Yukon

Mount Blackburn

0 Miles   50   100

0 Kilometers   100

Chitina

Copper River

Kuskulana R.

McCarthy Road

Chokosna River

Gilahina River

W R A N G E L L – S T. E L I A S

Chitina River

Lakina River

0 Miles   5   10   15

0 Kilometers   10   15

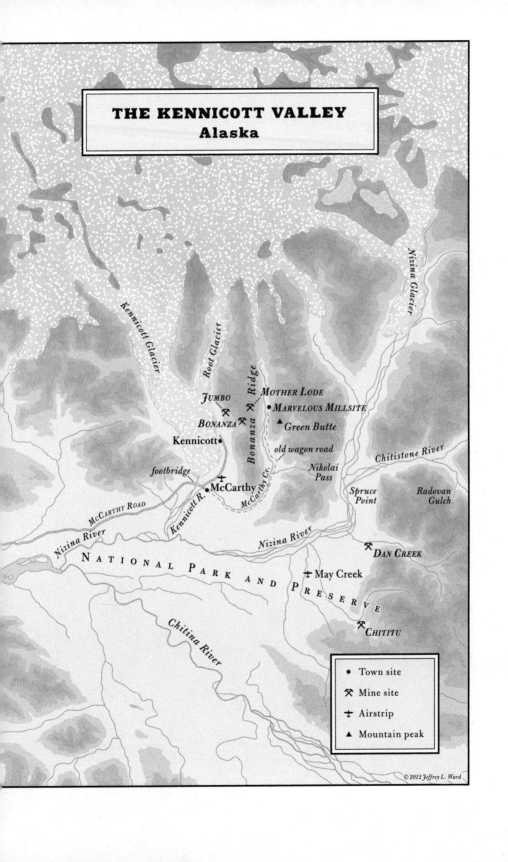

THE KENNICOTT VALLEY
Alaska

Nizina Glacier

Kennicott Glacier

Root Glacier

Ridge

MOTHER LODE

JUMBO ⚒ • MARVELOUS MILLSITE

BONANZA ⚒

Bonanza Gr.

▲ Green Butte

Kennicott •

old wagon road

Chitistone River

footbridge

Nikolai Pass

McCarthy

Kennicott R.

McCarthy Gr.

Spruce Point

Radovan Gulch

McCARTHY ROAD

Nizina River

Nizina River

⚒ DAN CREEK

N A T I O N A L   P A R K   A N D   P R E S E R V E

✝ May Creek

Chitina River

⚒ CHITITU

•	Town site
⚒	Mine site
✝	Airstrip
▲	Mountain peak

© 2012 Jeffrey L. Ward

PROLOGUE: THIRD MONTH

WHEN THE song of the snowmachine had faded down the valley, the sisters got ready to go. Elishaba moved quickly through the morning cold and snow in heavy boots, insulated pants beneath her prairie skirt, ferrying provisions from the cabin—raisins, sleeping bags, two white sheets. Jerusalem and Hosanna tore through the toolshed looking for a spark plug. The plugs had been pulled from the old Ski-Doo Tundra machines that morning.

It was late in the Third Month, and the days in Alaska were growing longer. The overcast was high, the temperature holding above zero. They knew they didn't have much time.

White mountains squeezed the sky above the old mining cabin. For weeks, Elishaba had been looking up, praying as if to the summits. But she knew the snow was too deep, she would be tracked easily. The only trail, the one that had brought their family the attention they once shunned, ran thirteen miles through the wilderness, slicing down the canyon through avalanche zones and back and forth across the frozen creek.

The trail ended at a ghost town. McCarthy had once been a boom-town of bootleggers and prostitutes. These days it was the only place in the Wrangell Mountains that could still be called a community, though most of the old buildings had fallen down and a mere hand-ful of settlers remained through the silent winter. At first that isolation had been the attraction. The Pilgrim Family had traveled thousands of miles to reach the end of the road in Alaska. They had parked their trucks at the river and crossed a footbridge into town and continued on horseback and snowmachine and bulldozer and foot to their new home.

Now McCarthy burned in her imagination not as the end of the road but as a beginning.

Psalms and Lamb and Abraham looked on in horror. Their big sisters had been put on silence. Yet here was Elishaba, calling out as she moved to and from the cabin, as if she no longer cared what would happen.

Elishaba was the oldest of the fifteen brothers and sisters, a pretty, dark-eyed, dark-haired young woman, strong from a lifetime of home-stead chores, from wrangling horses and hunting game. At twenty-nine, she was no longer a girl, though she had never lived away from her family, never whispered secrets at a friend's house or flirted with a boy. She had been raised in isolation, sheltered from the world and its television and books, schooled only in survival and a dark exegesis of God's portents. She was the special daughter, chosen according to the Bible's solemn instruction. Her legal name was Butterfly Sunstar.

She gave the children a brave and reassuring smile. They could see now that she was weeping and frightened and that she did indeed still care. She was committing the unforgivable sin. The Lord had held her, steadfast, in these cold mountains, and would not let her go. His grip was strong.

Her sisters looked happy, though. Hosanna had found a spark plug. Perhaps it was a sign their enterprise was favored after all.

Jerusalem—short, blond, and cherub-cheeked, at sixteen the second-oldest girl—had declared she would not let Elishaba go alone.

Elishaba and Jerusalem said swift good-byes and climbed together onto the little Tundra and sped down the trail.

They made it no farther than the open snow in the first muskeg swamp. The snowmachine lurched to a stop. The fan belt had snapped. Jerusalem used a wrench to pull the spark plug and stumped back up the packed trail, postholing through the snow. Elishaba tried to mend the belt with wire and pliers but gave up.

She looked about. The snow was too deep to flounder through, the trees too far away. It felt like one of those dreams where she tried to run and couldn't move. She sat listening for the sound of a snowmachine returning up the valley from town.

Instead she heard Jerusalem coming on the other Tundra.

They reloaded their gear and started off again. A pinhole in the fuel line was spewing gasoline, but if this, too, was a sign it went unseen. They flew too fast on a curve and nearly hit a tree and slowed down.

Jerusalem, holding on in back, started crying now, too. She was thinking about all they were leaving behind. In modern Alaska, with its four-lane highways and shopping malls, her family was famous, recognized wherever they went. People cheered when the Pilgrim Family Minstrels performed onstage. That beautiful old-time picture was gone forever.

The sisters prayed out loud. Where the snow-packed trail turned uphill, they stopped and listened. The valley was heavy with quiet. They started again and pushed up the hill and at the top they discovered the family's other big snowmachine, hidden in trees too far from the cabin for anyone on foot to find it. The sisters hesitated. They talked about switching, but the old Tundra was running well so they decided to continue. But right there the engine died, and that's when they discovered the fuel leak. Maybe the Lord was indeed helping them, they said. They felt a surge of hope as they transferred their gear and continued on the third machine.

There was so much about the world the sisters did not know. But there were things they did know and these were the skills they needed now. Where the trail climbed over the riverbank, Elishaba veered away behind the snowy berm, so that someone coming the other way might not see their track. She drove into the spruce trees and shut down. They could see the trail through the boughs. The telltale smell of two-cycle exhaust lingered in the still, cold air. They covered themselves in the snow with the two white sheets.

The faint whine of a snowmachine, growing louder, was coming up the valley.

Part One

Pilgrim's Trail

Here's for the plain old Adam, the simple genuine self against the whole world.

—Ralph Waldo Emerson, *Journals*

The Road to McCarthy

A PAIR OF old trucks crept down the street, pushing deep tracks through the snow. Neil Darish stopped shoveling the roof of the McCarthy Lodge to watch. In the back of one pickup, three or four hardy young people stood in the morning cold, looking around at the buildings left over from mining days. Strangers in McCarthy were rare in the middle of January, especially after a storm. It was eight hours from Anchorage through the mountains just to reach the end of the pavement, the last miles of asphalt crumbling and swaybacked by frost. At Chitina, you crossed the Copper River, and it was another

▲

McCarthy, 1983, shortly after creation of Wrangell–St. Elias National Park and Preserve

sixty miles into the heart of the Wrangell Mountains. The road from Chitina was gravel and followed the bed of a vanished railroad, a route frequently closed in winter by drifts or blocked by freeze-thaw flows of ice that locals attacked with chain saws and winches. At the end of the road was a turnaround and a footbridge. These tourists had apparently made the drive through the blizzard and been enterprising and presumptuous enough to push their trucks across the river ice and into town, rutting up the local snowmachine trails.

Unseen on the low roof, Darish stared as the trucks stopped and emptied their passengers: eight young people in their teens and early twenties, the boys with long hair spilling out from under vintage hats of wool and leather, a few wispy beards, the girls in tattered coats and long flowered skirts down to their snow boots. Darish felt vague misgivings as the strangers peered in the windows of the closed-up hotel across the street. He caught himself: He'd been in McCarthy only a short time, and already he'd picked up the local mistrust of visitors hunting souvenirs from the past.

The driver of the first pickup emerged. He was an older man, wiry and bespectacled, with pinched cheeks and a long, unruly beard. He gazed appraisingly at the weathered lodge and the few false-front buildings nearby.

"Papa, this is what we thought Fairbanks would look like," said one of the boys.

At this, Darish smiled. He knew Fairbanks was no longer anyone's romantic vision of the Last Frontier. Nor was Anchorage with its oil company high-rises, nor Wasilla with its busy highway and chain-store sprawl. McCarthy was another matter. And these new arrivals, he had to admit, looked like they belonged here—like they had just emerged, blinking, from the abandoned copper mines up the mountain.

The bearded father stopped taking the town's measure when he spotted Darish on the roof. At a wave, two youngsters grabbed shovels and scrambled up a ladder to pitch in. Darish tried to shoo them away. He could just picture one of these longhaired boys tumbling to the street. He had too much at stake here to invite a liability lawsuit. Buying the lodge, opening it in winter—Darish was trying to restore some can-do pioneer spirit to a melancholy town that had been shutting itself down for decades.

He caught himself for a second time rushing to judgment—he could hardly imagine a less litigious-looking family. It was a first impression he would recall ruefully, years later, as the family's appeal briefs were being filed before the U.S. Supreme Court.

Still, the boys wouldn't stop shoveling until he climbed down and invited them indoors to sit by the woodstove.

"I'm Pilgrim," the old man said in a deep and friendly drawl. "These are some of my children."

They were a striking brood, strong jawed and pink cheeked, handsome despite their ragged jackets and hand-me-down garments—an authentic, no-pretense look that wore well in rural Alaska. They stood by shyly as their father arranged himself at a table in the small dining room. His motions were deliberate, his eyes sharp and watchful.

The sound of hammering came through the walls. The innkeeper got the coffeepot. "So what brings you to the Wrangell Mountains, Pilgrim?" he asked.

It was a simple question—and with it Neil Darish became the first to hear a story that everyone in McCarthy would hear, sooner or later, told in that strange King James diction and plaintive Texas drawl, the pitch and timbre of the tale evolving over time as the teller came to comprehend the local pattern of feuds and factions and was thus better able to ascertain the Lord's purpose in bringing him here.

"My name is Pilgrim," he said, "because I'm a sojourner on this earth. The Bible says we are all strangers and pilgrims, and we live by faith until our Lord returns."

His story began with a big-bang religious awakening and a shaft of celestial light. Before that, things were vague—a backdrop of youthful affluence and pride. With God's direction, he had raised up his children on horseback in New Mexico mountains named for the Blood of Christ. There were fifteen of them, he said. Pilgrim was a trained midwife and had delivered each child at home. They had never seen a television nor experienced the temptations of the world. They were schooled at home, tended flocks of sheep in alpine meadows, made their own buckskin, and lived pretty much as their forebears did a century ago, innocent and capable and strong, spinning wool and making lye soap and each night singing songs of praise.

The Pilgrim children were silent and listened raptly to their father's words, as if uncertain how the story would turn out. The absence of teenaged restlessness among these bright and earnest offspring would strike many, on first meeting, as a healthy sign of what it must have been like to grow up within an oral tradition. People tried to remember if all children had been so attentive before they were handed cell phones.

The family had moved on from New Mexico when the Rockies grew too civilized, Pilgrim explained. Alaska was the sweet name whispered by God as their firstborn came of age. Later, he would show photographs of the caravan that carried them north—a small tour bus with a mountain of gear on the roof, two 1941 flatbed trucks bearing cabins of rough-cut lumber, antlers and snowshoes and frying pans lashed to the exterior walls, and an olive drab army-surplus six-by-six with a canvas tarp and a white star on the door, which the family had named "Armageddon." The four vehicles, each pulling a trailer and flying a navy-blue Alaska state flag with the gold Big Dipper, crept along at a top speed of 45 mph and turned heads all the way to the Canadian border and beyond. They were like a wagon train, Pilgrim liked to say, headed west when the land was free and wild.

For three years they had searched throughout Alaska, he said, a land truly blessed with *so many* riches. They knew somewhere a place was prepared for them. It had not been easy, because Fairbanks and Anchorage and the Kenai Peninsula turned out to be more tied to the modern cash economy than the subsistence mountains they'd left behind. Even now, Mama Country Rose and the younger children were waiting in the town of Kenai, along with their goats and horses and purebred mountain dogs. Everywhere they went, they encountered the welcoming arms of many new friends, but they never settled for long, as strangers did not know what to make of their countenance and their family-centered ways, and sometimes took advantage of their innocence and generous nature.

"We have truly followed a long, hard road to get this far," said Pilgrim, "and as we passed through the rock in Chitina last night, we all felt we had arrived at last at our home."

He asked Neil Darish if this ghost town had any property for sale.

PAPA PILGRIM had led his family into the mountains of Alaska looking for one of the last empty spaces on the continent. But he stumbled on something that would suit his purpose even better: a remnant settlement out of American history, teetering nostalgically between the open frontier of the nineteenth century and the protected wilderness of the twenty-first.

McCarthy had sprung to life a century earlier with the discovery of the richest vein of copper the world had ever known. Most mining camps of the Alaska Territory were lonely endeavors, but in these remote mountains the great capitalists of the Gilded Age, J. P. Morgan and the Guggenheims, invested millions to build a small city and a railroad up the canyons from the coast. The copper was pulled out of the mountain in blocks that were up to 80 percent pure, so rich that much of it could be loaded straight onto the trains without processing. One of the mines in the area consisted of nothing more than tunnels through glacier ice to extract the moraine, high-grade rocks that had been tumbling off a snaggletooth ridge for centuries. Copper from the

Wrangells electrified the nation, built mansions and museums in New York City, and gave the world the Kennecott Copper Corporation—named, along with the nearby river and vast glacier, for the early explorer of Russian America Robert Kennicott, though the name of the company somehow ended up with an extra "e" in place of the "i."

It didn't take long, though, to hollow out Bonanza Ridge. Alaska's first industrial boom lasted four short decades: from the afternoon in 1900 when a prospector named Tarantula Jack mistook the green oxides of exposed copper for alpine grass, to the sudden announcement that the last Kennecott train was pulling out on November 11, 1938, with twenty-four hours' notice, leaving bunkhouse beds made and the offices locked up as if for the weekend.

Down the mountain from the Kennecott mines and mill buildings, McCarthy had been staked in 1906 among the cottonwoods at the Kennicott Glacier terminus, an entrepreneurial service center providing saloons and hardware stores and whores' cabins by a creek. The town had a provisional air from the beginning, having been erected in the path of oncoming ice. The scrape and clatter of falling rocks, and floods dumped out of hidden summer reservoirs, kept the boomers alert to the talus-strewn face only hundreds of feet away. But instead of surging forward to push the outpost off its foundations, the glacier had retreated, baring a raw rubbly plain where green nature was slow to copy itself onto the blankness. With the closing of the copper mines, the false-front wooden stores and rooming houses weathered gray and began to puff and sag with rot. Roofs caved in under heavy winter snows. Fire razed the Alaska Hotel and the McCarthy Drug Store. Bushes fanned up in front of windows, and frail green poplars filled the streets and vacant lots, so that what remained of the town seemed to have been deftly hidden in the leaves where the rest of the world would not easily find it.

But there was, in fact, property for sale. Kennicott and McCarthy were never quite abandoned. In the decades after the mines closed, the valley became host to a small scavenger culture surviving off what the land provided—not just berries and moose and salmon, but also such nonrenewable resources as window frames of mullioned glass, china dishes, and spools of steel cable from aerial tram stations. It was not a bad place to eke out an Alaska bush living. The mining era had left rough, washed-out roads and a tattoo of private homesteads and claims on the landscape. Government didn't control every last acre here, as it did in most of rural Alaska. Nor did McCarthy have a complicating overlay of ancestral Native American occupancy. Winter temperatures plunged far below zero, but the summers were hot and there was enough gold in the creeks to pay for shipped-in groceries. For a while, you could even get back and forth to the highway at Chitina over sixty miles of old rails, riding a truck fitted with flanged steel wheels.

The iron rails were eventually pulled for scrap and replaced by a gravel road, a rattling washboard that ran flat and straight, splashing through beaver ponds and dipping past fallen trestles. Improved access in the early 1970s livened up McCarthy's otherworldly mix of homesteaders, marijuana growers, mountain climbers, sheep-hunting guides, college students researching the environment, and placer miners riding their bulldozers through town to get a beer at the lodge. Far from medical care, law enforcement, and the last filling station, it was no country for the casual tourist. Where the road ended on a rocky floodplain, visitors had to pull themselves into town on a tram car dangling from a cable above a murky glacial torrent in which boulders could be heard rolling angrily downstream. As in the old mining camps, there were no local authorities, and neighbors took care of problems themselves.

Two big events then drew attention to McCarthy and shaped what the town would become. One was the creation of Wrangell–St. Elias National Park and Preserve. The park was part of a sweeping act of Congress in 1980 known as the Alaska National Interest Lands Conservation Act, or ANILCA. Capping a frantic decade for Alaska that included settlement of Native land claims and construction of the Trans-Alaska Pipeline, ANILCA was the biggest act of wilderness preservation in the history of the world, protecting more than one hundred million acres of the forty-ninth state and doubling the size of the national park system. The new national park in the Wrangells, created to "maintain unimpaired the scenic beauty and quality" of the natural landscape, was the biggest park in North America—at thirteen million acres, six times the size of Yellowstone National Park. It was bigger than Massachusetts, Connecticut, and New Jersey combined. Tiny McCarthy, proud and unimpressed, was its only town.

The other event that put McCarthy on the map was the last thing anyone expected in such a get-away-from-it-all scene of natural splendor. One morning in March 1983, a quiet newcomer shot and killed six of his neighbors as they gathered to meet the weekly mail plane. Half the wintering-over population died. The killer, nabbed by state troopers as he fled the valley on a snowmachine, later told a court psychiatrist that Alaska was being spoiled like everywhere else and he wanted to purge nature of human beings—starting with residents of the wilderness town where he'd settled.

These two nearly simultaneous events, weirdly linked, had given McCarthy a defiant mind-set about its future. The survivors of the mail-day murders had been determined to rebuild their outback community. Settlers prepared for the rigors of self-sufficient bush life were welcomed. The modern world, with its big-government rules and general craziness, would be held at bay as long as possible.

To be sure, such a life was more complicated now that McCarthy was surrounded by a national park. The days of proper homesteading were over, and Neil Darish wanted Papa Pilgrim to understand this. It would be hard to imagine a family of seventeen moving their livestock into the heart of Yellowstone.

Alaska, however, was supposed to be different. Congress wrote special provisions into the 1980 conservation law to protect the lingering frontier lifestyles of rural Alaskans. Even in national parks, local residents could continue to live off the land, mine the creeks, and hunt moose. Federal management and promotion were to remain low-key. American dreamers could take heart: It seemed the nation, in protecting for perpetuity the great wilderness of the north, could not quite bear to say good-bye to the last of the Last Frontier—the small log cabin in the forest—or consign to mere inspirational metaphor the jumping-off point for the settler, the fur trapper, the gold panner, the young idealist dreaming of a better place, or the American Adam seeking to reinvent himself in a New World.

Exactly how the people of McCarthy were supposed to continue their eccentric pioneering ways without impairing the scenic beauty and quality of the natural landscape wasn't spelled out clearly. The Wrangells backcountry, moreover, would not yield readily to agrarian sodbusters and shepherds with their flocks. It was an unfinished country, tough to nestle in to, with its grizzly bears and wolf packs, crevasses and volcanoes, viscous rock glaciers grinding down the slopes, the bottom country slashed by brown, turbulent, unfordable rapids and gravel bars where trees fight to stand and are washed away. Hundreds of square miles of ice reaching into Canada are punctuated by nine of North America's tallest peaks, among them Mount Blackburn, whose 16,390-foot summit looms above McCarthy. Even the early Ahtna Indians, who staged fall hunts in these drainages and gave the suffix for river, "na," to many of the place names, preferred to live in easier terrain downriver toward the coast. As a panorama of nature, the Wrangell Mountains have never been a testament to ecological balance and a pastoral ideal. This country told the harsher truth of change—brutal, erosive change.

CHANGE WITHIN the community, though, had been slow. By the time the Pilgrim Family showed up in January 2002, the year-round population of McCarthy and the big country around was still only a few dozen families and individual households. The National Park Service, tactfully acknowledging feelings about government in a place that never had one, had not even stationed a ranger in town. Local charms were still rough-hewn. The hand-pulled tram across the river, so intimidating to visitors, had finally been replaced—but only by a footbridge, designed to keep out motorized vehicles. The town had a few new cabins, a lunch stand in summer, two bush pilots, and a passenger van for the five-mile taxi ride up to the abandoned mines at Kennicott, but the atmosphere when the Pilgrims arrived was still that of a place letting itself go back to nature.

It would not be easy, Neil Darish thought, for such a big family to settle here. In an empty country, paradoxically, every individual loomed large. Landowners would be wary of inflicting a family with fifteen kids on their neighbors; you practically needed letters of reference to get a town-site lot as it was. Likewise, some of the old buildings at Kennicott were in private hands, but the Park Service had started buying up the properties and calling everything "Kennecott," with an "e." Local people had always spelled it with an "i," unless referring specifically to the mining company. Now you had to choose a side when you chose your vowel.

Darish knew that many visitors fantasized about making McCarthy home. Few took the next step, and fewer still lasted through one winter.

Therefore he kept to polite generalizations and encouragements that first snowy day, until Pilgrim waved away his own real estate question and sent the children to the trucks. They returned with musical instruments—guitars, mandolins, fiddles, and a banjo. Pilgrim introduced the young people now by name: the oldest boys, Joseph and Joshua, and their teenaged brothers, Moses, David, and Israel. Elishaba, his dark-haired eldest daughter, lifted a violin to her chin and smiled, as if anticipating a pleasant surprise in store. Her sisters Jerusalem and Hosanna snapped open their instrument cases, attended by little four-year-old Psalms in a flower-print dress. Papa propped a guitar in his lap, tuned up, and started to strum.

In the coming years, everyone would agree on one point about the Pilgrims: The family could light up any space, living room or concert hall, once the old-time country gospel got rolling. "Hillbilly music," Pilgrim called it. They played slow or fast, on tempo and in harmony, traditional tunes and original compositions, with Pilgrim himself singing spirituals in a high, plangent twang.

From childhood I heard about Heaven,
Oh I wondered if it could be true
That there were sweet mansions Eternal,
Off somewhere out there beyond the blue.

The fingers of one daughter—Jerusalem or Hosanna, it was hard for Darish to keep the Bible names straight—flew lightly over the frets of a mandolin. Darish got on the phone. A show like this didn't come often to McCarthy.

The hammering next door stopped. Darish's partner, Doug Miller, stuck his head through a door to listen. Miller was extending the dark-wood bar he'd salvaged from the Golden Saloon. He had grown up in McCarthy, among antiques pulled from the ruins of Kennecott's bunkhouses. His parents once owned this very lodge—Miller had hung the moose antlers above the door as a boy. He had always wanted to get the lodge back. Now he and Darish had a business plan. Darish would deal with the public. Miller would do the remodeling and make sure everything about the place stayed authentic.

A small crowd gathered. Darish noticed how the mandolin player smiled when her big sister accidentally poked her with the fiddle bow. In his own family, such a provocation would have meant instant retaliation. He couldn't help but be impressed by the harmonizing and the genuine off-the-grid family warmth. The McCarthy audience clapped happily. The children were self-taught musicians, Pilgrim said. When they decided to take up music, he put the names of instruments in his cowboy hat, and the Lord guided their small hands as each child picked one.

The children stood politely as their papa named another tune and asked, "How about that one?" They always said yes.

They had learned to pick at mountain-man festivals down around Santa Fe, Pilgrim explained during another pause. Their family motto was "In our Lord Jesus, Music and Wilderness Livin'." They had been performing at a folk festival in Anchorage, in fact, when they first heard the name of McCarthy. Then the boys spied a large full-curl ram's head at a taxidermist's and were told it was shot in the Wrangells. So they drove out through the darkness of the previous day's snowstorm. And when they reached the place in Chitina where the pavement ends and the road passes in one lane through jagged walls of solid rock—it was the old Copper River and Northwestern Railway cut, just before the big bridge—the feeling was like something out of the Old Testament, like they were passing through a gate to a land of heavenly promise.

His audience could perhaps imagine the patriarch's sense of urgency, three years out from New Mexico: A pilgrim can wander alone, but a father of fifteen can't keep sojourning forever. Men in heavy parkas had been working on the road that evening, and Pilgrim described how they squinted at the strange family and asked where they thought they were going. Soon all those men saw through the blizzard were the red taillights of a family confident of the Lord's guidance as they headed at last into the true Alaska.

Doug Miller returned to hammering. The partner in charge of authenticity had seen enough.

The rest of the McCarthy audience couldn't have been happier, though. They wanted to hear more tunes, but instead Pilgrim inquired again about property. He was informed that January is a hard time to look at land, because the old mining roads are snowed shut. He declared the family would return with snowmachines in the Second Month.

As the musicians played merrily on, Neil Darish thought about writing up a little something for McCarthy's newspaper, which came out six times a year. The implications of a family this big moving to town were beginning to sink in. They would nearly double the winter population. He wondered—had he been too encouraging?

As the brief afternoon grew dark and the family prepared to head back across the frozen river to camp, Darish followed them to their trucks and drew Pilgrim aside. Darish was a follower of Ayn Rand's rational ethics of self-interest. An Objectivist perspective seemed usefully applied here. People would help the family if they came back, Darish explained. But it would be out of the shared values of self-help, not altruism or charity. The Pilgrims would have to show they were able to take care of themselves. Darish hoped he didn't insult the family patriarch as he spelled this out.

"You don't have to worry about that at all," Papa Pilgrim said, with a smile that showed he was a perceptive hillbilly who understood exactly where Neil was coming from. "All we want is a place to live our old-time way and be left in peace."

WITHIN WEEKS, the Pilgrims returned with six old snowmachines and fanned into the surrounding country. As the days lengthened and the snow softened by day and set firm at night, Papa Pilgrim and the older children pursued rumors of remote cabins and poked down private roads on their thirdhand one-cylinder Tundra snowmachines. The still-absent mother, Country Rose, hung back in the highway town of Glennallen, checking property deeds and looking up the names of absentee owners in file drawers of the Chitina District recording office. They called back and forth from the phone at the lodge.

Winter has always been the easiest time to travel in much of

Alaska. The unfordable rapids and vast swampy muskegs are frozen and covered in snow, open to travel at 60 mph with the latest technology, or half that on vintage Tundras. The Pilgrims rode out the Nizina River valley as far as the mouth of the Chitistone Canyon, where they checked out cabins that once housed a commune set up by California beatniks who reached the Wrangells by way of Tangiers. They looked in town at the Hippie Hole, a grown-over excavation for a marijuana-growing lodge, abandoned in 1971, but originally inspired by McCarthy's Prohibition-days reputation, when trains from the coast had a special whistle to warn of the approach of a revenue officer.

The family searched as far as Long Lake on the road back toward Chitina, and south to May Creek, probing the countryside with a bluntness of purpose that struck residents in the valley as obtuse, even rude. There was a protocol out here. You met a person in town and introduced yourself and hoped for an invitation. You didn't ride up to a stranger's place in the wilds. You certainly didn't turn and drive away when you were spotted, as the Pilgrims were doing. The community watched apprehensively as this furtive family went about its business. The Pilgrim offspring displayed a formal Old World politeness when approached in town but seemed easily spooked, eager to scamper away. It was as though they hadn't quite learned the niceties of community living. Still, people tried to reserve judgment. The newcomers were eccentric, without a doubt, but their novelty flattered the area's self-image as an oddball, open-to-anything part of the world.

By chance, another unusual visitor showed up in McCarthy around the same time: a best-selling British humorist. As a consequence, there exists a brief published account of the Pilgrims in their first weeks in the Wrangells, opening with a scene in which the Englishman, careening uncontrollably across the frozen Kennicott River on a borrowed snowmachine, encounters a sprawling riverbank camp full of Pilgrims that strikes him as something from *The Grapes of Wrath*.

Pete McCarthy's first book, a self-deprecating barstool memoir about his travels in western Ireland, had once soared to the top of England's best-seller lists. Now as a follow-up to *McCarthy's Bar,* the author was touring the Irish diaspora in search of connections to his Irish mother's surname, which he had taken for his own. He had hoped to drive out to McCarthy, but found "the worst road in Alaska" closed due to spring breakup conditions. His trip to Alaska nevertheless would provide a title for a new book—*The Road to McCarthy*—as well as a penultimate chapter in which, after some Mark Twain–style tall tales depicting the cheechako's white-knuckled small-plane flight over the mountains and an epiphany regarding the unfavorable ratio of grizzly bears to people in the valley, the explorer was pleased to discover fine beer and exquisite cuisine at the newly remodeled McCarthy Lodge, where he was the only guest. He marveled at the "meticulously designed pioneer-style rooms" assembled by the new owners, with their crisp linens, patchwork quilts, and hand-tinted photographs.

> I'd had visions of living like a brute for a week, then dumping my clothes in an incinerator back in Anchorage, hosing off the moose shit and going looking for food that didn't come out of a can. Instead I have been dropped into the Alaskan edition of *Homes and Interiors.* Doug and Neil have done a fine job. There are few more comforting experiences for the traveler than to journey great distances through unfamiliar and threatening landscapes, anticipating an austere and possibly squalid destination, only to discover that catering and interior design are not in the hands of heterosexuals.

Like any good travel writer, Pete McCarthy had trumped up a quest—in his case, to find out about a Wrangell Mountain prospector named James McCarthy. In 1899 this Irishman had loaned horses and provisions to a military surveyor exploring the upper Chitina and Nizina river valleys. In return, the surveyor named a local creek after McCarthy. A few years later, when the well-liked prospector drowned while crossing a river on horseback, the new town at the mouth of the creek was named after him as well.

McCarthy Creek winds twenty miles back into the mountains east of town, ending in a high glacial cirque. By chance, this cold and steep-walled defile became the very place the Pilgrims soon focused their hunt for land. What suited them especially, beyond the absence of neighbors, was the valley's geological and human history. McCarthy Creek had seen a lot of spillover copper-mining activity in Kennecott days, which meant there was likely to be remote private property. The family rode their snowmachines into the valley's upper reaches, where they found old habitations connected to an abandoned mine called the Mother Lode—a name surely never uttered in the presence of Pete McCarthy, who would not have resisted making another joke about the family with fifteen kids.

THE OLD mine that the Pilgrims would soon call home was on the back side of Bonanza Ridge. The green-and-white Mother Lode Mine had been the inverse of the red-and-white Guggenheim mines on the other side: speculative where Kennecott was spectacularly successful, obscure where Kennecott was famous. Some people once considered the Mother Lode cursed. The same seam that would enrich Kennecott's owners extended across shear zones and emerged high above McCarthy Creek, where backdoor claims had been snatched before the Guggenheims' Alaska Syndicate could get them. The first prospectors started sinking tunnels by hand, hoping to find a big deposit. The back side of the ridge did, in fact, contain the richest single vein of copper in the mountain, but the Mother Lode's original claimants never dug deep enough to find it.

Those early prospectors set up camp in the valley below and

climbed two hours every morning to reach their claims. They worked eight-hour days hammering and blasting and shoveling, then descended to camp, according to one account, in a "fifteen minute rush down the mountain over fine slide rock taking twenty or thirty foot strides and letting the finely crushed rock and gravel carry one along." Needless to say, these were young adventurers, not bearded codgers chasing a last dream.

They soon owned a sizable chunk of Alaska wilderness. The federal mining law of 1872 was generous in dispensing public land. In addition to the copper claims up high, the prospectors were granted a five-acre claim on the valley floor dubbed the Marvelous Millsite, where they built some cabins and a station for a tram to haul ore from above. Ocha Potter, a Michigan mining engineer who had guessed the mountain's secrets, then staked a 160-acre mining claim across the bottom of the McCarthy Creek valley. He imagined this would be the site of a future town. Without a show of pay to prove there were minerals present, however, the government would not grant title to the valley claim. No matter how many shafts he sank on the new claim, which he named Spokane, Potter couldn't find a single flake of gold. In an unpublished memoir left to his family, Potter described sending "one of the boys" to a friend's streambed placer mine across the Nizina River to buy ten dollars' worth of gold dust, which he salted across the bottom of a prospecting shaft. A visiting federal surveyor, "a very conscientious official," pulled up two buckets of gravel from the shaft and found a pretty tail of yellow in his pan both times.

After some time out for thought, down he went again. I began now to get worried. Looking down I could see him digging deep into the bottom, far below any possibility of superficial salting. But I had some loose fine gold dust in my pocket. As the bucket was drawn up I leaned casually over the shaft and let the last of my treasured gold dribble through my fingers. By the time the bucket reached the surface it, too, was thoroughly salted. When he saw the yellow tail from that sample, he asked me if I had staked the claims above, and when I said "no," he grabbed a pick and shovel, and disappeared upstream. When he came back to camp that night he looked at me rather sharply but nothing more was said about the validity of our "gold" claims. Months later he wrote asking how I had "put it over," but I never explained and my conscience has never bothered me.

In the end, though, the challenges of McCarthy Creek proved too great even for the resourceful Potter. Things kept going wrong. Ownership of the Mother Lode claims was thrown in doubt when one of the original claimants fell under the ice on the Chitina River. He was packing freight on a hot day in April when the ice collapsed beneath his sled. His friends ran to an open spot downstream and threw the fellow a rope as he popped out, saving his life, while his bug-eyed horse and sleigh vanished downstream under more ice. But the man went mad and headed south, disappearing back in the States; his partners had to wait seven years to declare him dead and clear his title.

Meanwhile, the miners battled daunting physical obstacles. They built a thirteen-mile wagon road down the valley to McCarthy, with bridges every mile and two rock tunnels, designed at a low grade with a future rail spur in mind. But they couldn't get financing to lay down tracks until they found a big ore body. A great bunkhouse for miners was built high on the mountain, teetering on a scree slope and cabled to limestone cliffs—in the words of national park historian Logan Hovis, "perched on the edge of nothing." Just below the bunkhouse, the mountain itself was moving, literally—the slope was the site of a rare rock glacier, a descending mass that is more rubble than ice. In winter, avalanches raked the mountainside. Snow shields behind the bunkhouse helped divert the crushing loads, but sometimes when vast gales of snow let loose the miners had to move inside the mine tunnels, emerging days later to see what remained. One snowslide tore away a high tram station. Another flattened the powder house, turning the rock glacier below into a minefield of scattered dynamite and blasting caps. Without better access or richer ore, capital for repairs was hard to raise.

In 1919 the Mother Lode investors finally sold out to Kennecott Copper. The big company drilled through from the other side of the mountain, went deeper, found an eighty-foot-wide plug of almost pure copper extending more than a thousand feet, pulled the ore out through the Bonanza Mine, and sent it down a tram to their own mill and train cars.

The McCarthy Creek valley began reverting to wilderness.

For a while, miners scratched at a deposit, across the valley and farther down, called the Green Butte. The road from town was kept open that far and became known as the Green Butte Road. But the ore pinched out and the mine buildings there were abandoned, too. After statehood in 1959, a Fairbanks miner named Walt Wigger bought the Mother Lode at an outcry auction and ran a bulldozer up the old wagon road. He erected two small cabins at the Marvelous Millsite camp, rebuilt some crude bridges, and scraped off a runway on Ocha Potter's never-used town site so he could fly in and out. Wigger drilled and pushed gravel for years but could find no riches that the earlier miners had missed. Then talk started up about a national park. Established mines supposedly would be allowed to keep working, under tighter environmental regulation, but Wigger, in his sixties, could see the end was near. He kept on flying until he crashed a heavily loaded plane by the creek. Rescuers found him alive in the Marvelous Millsite cabin, his face bashed in and several teeth missing. That was it for Wigger and the Mother Lode.

Again the wilderness closed back in.

In September 1980, a tropical typhoon drifted north and wrung itself out against the Wrangell Mountains. The rains fell for days. A few locals who happened to be sheltering in a McCarthy Creek cabin reported that the gravel slurry off the mountains was so loud at night, none of them could sleep. Geologists said a thousand years' worth of erosion occurred in the single storm. The meandering stream down the valley turned into a rocky flume, shouldering aside steep berms of cobbles. Long stretches of the wagon road washed away, along with the last traces of old bridges. God's untrodden vale was restored.

The transformation of McCarthy Creek was biblical not only in scale but in its timing. Three months after the deluge, Congress approved the Alaska National Interest Lands Conservation Act, and the Mother Lode valley became part of Wrangell–St. Elias National Park and Preserve.

THE PILGRIMS knew nothing of this history. But they liked what it had left behind: 420 acres of patented private holdings surrounded by miles and miles of protected public land.

They snowmachined up and down the valley to explore. They poked into the cavity in the mountain high overhead. They examined the overgrown gravel runway on the Spokane placer and the two livable cabins on the Marvelous Millsite. They returned to McCarthy and drove to Fairbanks to meet Walt Wigger in a restaurant. He told them the National Park Service had made an offer, looking to buy up potentially troublesome inholdings from willing sellers. But he refused to sell to the government. Wigger was impressed by the Pilgrim Family's size and single-minded drive, though he warned them the narrow mountain valley was a hungry country. The family patriarch didn't seem worried. He said God had chosen the valley to be their home. It dawned on the old miner that God might be willing for them to pay just about any price. They agreed on $450,000, twice the offer from the national park, which had been bound by strict agency appraisal rules.

Pilgrim had his own binding rules. The Book of Ezekiel, among others, speaks against extracting usury. He agreed to pay in annual increments of $30,000 without interest. They wrote out the deal on a table napkin. Pilgrim turned to a daughter, Hosanna, who produced a shoe box with the first payment in rolls of hundred-dollar bills. After three years, the big family's annual Alaska Permanent Fund Dividend payments from the state's investments of oil revenues—$1,963.86 per person the previous year—had accumulated nicely.

Papa Pilgrim was gleeful. The family returned to "Old McCarthy Town," as Pilgrim had started calling it, to celebrate with their new friends and neighbors. There would be music and dancing at the McCarthy Lodge. Snow still lingered but the days were getting longer, and the springtime sun was bright at eight that evening when the family appeared on the street, striding toward the saloon with their instruments. Pete McCarthy, still in town doing research, wrote that they looked like they were headed to a gunfight, though only Papa wore a pistol on his belt.

Neil and Doug had laid out food on the breakfast table because the Pilgrims would not enter the saloon. Pilgrim introduced his wife, Country Rose, a redoubtable woman with a tired half smile who sometimes played a stand-up bass, and then the children by name, the older musicians from before, and now the midsized sprouts, Job, Noah, and Abraham, and the little blond girls, Psalms, Lamb, and Bethlehem. He announced that their new home up McCarthy Creek would henceforth be known as Hillbilly Heaven. He said this with a Santa Claus sparkle in eyes that Pete McCarthy noticed were "extremely bright." The British writer, reveling in the strangeness of his namesake Alaska town, was utterly charmed.

The kids have spotted the cheese and fruit and cake and cookies, but make no attempt to eat until someone offers the food around. A couple of them have bare feet. I'm not sure whether they took their boots off at the door or whether they walked down here in the snow like that. They take the instruments out of their cases and sit in a semicircle. There are twenty-six people in the room, and sixteen of them are Pilgrims. Pa makes a little speech of welcome, and then they start playing. It's electrifying, moving and raw. Elishaba, the eldest, alternates lead vocals with nineteen-year-old Joshua as they trade licks on their violins. They have powerful, cutting voices, strengthened by singing outdoors, and sound like themselves rather than imitations of anyone else. Thirteen-year-old Jerusalem is a ferocious mandolin player, standing to take instrumental breaks then taking her seat again as her brothers and sisters, and Ma and Pa, continue the vocals. They've already written two songs about McCarthy, and they play them both tonight. At one point they put all the instruments down and sing a cappella in multipart harmony. Neil calls out a title, and they start doing requests. By now the three tiniest girls are holding hands and dancing in a circle, and the only ones not involved are two of the boys, about seven and nine years old at a guess—I think it would be hard to keep track even if you were their dad—who are lurking at the back. Suddenly they charge forward and start clog-dancing for all they're worth, legs jiggling and big green boots flailing beneath wild grins as the whole room comes alive with them. It's been a special evening. It's hard to believe they've only been playing for four years, and it'll be no surprise if in years to come some of these kids are earning a living playing in brighter lights than McCarthy can offer. By the time they finish, we are indeed in hillbilly heaven.

Talk turned to the new land. Pilgrim was told that traveling the thirteen miles to the Mother Lode camp would be tough. The family would never get their vehicles up the valley. The bridges are all gone, the road is washed away, the snow is melting with breakup at hand,

and where it survives the trail is so tangled in willows and alders that even summertime backpackers can't find their way.

"We're gonna be okay," Papa Pilgrim told the Englishman. "Don't make it in one day, we'll take two. Don't make it in two, then three. Whatever it takes. We got ropes, winches, all kinds of stuff. These kids can do most things." As if to prove the point, a woman came in looking for help with her snowmachine and one of the clever little boys ran out and switched out a family headlight so she could journey home.

Pete McCarthy adjourned "for a drop of the devil's brew" with Doug Miller at the bar, where they admired a photo of the singer John Denver and Doug's mother in McCarthy in 1975. Meanwhile, Neil Darish headed across the icy street with Pilgrim to inspect the latest improvements to Ma Johnson's Hotel. Late into the night, Darish and Pilgrim talked in the small hotel lobby about what lay ahead with the national park and tourism and Old McCarthy Town. Darish had grown excited about everything the Pilgrims would add to the local mix—their appearance, their handy skills, their resourcefulness, their optimism, their old-time religion. Their authenticity. There was just one thing about their old-fashioned ways that worried him, and finally he blurted it out.

"Papa, I just want you to hear it from me," he said. "You need to know that Doug and I are gay. That doesn't matter a bit to most people in McCarthy. Folks here live and let live. But I don't know how you might feel about it."

Papa Pilgrim replied slowly, his drawl emerging from his tangled gray beard as a kind of wistful sigh.

"Neil, you haven't judged me. We don't judge people either. We're here to mind our own business, to live quiet and peaceful lives, to work with our hands and sing our pleasant songs. Now I don't expect to see a street corner preacher here in McCarthy anytime soon, telling people how they ought to live. But if a preacher like that does show up, I can tell you that Pilgrim won't be here listening. He'll be home with his family at Hillbilly Heaven, telling them the truth."

It was as if Pilgrim's bright blue eyes had peered into Darish's heart. The accepting and nonjudgmental patriarch had made an important friend and ally.

Within days, the Pilgrims were battling their way up McCarthy Creek to their new home, and Pete McCarthy was headed out the gravel road to civilization. The road from McCarthy, he wrote, was "a tough drive through ruts and potholes and glacial debris, but I hope the Alaskan authorities never upgrade it. Easy access would change McCarthy forever."

From Alaska, it would be off to Ireland in a final search for the origins of his elusive namesake prospector. *The Road to McCarthy* would be Pete McCarthy's final book. Upon its release, its author was diagnosed with cancer. He died eight months later, at age fifty-two. He left behind a prediction about the Pilgrim Family that would prove, unusually for him, an understatement:

> It's almost midnight when I head across to Ma Johnson's to go to bed. Pa Pilgrim and Country Rose and Neil are sitting in the lobby talking, with a selection of children asleep in chairs and sofas all around them. They pick up a couple of the smallest kids, and the big kids pick up some of the medium-sized ones, and they say goodnight and head off into the darkness to their makeshift camp. I wonder how things will turn out for them and the town of McCarthy? Whatever happens, it seems unlikely to be dull. Seventeen people can't fail to make an impact.

2

History's Shadow

I F SOMETHING seemed a little strange about Papa Pilgrim's rustic charm, no one in McCarthy was inclined to press the matter. His origins were naturally a subject of curiosity. But an old frontier constraint against stirring the embers of a neighbor's past still prevailed in the Wrangell Mountains. It would be a long time, then, before the first of Pilgrim's secrets emerged—that the wandering hillbilly had grown up in the top echelons of Texas society, in an affluent Fort Worth neighborhood of well-kept lawns and shade trees, country clubs and sports cars. That he was the son of a Texas-size hero. And that his journey into the wilderness had started when his defiance of one of the most powerful men in Texas led to the death of a beautiful girl.

He was Bobby Hale in those high school days. His father, I. B. Hale, had been a three-hundred-pound, two-time all-American football tackle for Texas Christian University in Fort Worth. In 1938— the year Kennecott Copper closed its Alaska mines for good—TCU

▲

Bobby Hale and John Connally's daughter, Kathleen, 1959

was the undefeated national collegiate football champion. I. B. Hale was cocaptain of the team. His roommate was the Heisman Trophy-winning quarterback Davey O'Brien, the player for whom the national collegiate quarterback-of-the-year award is now named.

I. B. Hale was a first-round draft pick out of college by the Washington Redskins. But he turned down the pros to remain in Texas, where he signed up instead with the Federal Bureau of Investigation (along with his close friend O'Brien, who played briefly in the pros for the Philadelphia Eagles). Hale married beauty and wealth. He became head of the FBI's Dallas office and a friend of FBI chief J. Edgar Hoover. He left the bureau in 1951 to become security chief at the local General Dynamics fighter jet plant. He was admired in the community. But he was an inconstant husband and father, lavishing attention on public charities but not on his family. He was an enthusiastic dancer and bridge player at the local country club, where he had an affair with his wife's best friend that would end his marriage, and where he dropped dead of a heart attack in 1971 at age fifty-five.

Papa Pilgrim bragged privately to his children that he couldn't even get a speeding ticket when he was growing up because his father was so respected. But there was a sadness in the way he spoke of I.B., because for all the man's dashing qualities, he'd never had a lot of time for Bobby. He traveled a lot—he worked out of Kansas City for the bureau at one point, while his family remained in Texas—and when I.B. got home he usually had to sort out some trouble Bobby had gotten into. Nor did Bobby ever forgive his father for the affair, which he was forced to keep secret from his mother, Virginia, until it led to divorce and his father's second marriage. At least that was what Pilgrim later told his family—the assertion must be measured against the son's own complicated relations with women in the years to come.

Bobby did have the company of an identical twin brother, Billy. They were born in 1941. By the time they were college age, Bobby and Billy still looked enough alike to take tests for each other. One way to tell them apart was that Bobby had broken his nose many times. He was a trained boxer and an aggressive playground scrapper. He liked to drink and fight. He was headstrong—he once ran off and got an oilfield job against his father's orders—but he was good-looking and charming as well. He dressed sharply, drove a Thunderbird, and carried himself like he was something special. "As a kid, he could really snow you," his stepmother recalled.

Bobby's troubles got the twins sent away to an Episcopal prep school in Tennessee, but by the start of 1959 they were back as juniors at Arlington Heights High School, the affluent public school in west Fort Worth. One of their schoolmates was John Deutschendorf, a guitar player who later became famous as the singer John Denver and showed up in McCarthy, Alaska, in 1975 to make a pro-conservation movie. Singers Shawn Phillips and Delbert McClinton also attended in those years. Another schoolmate, when they were freshmen, was Lee Harvey Oswald, whose mother had just moved to a poor neighborhood in the district. And then there was the daughter of fast-rising Fort Worth lawyer and politician John Connally.

Her name was Kathleen, but Bobby called her by her nickname, KK. A young beauty, brown-eyed, chestnut-haired, an honors student, and popular with her peers, Kathleen was fifteen years old when she started sneaking out at night with Bobby Hale. Her father was legal counsel for the millionaire Fort Worth oilman Sid Richardson. He was also a close and longtime associate of Senate majority leader Lyndon Baines Johnson, having managed Johnson's first successful campaign for U.S. Senate in 1948. John Connally would go on to become a three-term governor of Texas, secretary of the Treasury for President Richard Nixon, and, most famously, the man wounded by Oswald in the front seat of John F. Kennedy's limousine in Dallas in 1963.

The Hale and Connally families knew each other socially. Kathleen, the oldest of four children, had always been a source of great pride to her family. But after she started helping Bobby with his homework and then dating him, she drew away. "We began to notice a subtle change in Kathleen. Suddenly a wall had gone up that we could not penetrate," Connally wrote in an autobiography published the year of his death in 1993. It was the only place he ever mentioned Bobby Hale in public. The name of his book was *In History's Shadow*.

First it was her behavior, her schoolwork, her time on the phone. Bobby was very good at making a girlfriend jealous, recalled Kathleen's friend and locker mate, Patsy Dorris, who was dating (and later married) Bobby's twin brother. Bobby would make sure KK saw him carrying another girl's books, but deny it meant anything. Then, after one of her parents' frequent trips to Washington, a teacher from school called to say Kathleen, now sixteen, had been sick in class—and it appeared to be morning sickness. The Connallys interrogated KK and Bobby, separately and together, with growing impatience. The teenagers insisted nothing was wrong. Kathleen was grounded. But one night in March 1959, she snuck out again anyway.

Connally recalled waiting up to meet her when she got home at midnight: "She repeated once again that nothing was wrong. And then I slapped her. Even as I did it, I wished that I hadn't. A thousand times since—maybe more—I have wanted to call back my hand. She was silent. The slap echoed in my ear. She turned and went to her room."

Connally flew off again the next day to the nation's capital, and that night Kathleen loaded her clothes in the family station wagon and left, ignoring her mother's tears. Bobby Hale and Kathleen drove to Ardmore, Oklahoma, where they could get married despite their youth, then on to Tallahassee, Florida. Once they had settled into a grim little second-story apartment and Bobby got a job in a shipyard, Kathleen wrote her parents. I. B. Hale and John Connally drove at once to Florida. Kathleen was indeed pregnant. The fathers were greeted warmly, but were rebuffed when they pleaded for the kids to come home. Connally was disturbed to hear from the landlady downstairs that the young couple argued frequently. Kathleen had even left the apartment for several days to stay in a hotel, but the newlyweds had reconciled. "Kathleen was determined to prove that what she had done was not a mistake, not a fiasco," Connally wrote. "She felt that what she had done was wrong, that she had disappointed us, but that she would somehow make it all turn out right."

The fathers drove home. A week later, on April 28, 1959, Kathleen was dead.

The teenagers had been married for forty-four days.

The Connallys and Hales rushed to Tallahassee in Sid Richardson's corporate plane. Bobby had been placed in protective custody overnight after threatening to throw himself off the apartment balcony in grief.

He had been the only one present when the shotgun went off.

A coroner's inquest was held the very next day. Given the prominence of the parents, it was front-page news in Texas and Florida.

Bobby conceded they'd been fighting. Earlier they had fought over a bathtub ring that KK failed to clean properly, he said. When she died, it was something even less important—really just a discussion, he said. But she had walked out and disappeared overnight. He searched all over town, little suspecting she was hiding in the landlady's apartment downstairs. The landlady said Kathleen was "thoroughly frightened." A police officer said she'd come by the local station that morning. KK wrote Bobby a letter saying she was hurt in mind and soul. She felt he didn't love her anymore.

Bobby testified before the inquest jury that when he returned to the apartment at noon, his sixteen-year-old bride was sitting on the couch, holding his 20-gauge shotgun. She had it pointed at her head, her finger on the trigger. He didn't even know she could load it. He said he got on his knees and tried to talk her into putting down the gun. Then he stood as if to casually stub out a cigarette.

"At the last desperate moment I lunged at the gun. I hit it as hard as I could. It hit the wall and she was still . . ." His voice trailed away, and he sat, mute and wide-eyed. I. B. Hale, sitting in the audience, wept.

After several moments, the judge asked, "Did the gun go off before you hit it?"

"I don't know. She opened her eyes once, looked at me, and fell to the floor. I caught her and said 'KK.' "

The circumstances were certainly suspicious. The shotgun wound was behind her right ear. No fingerprints were found on the gun, according to extensive press coverage. There was testimony about how she tried to get away. Her friends back home couldn't believe Kathleen would ever threaten to kill herself. But Bobby's story was supported by a lie-detector test.

The inquest took less than a day. The coroner's jury ruled the shooting an accident. The families flew straight back to Texas. Nobody seemed interested in a drawn-out investigation.

Senator Lyndon Johnson—KK's "Uncle Lindy"—canceled a lunch in Washington with former president Harry Truman and flew back to Texas to serve as a pallbearer at the funeral. The sanctuary of the First Methodist Church was filled with political friends of the Connallys and teenaged friends of the young couple. Bobby entered on the arm of I. B. Hale.

"I have not spoken to Bobby since then," Connally wrote in the chapter of his autobiography titled "Kathleen." "Over the years, he has attempted to call me. I have never taken his call, nor will I. If this seems flinty and cold, so be it. Our daughter was gone and so was Bobby Hale, as far as I was concerned."

Connally wrote that the death of his vivacious daughter left a burden of sorrow more profound than any tragedy in his life—his later bribery trial, his bankruptcy, even the assassination of a president.

"This is the first time I have ever discussed it in any detail," he concluded, "and it will also be the last."

3

The Bollard Wars

NOT LONG after the concert at the McCarthy Lodge celebrating the Pilgrims' new home, the National Park Service stepped forth to welcome the family to the McCarthy Creek valley.

One generation earlier, when Wrangell–St. Elias National Park was first created, such a gesture from emissaries of the federal government would have seemed presumptuous, if not rashly provocative. The new parks had been controversial in Alaska. Park rangers were being refused service in restaurants and stores in the regional crossroads town of Glennallen. They were booted from their motel rooms

The Pilgrim Family band, Fourth of July parade in McCarthy, 2002

and had their office lease revoked. In 1979, somebody even torched the rangers' Cessna 180 at the Tazlina Glacier Lodge airstrip.

But these days a friendly welcome struck the park's managers as appropriate. Twenty years had passed. The government's presence in the mountain range was indisputably established. The Pilgrims were the newcomers.

There was, to be sure, some urgency to the park rangers' overture. This big family was moving lock, stock, and barrel into a valley that had seen little human disturbance since the park was established. The three Pilgrim properties were, moreover, noncontiguous. In the old days, miners had never worried how they got from one place to another. But now arrangements would be necessary. Even in Alaska, a person could get in real trouble driving cross-country through a national park.

On May 3, 2002, assistant superintendent Hunter Sharp, who was also the park's chief law enforcement ranger, stopped by Walt Wigger's one-room shack in town, a wooden gypsy wanigan on wheels with a smokestack. The family was setting up a kind of base camp, stacking lumber and supplies and staking out their horses. Accompanying Sharp was Marshall Neeck, the park ranger based at Kennecott—or "Kennicott," as the locals persisted in spelling it.

Pilgrim was not home. The older sons would not make eye contact with the rangers or speak, except to caution that the big mountain dogs were biters.

Three days later, Sharp tried again, this time in writing.

Dear Mr. Pilgrim,

I am writing you to welcome you and your family to McCarthy Creek. You have selected a beautiful place for your home. I have heard from some of the people you have met around McCarthy that you and your family are very talented musicians. I am sure that your family will have much to offer to the community. . . .

I was hoping that we would have a chance to talk at some point. I stopped by your lot in McCarthy on Friday to welcome your family to the area. The two young men there told me to stay off the property, a request that I complied with.

He said he hoped to avoid any problems.

I know from my own experience that living with a National Park is different than living next to some of the other public lands such as National Forest lands or State of Alaska lands because the land use regulations are different. Owning land within a National Park does not necessarily mean that you cannot do what you want with the land that you own. However, I am convinced that we will both have an easier time if we can discuss some of the restrictions that may apply to the use of the public lands before any issues come up to create barriers between us.

At the McCarthy airstrip, the envelope from the Park Service went unclaimed in the mail shack.

Later, Neil Darish approached Hunter Sharp and said he'd been asked to inform the park ranger that the Pilgrims intended to read the park regulations for themselves and did not wish to be contacted for any reason.

The Park Service looked up the new deed for the Wigger place and found the surnames "Sunstar" and "Hale." They began making calls to other agencies. A ranger flew a small plane up McCarthy Creek and took photos of a fresh clearing around Wigger's cabins. A bulldozer had opened a road across a few hundred yards of public land to the Spokane placer airstrip, and there appeared to be new switchbacks up the rockslides toward the Mother Lode Mine.

In June, Chief Ranger Sharp sent a terser letter, this time to Mr. Robert Hale. He said the National Park Service was undertaking a program to secure openings to the abandoned underground workings connected to the Kennecott Mines National Historic Landmark. A park crew would be arriving by helicopter in July to install metal gates and plugs at mine shafts proximal to the Mother Lode claims. The crew also intended to make a boundary survey of the Spokane placer site and Marvelous Millsite. Mr. Hale was encouraged to get in touch with District Ranger Neeck if he had any questions.

The letter was left unopened at the mail shack with a boot mark on it. The Park Service then posted the same information in a public notice in the shack. They returned to find a sheet titled "AKA Pilgrim's Public Notice #1" nailed directly over theirs.

The Park Service officials have pursued our family with harassment and threats. We want the folks of McCarthy and Kennicott to understand that the park's attitude and actions are unwarranted, and legally unfounded.

The Pilgrim Family declared they would henceforth enforce their claim to all long-standing and existing rights-of-way connected to their mining properties, and deny access to park rangers for any survey or mine closure.

Representatives of the National Park Service have been noted publicly in the past to deny any recognition or legality of previous right-of-ways within the park, including even our beloved McCarthy Road a lifeline for it's people.

We feel it is important for us to "disclaim" ANY AND ALL of their false claims and disallow their continual course of threats, harassment's, and proposals about our private land holdings.

✛

ON A sunny day soon after Hunter Sharp delivered his terse letter to the Pilgrims, everyone in McCarthy headed up the mountain to attend a memorial at Kennicott. The Pilgrims went along, too. There would be food and music and speeches. People were calling it a big event—the end of an era.

The memorial was for Chris Richards, a slight, animated man with a broom-straw beard and wire-rim glasses who had died in a fire the previous winter. Richards had been known informally as the Mayor of Kennicott. Now people were also referring to him as the seventh and last victim of the mail-day massacre. The older Pilgrim children had heard stories about the murders of six people in McCarthy, back in the early days of the park. Papa told them it was not a fit topic for discussion.

A hundred people, including Chris Richards's family from down south, gathered in Kennicott that day above a glacial moraine covered with picturesquely rusting industrial junk. Several Park Service employees were present as well. The agency had been giving the old mining and mill complex a lot of attention lately. In a park created in part to protect the continent's last wilderness from mineral exploitation, it turned out that visitors were especially fascinated to encounter the lost industrial city, the massive falling-down buildings of the private company town whose red paint and white trim, peeling with age, provided a ready emblem for the "rape-ruin-and-run" development that environmentalists had warned against during the fight to establish the park.

Tourists liked to explore the fourteen-story crushing mill and leaching plant that stepped down the mountainside in terraces of heavy timbers. They poked through the power station and the bosses' homes built on a short loop of gravel dubbed "Silk Stocking Row." There was a hospital, a school, a store and assay office, even a small gymnasium with a knot-free hardwood floor. The way everyone disappeared overnight when the mines closed in 1938 added to the mystique.

The park was tightening things up, but for the longest time, anyone could wander through the buildings, picking up hospital records or a handful of bolts left in bins at the company store. They could climb the mountain on a half-day hike to the abandoned mines—the Bonanza, the Jumbo, the Erie. The ground at Kennicott was still littered with spilled chunks of blue copper azurite and green malachite. Some of the structures were collapsing, with alders growing up through the floorboards. It was, in short, not only the implacable beauty of the mountain wilderness but the atmosphere of decline and fall, the passing of bygone dreams, that gave shape to the visitor's experience in America's biggest national park.

Chris Richards's little red millworker's cabin at Kennicott was where the violence had started that morning in 1983. His new neighbor, a bald, bushy-bearded computer programmer named Lou Hastings, showed up at the cabin on mail day and started shooting. They were the only two people in Kennicott at the time. Richards was full of questions afterward. Why did Hastings take out his hatred of the world on people who had come so far to get away from it? And why put on a silencer to kill the only other person in a ghost town? Richards managed to plunge a kitchen knife into Hastings's thigh and escaped into the snow in his sock feet, bleeding from a hole in his cheek. He was flown to safety by a local pilot, who warned away the approaching mail plane and summoned the troopers. Six others meeting the mail plane that day, including a young newlywed couple who helped Richards onto the plane and stayed to warn the rest, were shot from ambush and killed.

In the two decades since the murders, Richards had stayed on in his little tinder-dry cabin with no electricity, hauling water in plastic jugs, living altogether more primitively than Kennecott employees had in the 1920s. His black pirate flag didn't scare anyone. Tourists peered in his windows. He had fled a broken heart to "the middle of nowhere" and now, he complained, he was living in a fishbowl. But he liked to tell visitors about the history of the mines. Some days he would also tell about getting shot in the face by the mail-day killer. He said it was like Hastings had taken a piece of his own insanity and shoved it in Richards's brain. "My doctor said I should marry an ophthalmologist," was one punch line. "I asked if she could be a lawyer-nymphomaniac, too." Friends knew him as lovable and vulnerable except when he was drinking. One time some tourists were afraid to cross the footbridge in McCarthy because Richards was standing on the far side, waving a pistol in one hand and a bottle in the other. The winter the Pilgrims arrived, he had been struggling to dry out— not for the first time. His cabin was plagued by skittering insects that only he could see. Friends had warned him about excessively spraying wasp killer around the hot woodstove.

He died on the night of the Christmas pageant at McCarthy's little missionary church. The local pastor almost canceled the event when temperatures dropped to forty below for a week and not even snowmachines would run. But the cold let up and a few dozen friends and neighbors made it after all, mingling for a potluck supper and still talking, in a place that often featured weeks-long gaps in conversations, about the fallen twin towers from that September. Even far from New York City, they said, it felt especially important to come together that year as a community. So with heavy winter coveralls and boots piled downstairs, the people of McCarthy stood side by side in their sock feet, fervent Christians and nonbelievers, and sang "Silent Night" while outside the generator rumbled through the darkest hours of an Alaska winter.

They saw the light up at Kennicott as they walked back across the footbridge to their trucks. Miles across the glacier, it burned bright like a Christmas star, a single pinprick in the silent sweep of stars and ice. The glow flickered and brightened, throwing shadows up the mountain. A call to Kennicott on the new phone at the church confirmed that it was a fire and made the families on the bridge feel helpless and guilty after the neighborly warmth in the church. The good news was that years earlier Chris Richards's cabin had been dragged away from the other historic buildings into a leveled yard of mine tailings. The bad news was that his white husky mix was whining outside the cabin door.

At the memorial six months later in June, people said it was going to be hard to imagine Kennicott without Chris Richards. In a way, his loss marked the end of McCarthy's transition from hideout to tourist attraction. Richards had been so much a part of the contradictory spirit of that transition, both embracing and resisting the national park's plans to fix up the ruins, embracing and resisting the visitors who paid him for tours through the sagging red buildings and across collapsing foundations, his acid historical narrative veering into more recent anecdotes of tourists who tried to walk off with souvenirs from his porch.

Then again, eras were always ending here. It was the natural sadness of living on a frontier, a counterpoint to the great excitement of opening something new.

And new things were indeed starting to happen. Three weeks after the Kennicott fire, the Pilgrim Family had showed up in McCarthy.

THE FOURTH of July was a big occasion in McCarthy in copper-mining days, when it was the only day, other than Christmas, that the miners got off work. The streets would be decorated with red, white, and blue bunting for parades featuring marching bands, followed by baseball games between the McCarthy Tigers and the Kennecott Bear Cats and sometimes a team off the train from Cordova, the town at the steamship docks on the other end of the line. These days, the Fourth is still a big deal. A hundred visitors might show up in McCarthy for the improvised events—a parade of the oldest surviving trucks in town, mud wrestling by female mountain guides, a slowest-bicycle race.

In 2002, the parade featured the newly arrived Pilgrim Family band, performing in the back of a pickup truck that crept past the lodge followed by Papa on horseback.

The nation's birthday served to remind the area's lone full-time government employee that there had still been no official contact with the new family up McCarthy Creek. The date for shutting off the Mother Lode entrance and surveying the Pilgrims' property lines was growing near.

Marshall Neeck took off his NPS uniform and drove his four-wheeler down from Kennicott. Outside McCarthy's red railroad depot, which now housed a small museum, he saw the town's last gold miner, Randy Elliott, in conversation with Papa Pilgrim and three sons. In his incident report, Neeck noted that one of the sons wore a pistol.

"I'm looking for a Mr. Hale," the ranger said, sitting on his four-wheeler in the street.

"There's no one here by that name," said Elliott.

"I'm hoping I can talk to someone in the Pilgrim Family?"

Elliott gestured at the older man standing next to a pickup truck. "That's him."

"I'm Marshall Neeck, and I want to apologize for any misunderstandings that . . ."

"You can stop right there," Pilgrim said. "I've said all I'm going to say."

"I was hoping that you can tell me how we can communicate," Neeck said.

"If you keep speaking, I'll get in my truck and drive off. I hope you can respect that."

"I do respect that," Neeck said, "and I respect your privacy and way of life. I was just asking how we can communicate."

"That's it," said Pilgrim, getting into his truck. The sons stirred, glaring at the ranger.

Neeck did not want to start anything. He drove away.

☨

ABOUT ONE thing, the Pilgrims' neighbors had been right. Getting to the land at Hillbilly Heaven proved a vexing logistical problem. That first spring, the family had all snowmachined up to the homestead. But when Country Rose and the oldest boys went back to the road system to get supplies, the snow deteriorated quickly. Alders poked through where they choked off the old mining road. Papa and the girls and young children were trapped. The boys arranged for a local pilot, Gary Green, to airdrop boxes of groceries.

A feeling of desperation settled in. It was left to Elishaba, the oldest daughter, to find meat. She scaled the mountainside above the cabin with a rifle slung over her shoulder and her little brother Israel following. When she found herself hanging from a bush on a cliff, she ordered Israel not to look down. The mountain goat she shot tumbled nearly back to the valley floor. It was badly pounded and she had no license and the season was closed, but it was the first meat they'd seen and her father praised her when she carried it through the cabin door.

Once the snow melted, travel up the valley on horseback required crossing the creek again and again. They scraped off the airstrip but hiring local bush pilots to fly them from McCarthy was eating through their savings.

In midsummer, the two oldest Pilgrim sons, Joseph and Joshua, spent a week at Wigger's wanigan in town rebuilding a tracked vehicle that they hoped to use over the trail to the Mother Lode. The journey turned out to be exceptionally arduous, however, with willows leafed out and alders grown thick, and steep gravel climbs at every stream crossing.

Joseph and Joshua had made it partway home when they heard the rumble of heavy equipment and came around a corner to find their father at the controls of the D5 Caterpillar left at Wigger's mining claims. He had come from the homestead, clearing the wagon road as he traveled.

How was the trip from town, boys? he asked.

Really tough, they said.

"You'll have it easy the rest of the way," Pilgrim said with a big smile.

For the next three days, the boys helped their father push the bulldozer's eight-foot blade toward McCarthy, carving through berms of river rock and cutting new trail where the bank had washed away. Pilgrim told his sons they were doing maintenance of the Green Butte Road. But each night, he covered the Cat with a camouflage tarp under trees so the Park Service could not see it from the air. When they got close to town, they left the last stretch disguised as rough trail and turned back up the valley.

McCARTHY DID not split into pro-Pilgrim and anti-Pilgrim factions right away. At first, the newcomers mystified one and all. They made a curious sight in town that first summer, clustered together in their pioneer garb and talking among themselves, like travelers who didn't speak the local language. The youngest children met tourists at the footbridge and offered rides to Kennicott in a horse-drawn wagon. A few visitors wondered if they might be Amish. This quaint effort siphoned off a little business from the existing van shuttle service, but the van's owner was sympathetic and didn't object.

Then the Bollard Wars broke out again.

The bollards were steel and concrete posts, sunk deep into the riverside gravel at either end of the footbridge across the Kennicott River. They were put in place to keep motorized vehicles from crossing the sturdy metal grating into town. To some, the bollards were a symbol of the community's effort to hold the world at bay. But dissenters had come to see them as a rebuke to the very frontier freedoms that McCarthy's yesteryear charm was supposed to evoke. Persons unknown had cut them down three times already. The previous summer, with a state trooper investigation under way, highway workers had set out to make the obstructions bombproof, installing ten-inch-diameter steel pipes filled with steel beams and concrete, welded to three-foot-square plates buried five feet deep in the gravel.

This time the bollard busters had used a torch and bulldozer to clear the way.

This dispute over access had been building in McCarthy for some time. Those who accepted traditional notions of frontier progress believed better access—a faster road, a bigger bridge—was the key to McCarthy's future. Others saw nothing wrong with a few roadblocks. The pro-footbridge association of local residents, the McCarthy Area Council, or MAC, was now opposed by a second group, the Coalition for Access to McCarthy, or CAM. When the two groups were invited to pose questions to state transportation planners regarding improved access to McCarthy, the final merged list of 122 queries, ranging from the eminently practical to the nigglingly constitutional, read like found poetry, a free-verse ode to rural Alaskan cantankerousness.

Nobody knew which side the Pilgrims would be on. If anything, people assumed the reclusive family would be opposed to "progress" of any kind, including bridge improvements.

As that summer of 2002 drew to an end, however, a surprising letter appeared in the pages of the *Wrangell St. Elias News,* the bimonthly newspaper published in a cabin across the river from town. It started off in a familiar ingratiating voice:

> We really love and appreciate the courage of all the folks of McCarthy, and I would say that we can see everybody's deep plight concerning the road and the bridge. Although it may not touch my family as close as most, as we are sort of "bent" towards the joy that extreme hardship brings, we in every way share in our hearts with you the needs and frustrations that are upon us all.

We also have been faced with challenges by Park Service threats of road, bridge and mine closures. It seems they would as soon be rid of us permanently so they could have their own way.

Papa Pilgrim then unleashed a long anathema on the Park Service, whom he accused of using deception and falsehood—and control of access and the footbridge—to divide the "in-dwellers," one against the other.

Don't they want us? Need us? Aren't we the people that represent the park and its history? Is it not the devotion of the bush pilots, hotel and lodge keepers, the miners, the families that carved out a living 200 miles from town, that form that personal and living touch that visitors come to see here in Historic Alaska?

The inholders are the real people of the Alaskan bush. After those few months of serving the park's visitors, they alone are left, as the cold winter wind is blowing, and the snow reaches the bridle of a horse. They find the joy of the silent northern lights running wild. A hot cup of coffee at the lodge to help out along the winter trail home. Where, then, are the park officials? The Department of Transportation bridge builders?

They will think of us again when winter turns to spring and break-up roars off the rivers.

They will make their secret plans to clean house in a big sweep, through harassment, fraud and deceit, as they strive for total power and control.

Once they get rid of us, then the roads will open up and become paved, bridges will be built, and fancy parking lots and motor home parks, where you'll get arrested if you leave the designated walkway or park at the wrong angle with your car.

Yes, even though I am new to all of this, it's easy to see down the trail a little ways.

Pilgrim warned his neighbors of an "onslaught of evil" before turning, like a practiced preacher, toward the bridge as a symbol of unity and a better day.

We need to see the light and realize where the battle really is—
IT IS INSIDE US!

The challenge is great, but we know that "what we sow, we will reap." Where bitter seeds are planted, hearts will harden, but a helping hand will make the harvest sweet.

The National Park Service has betrayed Alaska. This cannot be good.

But you are my neighbor—thank God you're there—let's get together. . . . We could say, "Remember the Alamo," or even better, "What must I do Lord to be saved?" I do know love is real. It works and never fails. Our survival as a community is challenged, and we love you.

In Jesus,
The Pilgrims

PILGRIM'S SURPRISING down-from-the-mountain sermon was as welcome to the pastor of McCarthy's little church as it was to the editor of the local newspaper, for they were one and the same person. Rick Kenyon was a self-made frontiersman, no more trained in journalism when he started the paper than he had been in ministry when he started his Bible study classes in McCarthy—or for that matter, in carpentry when he built his first log cabin, after moving north from Florida. But he was a fast learner and a natural crusader, ready to use any pulpit available and to hammer together additional pulpits as necessary. He was delighted to discover a new ally whose finely honed sense of political grievance and vigorous begetting seemed certain to tilt the hand count at community meetings in Kenyon's favor.

The *Wrangell St. Elias News* coverage of the Bollard Wars had not been entirely fair and balanced. It was characterized by a certain vagueness regarding the laws against criminal vandalism, the possible identity of the perpetrators, or indeed the existence of any local support whatsoever for the bollards. The bollard busters could as easily be called patriots as vandals, the paper opined. Reporting focused on the government bureaucrats trying to choke off access to McCarthy—state Department of Transportation officials whose inertia had long prevented major improvements to the gravel road from Chitina, and now, increasingly, officials with the national park, in thrall to distant urban elites and unmoved by the struggles of Americans living on the wrong side of the Kennicott River, like the Kenyons, who were forced by the bollards to park at the footbridge and walk to their own church.

"Some people are starting to think of NPS as DOT with a badge and a gun. Now there is a scary thought," Kenyon wrote.

McCarthy had several boosterish newspapers back in mining days but never a church until the Kenyons arrived—not even during the height of the copper boom, when the town had nearly three hundred residents, saloons selling bootleg white mule from stills out at the creeks, and a row of fourteen little cabins for working girls with names such as Tin Can Annie, the Beef Trust, and the valley's first black female, Blanche. Long after the mines closed, however, the area did attract an end-of-the-world sect when a religious leader named Brother Ivy moved to Chitina with his followers, bought the Chitina Cash Store and renamed it the Light House Mission, and assembled a windowless log house in anticipation of the big finale in April 1976. The saga of the Ivy Sect's disappointment was still remembered by a few old-timers, its conclusion spelled out in the unpublished memoir of Curtis Green, a blue-collar hermit who holed up in McCarthy those same years reading Whitman and Thoreau through the winter:

When the world did not end as scheduled, the clan members gradually faded away. Brother Ivy and his wife remained and

eventually opened a small grocery store/gas station on the edge
of town . . . and Brother Ivy developed a bizarre, nay grotesque,
physical condition. Testicular elephantiasis? Goiter of the go-
nads? Who knows? He never had it diagnosed, as he would
have nothing to do with doctors—I can't knock him for that, but
there is a limit—claiming that the Lord would heal him. Now,
that's faith—even after the Lord failed to end the world when
He was supposed to. His balls grew to truly gargantuan propor-
tions, so that he could no longer wear trousers, wearing instead
a long robe that reached to his feet. When you would come into
the store, he would waddle out from the living area (his wife was
a recluse and never waited on customers), you could not help
but notice this massive bulge that reached to his knees, swaying ponderously beneath the folds of his robe as he walked. I am
not exaggerating, nor do I wish to poke fun at his unfortunate
condition, that is simply the way it was. Actually, I kind of liked
Brother Ivy, he mellowed out and I will have to say that he never
once tried to push his religion. But his balls were famous state-
wide and for a while were Chitina's biggest tourist attraction.

Just as the Ivy Sect was disintegrating, Rick Kenyon, a Florida gunsmith, felt called to Alaska to do the Lord's work. His wife,
Bonnie, wasn't convinced—"I would have to hear God tell me that
in an audible voice," she told her husband, thinking she had ended
the discussion about leaving Florida. A few weeks later, she turned
on an Oral Roberts television special, and on the screen was Lowell
Thomas, Jr., a bush pilot and the forty-ninth state's lieutenant governor, pointing at the camera and saying, "If you want to get close to
God, go to Alaska." Bonnie wept and started packing.

After twenty-three years in McCarthy, Rick and Bonnie Kenyon
were warm and welcoming neighbors, affable in person, as ready to
help pull a traveler from a ditch or offer a fresh slice of pie as they were

to advise in print on the proper functioning of a well-regulated militia. They were busy fillers of economic niches, running a bed-and-breakfast, selling propane, and taking daily weather readings for the federal government. Despite a subscriber list boosted by summer residents and Alaska history buffs, it was no small commitment to put out a bimonthly newspaper in a community whose residents numbered in the dozens. The *Wrangell St. Elias News* had its small-town charms: "Items of Interest," an intimate kind of pre-Facebook posting of community comings and goings; long articles about Kennicott history and rampaging bears; and "Good News from the Wrangells," a homey religious column ("If God had a refrigerator, your picture would be on it").

Lately, however, the pastor/editor's antigovernment fervor had been heating up. Anticipating national politics by half a decade, he was invoking the Boston Tea Party to explain the Bollard Wars. Now here came the Pilgrims with reinforcements. In truth, Rick Kenyon had misgivings about the family at first. For all their apparent devotion to the Bible's word, they had not seen fit to join his congregation at the McCarthy-Kennicott Community Church. And despite their evident poverty and many mouths to feed, Papa Pilgrim insisted on rounding his propane charges up to the nearest five dollars rather than handle the "satanic" pyramids on one-dollar bills. But Kenyon remembered how the park had tried to buy Wigger's land and got turned down. He had seen the public notices about the Pilgrims around town. It made sense to him that a finger-wagging park administration would try to run this meek and eccentric Christian family off and take their land. Kenyon's light-in-the-forest evangelism had always thrived best in the face of adversity and struggle. He realized, as he prepared Pilgrim's letter about the Bollard Wars for publication, that the crusade against oppressive government in McCarthy might have found something even more important than a new and multitudinous ally. It had found a new cause.

☦

THERE WAS more to McCarthy than the community depicted in Kenyon's newspaper—a statement to which some of Kenyon's more acerbic and fed-up local readers might have added, "Praise the Lord." There were neighbors, for instance, who considered the bollards a useful innovation in social engineering, and some who saw the wilderness inside the national park as their natural place of worship.

Within weeks of his family's arrival, Pilgrim had a run-in with a summer institute that had been bringing small numbers of college students to McCarthy for thirty years.

Pilgrim told the Wrangell Mountains Center that students were no longer welcome to make their annual backpacking trek up McCarthy Creek. The reason he gave was that he'd heard the college students sometimes camped in the nude. His own children had never been exposed to the naked human body, he said. In fact, they remained fully dressed even when they bathed, a practice that kept them from temptation and sin.

The institute's leaders approached Ben Shaine, the emeritus teacher and one-man think tank who had helped start the college program years ago, wondering how to respond to Pilgrim's edict. Shaine relished the teachable moment—could there be a better illustration of the conservationists' argument that private ownership, not public parks, was the ultimate "lock-up" of land? Rick Kenyon's newspaper was fulminating about bollards and access, but the environmental studies program was the only group whose access was actually getting cut off. He loved the way students arrived in McCarthy every year expecting a summer of rural repose and left with their heads spinning at the complexities of life on the modern frontier.

Shaine's second thought was that this was probably about something more than allegations of nudity. Even fully clothed, college-age young people were likely to be distracting for Pilgrim's older offspring, who were taking noticeable detours to avoid the old false-fronted Hardware Store where the program was based. It was certainly true that the visiting students were curious in turn about this strange family, with its radical rejection of society and commitment to live by its ideals. Then again, Shaine recalled an incident years earlier when a group of college-age campers, hot and sweaty after a backpacking trip, had defied mosquitoes as well as social convention to shock a few locals on their triumphal march into town.

It was no surprise that the father of daughters named Jerusalem and Hosanna would not see eye to eye with a father who had named a daughter after the earth goddess Gaia. But Papa Pilgrim and Ben Shaine had developed a nodding acquaintance around town that first summer. One afternoon, Shaine had chatted with several Pilgrim sons by the footbridge, pointing out in his soft professorial manner that ice they could see now on the nearby glacier had started down Mount Blackburn at the time of the American Revolution. Papa gave Shaine a smiling wink, presumably for having shared a geological example within the range of biblical literalism, rather than pointing to summit ridges of limestone formed on the bottom of the Pacific Ocean two hundred million years ago.

Shaine winced, then, upon reading Pilgrim's angry letter to the newspaper about the footbridge and the national park. He sensed that an important emerging consensus about access and the future of McCarthy had encountered a formidable adversary.

Shaine had been working on building that consensus since 1971, when he first came to the Wrangells to lead an undergraduate field research project for the University of California at Santa Cruz. A geography professor at Santa Cruz, Richard Cooley, was teaching a class at the time about Alaska, asking students whether hard-won environmental lessons from the lower forty-eight could be applied to the unspoiled new state. Every year, Cooley threw open the subject of Alaska's future as if it were a window into the American soul. The university wanted to start a summer program, and McCarthy had seemed a perfect location. Oil development and Native land claims were starting to redraw the map of Alaska, and environmental groups were calling for a national park in the Wrangells. The icy landscape framed natural questions about wilderness and the role of human communities.

Shaine was soon part of the community himself, staying on for winters with his wife, Marci, a former Santa Cruz student, learning homesteader skills, and building, with experienced helpers, a house of their own on the mountainside near Kennicott. When it came time for Congress to act on the Alaska conservation bill, Shaine flew to Washington, D.C., and helped the national environmental coalition draw lines on a map of the Wrangells. He also helped ensure that the bill's provision for rural subsistence extended to the self-reliant settlers he had learned to admire around McCarthy.

As much as he appreciated the local way of life, however, he could see that too many immigrants would overwhelm it. Park protection would limit their numbers. So would difficult access. That was why Pilgrim's letter distressed him. The Wrangells were still primitive because getting there had never been easy. Even the Copper River and Northwestern Railway, that iron symbol of capitalist ambition, had declined to build a permanent bridge across the Copper River at Chitina, calculating it was cheaper to remove the rails before the violent ice breakup every spring and then rebuild a wooden trestle. In its day, there was no denying that the CR&NW—nicknamed "Can't Run and Never Will" by doubters—was an impressive engineering achievement, climbing 196 miles from Cordova on the coast, much of the way atop wooden trestles. It cost a fortune, and it generated a much larger one. But when the copper was gone, the iron was torn out for scrap. Access served its purpose, and then it went away. The last load of rails, pulled from the approach to McCarthy, was awaiting shipment on a dock at Valdez in 1964 when the big earthquake struck, spilling the iron forever into the sea.

The first summer Shaine came to the Wrangells, in 1971, he attended the ribbon-cutting ceremony for a new state highway bridge at Chitina. The poured-concrete bridge promised altogether more permanent access to McCarthy. A wide paved driveway would quickly spell an end to the magic of the place, he felt. Within two years, a crude sixty-mile gravel road had been roughed in over the CR&NW rail bed, with a bridge extended across the Kennicott River into town. McCarthy residents did double takes as strange camper trucks rolled past their windows that first summer bearing booty from the Kennecott company ruins. The state engineers, however, had not taken into account an important quirk of local geology. Every summer, a lake ten miles up the Kennicott Glacier fills slowly with meltwater and then dumps all at once, flooding the banks and scouring everything in the river's path. The highway bridge lasted only one season. Weakened, reduced to a footbridge for a few years, it eventually washed away.

After that, road improvements were stalled by controversy. Shaine and his fellow environmentalists argued that a rough gravel approach, challenging but manageable, was appropriate for the prospective frontier park. The splintery forty-year-old hand-pulled tram car across the Kennicott River, pressed into service with the loss of the makeshift footbridge, was another useful impediment. It resembled other cable trams used by prospectors in the Wrangells backcountry, where the ice-cold silty rivers were notoriously unsafe to cross on foot. For several years, the old tram into McCarthy was a primitive affair, with no rope and pulley for hauling the car back and forth. You grabbed the steel cable and worked your way across. If you were unlucky enough to show up when the platform was on the wrong side of the river, you had a choice of waiting hours for someone to show up on the far shore, firing three shots in the air to attract attention, or hiking up to where the river poured from under the glacier and crossing atop the ice.

When residents tired of wet boots, mangled fingers, and metal splinters from the badly sagging cable, they replaced the tram in

1983—with a better tram, one on which you could pull yourself and bigger loads of supplies on a loop of rope. "Kennicott Cross Purposes," residents called themselves in merry self-deprecation when they formed a nonprofit to rebuild the tram with state funds and local labor. Each of them had built a cabin or two and had a different idea about how the new tram should be designed. But they all had come to see a hand-powered device as a shrewd solution for controlling the trickle of summer tourists drawn to the new national park. A tram was a perfect "self-administering admissions interview," according to those who fretted what easy road access would bring. "If you could drive to McCarthy," said Curtis Green's brother, Loy, "it wouldn't be here."

As Shaine looked back, he remembered those days just after the mail-day murders in 1983 as a time of unusual common purpose. The town had once been divided about creating a new national park in the Wrangells. The graffito SIERRA CLUB GO HOME, bulldozed in the gravel bars of the Chitistone River by an angry prospector, was an essential scenic flyover for VIP tours of all political persuasions, until the braided river washed it away. But the murders focused everyone in a common resolve to protect their community—from nut cases, pushy park bureaucrats, and kitschy tourism developers. McCarthy would remain a refuge. Now, however, dissension over access choices and park policies had started to tear at the town. Community meetings were becoming unpleasant. From the evidence of this angry letter, the arrival of the Pilgrims was going to make things worse.

But living so long in the Wrangells had taught Shaine to take a longer view. His rusty beard was graying now, his daughters Gaia and Ardea were grown, and the classes at the Hardware Store had been taken over by a nonprofit institute. He was the only person left to have lived in the Pilgrims' chosen valley himself, having spent several winters with Marci in abandoned cabins along McCarthy Creek, exploring and hiking to the valley's nether reaches. He knew how hard life would be for the Pilgrims. Wild game was scarce, and the only agriculture he'd ever seen was a friend's marijuana plants growing in five-gallon buckets on the roof of the old Green Butte bunkhouse. Access up the old mining road, never easy, was impossible after the ravaging 1980 floods.

Shaine once wrote a novel, *Alaska Dragon,* about a fictionalized McCarthy, murders and all. His geography imagined a hidden valley like McCarthy Creek, populated by a hermit who listened to Mahler on cassettes, a geologist whose view of time was so deep that glaciers were mere ephemera, and a priest waiting to be carried off to heaven by angels. In fact, as in fiction, something about the Mother Lode valley always seemed to attract mystical adventurers and scammers whose plans didn't pan out. He urged the Wrangell Mountains Center not to press their own access issue with the Pilgrims. Better than anyone in McCarthy, Shaine knew the newcomers might not last. Few did.

WHILE PEOPLE around McCarthy struggled to size up the Pilgrim Family that first summer, the Park Service was expanding its law enforcement file. As early as May 2002, Chief Ranger Hunter Sharp had written in a memo: "I believe that there is the potential for conflict with this group in the future."

In the two decades since passage of the Alaska conservation act, disputes with so-called inholders—people who own land within national park boundaries—had been handled by administrators and resource managers, not armed park rangers. This time, however, negotiation seemed impossible. The park's superintendent resolved to make the Mother Lode owners' lack of compliance a law enforcement issue.

There was another incident in late July 2002. A Park Service helicopter flew over Bonanza Ridge to close down the last tunnel entrance to the Mother Lode mine. The Pilgrims knew they were coming. Only one flat ledge on the finback ridge could be used for helicopter landings. Park personnel found the ledge blocked by a canvas tent belonging to the Pilgrims. The mission had to be aborted.

Pilgrim's letter about the bollards in the *Wrangell St. Elias News* was added to the file. Investigators highlighted the phrase: "I DO NOT consider the park service as a person, but rather a ruthless, relentless and uncaring political system of deceptive and harmful motives."

On September 17, 2002, Hunter Sharp sent one last letter to Robert Hale, now sterner, saying they planned to proceed with a survey of his property line and insisting on his cooperation. The park had a pretty good idea of the corners, but cutting a survey line would forcefully make the point that parkland was not open to homesteading.

> *Your family has accomplished considerable ground clearing work near the Marvelous Mill Site. . . . Some of your recent ground clearing work appears to have been performed on land to which you do not hold title or to which you do not have a valid right-of-way permit, and thus is a violation of law. Please stop your clearing and ground disturbing actions on federal parklands immediately. . . .*
>
> *Mr. Hale, you have refused and rebuffed all of our attempts to communicate with you. You have publicly characterized our attempts to communicate as harassment. You have persisted in taking actions that we have reluctantly concluded to be deliberate violations of law. Many of these serious issues might have been avoided if you had cooperated with our initial attempts to establish communications with your family. Please consider this letter another attempt.*

Just as Sharp's letter was being sent, a backpacker from California started up McCarthy Creek on foot. Along with several visiting friends, Anne Beaulaurier planned to follow an old trail up the valley to Nikolai Pass. She had spent the summer hiking in the pristine, trail-free vistas of Denali National Park, fell in love with Alaska, and found work so she could stay. Denali was one of the original parks in Alaska, and friends had recommended she visit one of the new parks created in 1980.

So far, however, with its PRIVATE PROPERTY signs along the road from Chitina, coughing rusted-out trucks around town, and rowdy hunters partying at the local saloon, McCarthy and environs seemed more like the Wild West than a sacred natural treasure.

The backpackers crossed the stream on a log bridge and had hiked only a short way up McCarthy Creek when the trail opened unexpectedly into a road. Freshly cut alder and willow lay everywhere, tangling their ankles. The difficulty seemed to go on forever, Beaulaurier later told the Park Service. Finally the trail crossed the creek, and when they waded out the other side they found raw bulldozer tracks over a muddy and torn landscape. Trees alongside had been cut down, the sawdust still white and fragrant. After another mile or so, the depressed hikers turned around.

Back in McCarthy, they griped about the mess they'd seen along McCarthy Creek. No one knew what they were talking about.

It was early winter before a ranger flew another reconnaissance mission up the valley. He reported back to the superintendent that Papa Pilgrim had bulldozed his own access road from the Mother Lode to McCarthy, thirteen miles through the national park.

4

Sunlight and Firefly

I N THE years after the death of his teenage bride, Bobby Hale became a wanderer. He never returned to high school at Arlington Heights. He got a degree from a local alternative technical school and tried college on several campuses, studied marketing for a while, without ever lasting long. At one point he was enrolled at Texas Christian University, where his father was still a hero, but flamed out spectacularly, according to his twin brother's wife, Patsy Dorris Hale. Bobby,

▲

Billy Hale, left, visiting his brother, Bobby, in the New Mexico mountains in the 1990s

still supremely confident as a scrapper, challenged a hulking football lineman to a public fight for flirting with Bobby's latest girlfriend. This oedipal challenge ended with the lineman demolishing Bobby in front of a fraternity crowd. Battered, swollen, and humiliated, Bobby went into hiding, leaving behind his classwork and other responsibilities. That was his way of dealing with shame, Patsy Hale said, after Kathleen Connally's death and now this.

Finally he left home altogether in a fog of marijuana smoke, motorcycle exhaust, and parental frustration. It was America in the 1960s. He popped up in San Francisco for the 1967 Summer of Love and in rural communes from Oregon to the Mojave Desert, pursuing women and gurus and hallucinogenic enlightenment. In later years, he referred to this period as a search for Truth. It was a search that began in Fort Worth, whose motto is "Where the West Begins," and his choices thereafter skewed to the old frontier: In Oregon and California and New Mexico, as later in Alaska, he drifted into abandoned mining claims and shepherd cabins, finding comfort as well as convenience in recycling the work of earlier pioneers. He rode horses and drove old trucks that were hard to find parts for. He told more than one person he'd been born one hundred years too late.

Before he left Texas, however, in the summer of 1962, his name showed up in FBI files, in the curious case of President Kennedy's mob mistress.

In Los Angeles, J. Edgar Hoover's men had staked out an apartment belonging to a woman named Judith Campbell, a ravishing dark-haired beauty involved romantically with both President Kennedy and Chicago mob boss Sam Giancana. On August 7, 1962, the FBI watched two young men break into Campbell's apartment through a sliding-glass balcony door. Two FBI reports identified the burglars' getaway car, a blue Chevrolet Corvette, as registered to I. B. Hale, a former special agent who by 1962 worked in security for the General Dynamics fighter jet plant in Fort Worth. The FBI noted that the description of the burglars—around twenty-one years old, between five-nine and five-eleven, around 165 pounds—matched that of Hale's twin sons, Bobby and Billy. The report also noted, as a matter of passing interest, the story of Bobby Hale and John Connally's daughter, and added further circumstantial evidence: "An associate of I. B. Hale has indicated to the Dallas Office that one of Hale's sons had obtained a Chevrolet sports car and was possibly in California."

The story was unearthed by investigative reporter Seymour Hersh for his 1997 book about Kennedy, *The Dark Side of Camelot*. Hersh, who won a Pulitzer Prize in 1970 for uncovering the My Lai massacre, labored in his book to corroborate the claims of Judith Campbell Exner, made decades after the fact, that she once served as personal courier for money and messages between Kennedy and the mob leader related to vote buying in Chicago and CIA plots to assassinate Fidel Castro. Many historians of the era remain unconvinced, calling Exner's claims unsubstantiated and improbable. But there is no question about the president's compromising relationship with her. The FBI never reported the August 1962 break-in to the Los Angeles police for fear of compromising their own investigation. Exner claimed her phone was tapped by the feds; the FBI agent at the scene guessed that the burglars, who appeared to take nothing, had placed their own wiretap on her phone, for reasons unknown.

In his book, Hersh speculates that General Dynamics, a company in "desperate" financial straits at the time, used evidence gathered from the break-in to blackmail the president. It was not long before the White House overruled the Pentagon on the largest U.S. military aircraft contract in history up to then, a $6.5 billion deal to build the experimental TFX fighter jet, later renamed the F-111. The contract award to the General Dynamics Fort Worth plant shocked the military and Congress at the time, since General Dynamics had been a distant second to Boeing in procurement studies leading up to the decision. Congress convened an investigation, which initially turned up no collusion between the company and White House officials. But, Hersh wrote, FBI chief Hoover never revealed to Congress the report of the break-in at Campbell's apartment naming his old friend, former special agent Hale. The congressional investigation was called off after Kennedy's assassination in 1963.

Hersh's own investigation reached a dead end. I. B. Hale was long dead, Billy Hale could not be found, and efforts to contact Bobby Hale, living in rural isolation in New Mexico in the 1990s, were rebuffed. Asked about this episode years later, Papa Pilgrim dismissed the allegations as preposterous. (General Dynamics and Lockheed Martin, the company that took over the Fort Worth fighter jet plant in 1993, declined to comment on the Hersh allegations for this book.) But Patsy Hale, Billy's girlfriend in 1962 and later his wife, said there may indeed have been something to the connections Hersh drew. Bobby had been out in Los Angeles that summer, she said, obsessed with Marilyn Monroe and trying to arrange a personal meeting in the weeks before the movie star died. The boys' father was in California, too, on some business or other. When everyone got back to Texas, I. B. Hale summoned the boys urgently one night and they drove off in the blue Corvette at midnight. They told Patsy they were going to California to sell the car—which struck her as odd, given how easily they could have sold it in Dallas. When she picked up Billy after he hitchhiked home from California, he of course said nothing about a break-in. It was only many years later, after Hersh tracked her down, that she learned of the FBI reports and recalled something the twins' mother had said before she died: that even after going to work for General Dynamics, I.B. still went away from time to time to handle secret special projects for Mr. Hoover.

So the mystery surrounding I. B. Hale's sons and the FBI reports remains. Inevitably, under such circumstances, the names of I.B. and Bobby Hale twinkle dimly within the labyrinth of Kennedy assassination conspiracy theories. Various coincidences have been examined:

the ties to John Connally, General Dynamics, and J. Edgar Hoover, and the fact that Lee Harvey Oswald attended the same high school as the Hale twins before dropping out to join the Marines. Virginia Hale, working for the Texas Employment Commission after separating from I.B., helped Oswald get a welding job and make some Russian-speaking contacts in 1962, according to the Warren Commission Report. Papa Pilgrim insisted that I. B. Hale rode in the motorcade that day, though he is not listed in the investigation. These strands lead to dead ends, however, as conspiracy theorists have struggled to explain, for example, how the 1959 shotgun death of Connally's daughter could have had any bearing on the assassination four years later—or be linked perhaps to the 1969 20-gauge shotgun suicide of the daughter of Fred Korth ("This was the way that a large number of people who knew too much about the assassination died," mused one conspiracy buff in an online discussion group), who succeeded Connally as secretary of the navy and was also involved in procurement of the F-111 fighter from General Dynamics. . . .

IN THE summer of 1974, Bobby Hale met Kurina Rose Bresler at a hot spring in Southern California. For years afterward, he liked to describe how the Lord appeared in a haze of rainbows and waterfalls and told him that Rose would give him twenty-one children. Twenty-one was an important number to him, since it is a multiple of the sacred number seven, which comes up repeatedly in the Bible, as when Jesus told Peter to forgive another's sin not seven times, but seventy times seven. The Book of Revelation also features a seven-headed beast, seven seals, seven trumpets, and seven mentions of the wrath of God.

Another number of possible significance was sixteen—Rose's age at the time, as it had been Kathleen Connally's when they eloped. Hale was now thirty-three. He had been married two more times since his first bride's death and had already fathered four children of his own.

There had been other women, too, including one who led Bobby Hale to Haight-Ashbury in 1967. On their way to New Orleans the following winter, the couple stopped in Los Angeles and had dinner with a Scripture-quoting man doted on by several dazed female followers. According to the girlfriend and to Patsy Hale, who heard about the visit from her brother-in-law, it was a passing encounter with Charles Manson, one year before the murders that gripped the nation.

Three years later, Bobby Hale had moved with a new girlfriend and baby to a commune in the wooded hills above the southern Oregon coast. Sunnyridge was a genial, open-ended community on a federal mining claim, where back-to-the-landers paid a small annual fee to the government, under the mining laws of the West, supposedly for the right to look for gold. It was a family-friendly place along an old logging road, with a number of college-educated refugees and a central lodge built of salvaged barn wood and straightened nails, according to Ellen Sue and Ted Pilger, ex-residents who maintain a website recalling the commune's halcyon days. Hale remained on the social margin, the Pilgers say. He was tall and lean, with long black hair and a black beard, good-looking but self-impressed. He taught Transcendental Meditation and carried himself with an implacable self-confidence that some women found attractive but men couldn't stand. Sunnyridge flourished for a half dozen years and then broke apart, the Pilgers say, as families grew up and everyone felt the faint disillusion that follows hope for a perfect place.

Hale had moved on by then, traveling to Europe to help run a lecture tour for the Maharishi Mahesh Yogi, the founder of the Transcendental Meditation movement. He was now deeply immersed in TM, with its promise to connect with the "creative intelligence" of the universe. And then, he later told Rose, he was turned off in an instant by an overheard conversation between two leaders, regarding ways to keep crowds coming back by dangling promises of cosmic consciousness. He said he took the Maharishi's limo straight to the airport and flew back to California.

His spiritual beliefs evolved into a blend of Christianity and a worship of the planets. In 1973 he headed to South America to escape the Comet Kohoutek. The comet's sudden discovery had some people predicting that a great doomsday event would strike North America in January 1974—it would be "brighter than seven moons," one cult leader foretold. Hale departed from Geyserville, north of San Francisco, with a girlfriend later known to Kurina Rose as "the one-legged lady." (Hale drilled a hole in her wooden leg to hide their cash, which came in handy after their backpacks were stolen.) As Rose recalled her husband's tale, the pair rode horses through Ecuador and Bolivia, consumed copious amounts of LSD, and encountered many cosmic signs—trees bending in homage, voices from the high Andes—that convinced Hale he himself might be some kind of prophet. Eventually the Americans were deported, but not before Kohoutek had safely passed the perihelion in its orbit, relieving anxieties about doomsday while leaving in its wake a new earthbound metaphor for dim anticlimax.

Meanwhile, Kurina Rose was struggling through her teen years. Her parents were divorced. Her mother, a singer and actress who had played a nun in a touring production of *The Sound of Music,* had remarried a movie producer whose films included *Shaft* and *The Heart Is a Lonely Hunter.* Growing up in a Beverly Hills canyon, frequently in the care of her grandmother, Rose rebelled against the materialism of Los Angeles, drawn instead to the freedom that beckoned in the countryside. She swooned watching *Little House on the Prairie* on television, and dreamed of going back to the land. She left school and ran off to a hot spring outside Apple Valley, in the dry creosote and piñon pine mountains west of Los Angeles, where she met Bobby Hale.

He was going by the name "Ram," which was short, she understood, for something Hindu. She recalled that he was tripping when they met, and God appeared to herald the moment. He called the pretty teenager Sunlight. She gave him the name Firefly. They changed their names legally, and took the name of his star-spangled faded-lemon vintage truck as their surname. He followed her home to Beverly Hills, and when her parents told him to get lost, Sunlight snuck out in the night, just like Kathleen Connally had, and ran away with Firefly. She did not see her parents again until she was pregnant with a daughter whose legal name would be Butterfly Sunstar.

FIREFLY SUNSTAR was energetic and clever, and he made his new mate comfortable in their tumbleweed camps and squatter homes. They worked to build a self-contained world, and Firefly, older than anyone else around, was a natural leader. He had a brilliant way of divining what was going on in people's heads, though Sunlight discovered this did not automatically endear him to those whose heads were being thus invaded. He could be volatile and inconsistent. He would charm people and draw them in, then turn on them and drive them away. It did not take Sunlight long to figure out that alcohol and psychedelics could make him angry and jealous. He was like Jekyll and Hyde, she told him. But she was determined to prove that she hadn't made a bad choice—that her relationship would not break up like her parents'.

One night in a rage he flung burning coals on Sunlight and baby Butterfly as they sat naked by a campfire. When she threatened to go seek medical care for the baby's third-degree burns, he apologized, piteously and at length. He said he was tortured by things from his past. He told Sunlight the story of eloping as a teenager. He couldn't forgive himself for driving his sweet bride to her death. It was years before he could even hug his own mother again. He was convinced he had a devil in him. His brother, Billy, was the good son. He was the bad seed, rejected by the world, unreachable by pity or love.

Then on a visit to Texas they attended a Baptist church with Billy. People remembered I. B. Hale and the story of the Connallys. They told Bobby they'd been praying for him for twenty years. Firefly and Sunlight went to one service after another. Firefly couldn't sleep; he was up all night driving around Fort Worth thinking about what he should do. In church he stared at his Bible, sifting for his soul while the preacher spoke rapturously of salvation, and finally he rose up. Sunlight grabbed his arm. He was never one for doing things half-way, and she feared where this might lead. He tore free and strode to the front of the church to receive Jesus. He saw that all the voices and signs he'd been sensing, which he thought were communication from God, had been the devil fighting to keep him.

He removed his bag of marijuana from the bus and sprinkled it over a field. He cut his hair and shaved his beard and renounced the name Sunstar and lit a bonfire to burn their eagle feathers and tarot cards.

Kurina Rose joined him in Jesus after he broke down in tears. He told her he hadn't cried so hard since KK died.

5

Motorheads

I T MAY be that few McCarthy neighbors, busy with preparations for the long cold season ahead, took time to read all the way
through the ardent handwritten epistle delivered around town in the
Tenth Month of Papa Pilgrim's first year in the Wrangells. If anyone managed to penetrate the blaze of incandescent self-regard, they
found the four pages of cramped lettering to be a birth announcement.
A child had been born at the Mother Lode, the first birth in that part
of the Wrangells since the copper mines closed. The letter was also
an account of a desperate motorized trip up McCarthy Creek that fall,

Winter tourists and snowmachines at the McCarthy Lodge, 2003

over a route still impassable to vehicles as far as most people knew, but nobody seemed to pick up on the improved access.

Maybe no one in McCarthy even made it past the song verses, decorated with musical notes, that opened the letter like theme music for a television show:

> *Oh what a Love that will Bind the wounds of Loss and Heal*
> *   my Breast—*
> *Oh what a love that will cast away the pain*
> *Oh   "   "   "   that will Bear for me the Cross of a brand*
> *   new start*
> *Oh what a love that will let me begin again . . .*

A song was given that desperate night I made my way that day and night to my beloved wife, Country Rose—Now in Labor with our child!

Our 16th child to "part the womb" —one land, one family, one birth to bless us —every child a new plan and vision of looking forward to the Beyond.

Having wandered threw out Alaska so many years, it was filled with trials, wanting to except neighbors, wanting to find our place—only to be slandered, robbed, and beaten, praised, accepted and Loved. But the reward came that Patience reaps, and the "End of the Road" McCarthy Town became the Beginning for a Pilgrim Family. Our first visit produced a family list of 177 reasons to be here, and not one "No"!—It was God Given.

Pilgrim wrote of driving home that fall after seeing a doctor in Anchorage, keeping in touch with the Mother Lode properties via a new remote phone at the cabin.

My knee at times in "screaming pain"; —Time was short, for Mama Country Rose was "overdue" with child — Trusting in

God that He would not let us down after all He's done for us. Threw Anchorage headed home — Truck and Trailer with food, clothing, bedding, tools we pulled into Palmer . . .

Just as I headed out the hwy I received "that" call that said — "Don't stop now my husband, the child is coming." —I'm set free and Homeward bound. 50 years of driving faultlessly had prepared me for this day as I climbed into the driver's seat and told my right leg to work for me now, as we sped down the hwy the tears in my eyes gave the road a shimmer —and a call to mama to let her know, "I'm threw the Hills now and open country is before me —yes baby the hammer's on the floor, just believe." On the road I stopped along the hwy at a Christian home. I pulled up —they were gathered outside —Pilgrim! Hello! —Pray, Pray my brothers, my wife is in labor and hundreds of miles of blacktop, 60 miles of dirt, 17 river crossings lie ahead —Oh Pray! as my engine sound disappeared into the darkness.

I reached the bridge and the bollards, and no sons were there yet —They had had trouble? —I slumped over the wheel as the tears and the pain put me asleep —

I awoke surrounded by family —A call to mama revealed she was in strong labor, as my sons wisked me across the bridge —Into a track R.V. —A blurr through Old Town McCarthy —Oh Lord Jesus, so far to go! The next hours were so hard, holding my body together threw the trail and sometimes submerged in water —yet we all had only one purpose —

To Be There On Time —It was unconceivable that we wouldn't be there. I remember asking the sons to stop just a moment —I felt I was falling apart and the pain made me think of a warrior wounded in the battle field with no relief. Then I heard Joseph say as he put his arm around my broken body —We're almost there —you'll see the lamp in the window soon papa. Then I was carried in, and as I stood there I saw mama — She saw my

brokenness, I saw her love, as she sat so honorable on the couch
—We embraced —we wept —we were finally all together and our
prayer and great need answered.

The children, he wrote, needed to know why their mother cried
in pain. It was because of mankind's sin, but God would save those
who lived in faith. He described the birth itself in melodramatic detail, and then how he received the child: "Thoughts pierced my heart
as I saw this child, my fingers caressing its head, so small, so new, so
holy, such promise, such love." A boy!

Now was the moment—I lifted him to God in Prayer and
Thanks—As before, I waited for to hear his name—Three Times
it came to me—He shall be called Jonathan—Gasp and tears
were heard threw out the family—What a lovely name.
　　Then we celebrated with all that God had provided—Leg of
Lamb, berries, cheese, home grown everything—We searched
the meaning of His Name in the Hebrew = JEHOVA GIVEN.
We understood so deeply, and more to learn. This Land and
its people, our Home and all He's done here is purely GOD
GIVEN—We know this and now can for a surety look forward
with the promise of a New Love, New life, New Song in our
hearts—We wanted to tell you because we love you so much with
His Love that looks to the beyond—
　　—In Jesus The Pilgrims and Baby Pilgrim "Jonathan"

PEOPLE ASSUMED the Pilgrim Family had gone into the wilderness, like their namesakes in New England, looking for space to establish their own theocracy. Like those other Puritans, though, the
family's motivations soon shifted toward the mercantile.
　　Neil Darish at the McCarthy Lodge was probably the first to learn

Pilgrim was thinking about bringing tourists to the Mother Lode. In a way it made sense—even in the 1950s, a bush pilot had a pretty good business flying tourists from Anchorage out to see the old Alaska ghost town, until Kennecott's lawyers barred the door. Actual mining wasn't an option. Before the national park, new owners at Kennicott had tried picking up the blue and green copper ore left on the ground. They gathered tram spillage in bags of jute and shipped the bags by plane and truck to Tacoma. The ore caused such a stir in Tacoma that smelter operations paused—no one had seen copper that rich in decades, not since the Alaska mines shut down. But the venture didn't pay, and the owners soon turned from high-grading ore to high-grading antiques out of the ruins. These days visitors were the only real source of outside income.

Pilgrim stopped by the lodge frequently to ask advice of Darish. The lodge owner found it flattering to have the welfare of such an industrious yet innocent family placed in his trust. Papa was an engaging conversationalist, quick to pick up on the community's dynamics, keen to want the same things Darish wanted and full of questions. Papa was concerned that the family's horseback ride business, so picturesque and appealing to tourists, was raising objections among locals because the horses chewed bark off the cottonwoods and left steaming piles in the streets.

Darish flew up to see the family's new homestead. He and Pilgrim agreed the mountaintop Mother Lode mine could be quite an asset. Tours through the caverns would tap a deep treasure-hunt craving in visitors, and the liability-averse Park Service would surely never agree to such a venture on their side of the mountain. Darish explained the big picture: In his view, visitors were drawn to McCarthy as a genuine lived-in place, not some fake reproduction of the old frontier. Not only did Pilgrim see the beauty of that, he said tourists could not find more genuine country ways than his family's. He elaborated on this in a couple of early letters to Darish from the homestead, printed out with unpracticed spelling on the back of sample logs from the mine, in which he imagined a future visit to "Hillbilly Heaven Mountain Lodge":

> They have over 400 ac of private land, a wonderous location all set up for guest to come and experience Real Alaska Living. . . . Take walks on the glaciers, climb threw Diamond Creek, find hidden valleys—watch the big ram sheep, and enjoy the numerous bears that climb the distant cliffs—dont worry they all carry .454 to protect folks if needed. . . . The famous "Mother Lode" mine—The Last open copper mine in private hands, is in the near future being prepared even now for limited tours. Chip a peice of ore from the walls of this mine—while your up there you'll be amazed as you'll seem to be on top of the world looking out over the World's Largest National Park. You'll see giant ariel tram that brought the ore down and you'll walk along the top of Bonnanza Ridge—its towers, hidden valley and pinicles point towards Heaven.

As he wrote that first letter, Pilgrim was experiencing his first spring breakup in the valley, with snow melting to reveal Wigger's D5 bulldozer and a rock drill and the fullness of the Lord's love for the family. Whenever his sons managed to get back, they would commence rebuilding the interior of the main cabin, which had been trashed when they got there, insulation and grizzly bear scat strewn everywhere. "Old Slew Foot," as Papa called the giant bear, showed up one of their first mornings at dawn, rousing the dogs. They got off a wounding shot, and five sons with rifles tracked the grizzly up the mountain. From an alder thicket Old Slew Foot made his final charge and they loaded him with bullets. They saved the skin and said nothing to the park. Thus was McCarthy Creek reclaimed for God's glory.

"I sit helplessly amid torrents of water, Ice break-ups, unwalkable snowy trails, mt. trails closed by Avalanche danger, a Joyous prisoner to God's Love, and so at peace with all my youngest children, in this wonderful valley we know now as home," Pilgrim wrote. The letters came as a surprise to Darish, both for their lightheartedness and because he had figured, above all, that the Pilgrims would want to keep people away. "We treasure our solitude," Pilgrim explained, "for the Bible tells us that the family shall dwell in Solitary." But his family intended to strike a beautiful balance, he explained.

> In the evening they'll play some of their unique versions of mt. music, they have "dubbed" "Gospel Grass" music. I do think I heard one of them fiddlers say "God loves fiddlen around and playing to Him." The young one's dance the old celtic "clog." The meals are free, Mama Country has obviously been use to cooking for these past 30 yrs. . . . After good simple food—mountain music—you'll be ready to take the trail to your "Pappy cabin," light the lamp and look out up the mts. or glaciers or the river and count the beauty and blessings of a experience that is guarenteed to change your Life—This is their first season, and Limited Availability is open—Make soap with Mama or try your hand at the spinning wheel—They love to teach, or watch the Tanning of hides, Native style, or watch the boys make you something at the forge or anvil—or! Learn to load a black powder rifle, and how sweet it shoots—

Pilgrim even offered a general description of the town for Darish to use on his "web sight."

> Come on down to "Old Town McCarthy"—the town that was the biggest little town in Alaska—where copper and gold flowed out of glaciers—the Wild West of Alaska, where "churches" were out-lawed—and sin, riches and harlotry were coveted!—A few

families left from those boom days have held onto what Alaska really stands for—"Preachers"? well not exactly, to say the least, but rugged, ready and caring people that have begun to build the town back. . . .

Darish advised Papa to approach his lodge idea like a sensible business. Buy insurance, for one thing, and work with the national park to get the proper permits. Pilgrim seemed so naïve in some ways.

I have a question—How do we get paid? Let's say they send 6 months advance for full, to stay 3 nights. . . . Well if nobody has cash any more, can I have one of those little credit card things, that pulls over the card & "Bill"—they sign it—I give them a copy—I send one in—& I keep one—or I could advertise— "Cash only! I can't trade your signature for Hay!?"

I wouldn't be that concerned about people, at least what kind—There would be a few things, but they would naturally take care of themselves—foul speaking & Nudity are out, but that's never been a problem, even when we're in someone else's world—

Robbers—murderers—hurtfull people—Park Rangers, and state troopers, drunk child welfare protection workers, and any one that has a purpose to harm or do evil to others are not acceptable —

And or if a problem arose, I believe we can very nicely get them a quick departure date, so that only good things happen. But whatever position you take to help us, it will be honored, and each Act and Labor has its Reward —

There won't be Trouble—God's bigger than that, and we won't be passing out saw-off shotguns to be sure—of which we have none! And all Jews are welcome! By the way!

We have one thing to endever together, to mind our own business, to live quite and peaceful lifes, and to work with our hands, singing a pleasant song.

BY THE time Jonathan was born in October 2002, they were fixing up a guest shack they called the Happy Cabin. The family lived in two cabins left from Wigger's prospecting days. Then the smaller and nicer of the two cabins burned down. It happened after a night when the temperature hit thirty below. The woodstove had been loaded extra full and the winds had howled down the valley with unusual force, the bellows of winter. The next morning, the valley was silent as Country Rose went to the window and saw smoke under the eaves. Fifteen-year-old Israel risked his life to dash back in the cabin for an armload of rifles, then ran barefoot through the snow to disconnect a propane tank and pull it away from the flames. They saved the livestock penned next door, but after that everyone slept in the living room of the drafty main cabin.

The fire aroused sympathy in town. Darish sent tourist business their way—a group of snowmachiners from the city who had showed up in McCarthy looking for something a little different.

They called themselves Motorheads, though they weren't the kind of Alaskans whose enjoyment of the wild usually involved noise and speed and prodigious consumption of fossil fuels. White-collar lawyers, accountants, a few members of the opinion staff at the *Anchorage Daily News,* they were more likely to be taken for cross-country skiers, fly fishermen, and kayakers. Conservatives and liberals both, the longtime friends didn't, for the most part, own big trucks and four-wheel off-road vehicles. Every winter, though, a dozen or so headed off for a boys' adventure on borrowed or rented snowmachines. They told friends they saw a lot more beautiful country that way than they ever would on skis.

One year, their destination was a lodge that stayed open all winter along the unplowed Denali Highway. The next year, in early 2003, they decided to go to McCarthy.

When they got home, all they could talk about was the Pilgrim Family.

The original plan, worked out over the phone with Darish, had been to drive to Chitina and then travel by snowmachine along the old train route to McCarthy. But when they got to Chitina, it hadn't snowed in a while and the road was plowed. They decided to keep driving and make McCarthy their starting point rather than their destination. They parked by the river at the end of the road, near the footbridge built to keep out those rough riders of summer Alaska tourism, the true motorheads.

Right away they got in trouble. On the hard-packed trail to town, several of the brand-new 700 cc rented snowmachines overheated and had to be left for retrieval later. The next day, traveling up the icy trail to see Kennicott, a machine overheated and leaked radiator fluid, and when they stopped a cabin owner yelled at them because his dog team might lick up the dribble of poisonous antifreeze along the trail. The Motorheads were mortified and spent the next hour working with shovels and plastic bags to remove traces of green snow.

Back at the lodge, disheartened by their mechanical troubles, they learned from Darish of a family, new to town, who could help. Two young men with long hair and beards and floppy hats stopped by the lodge and went to work fixing the damaged snowmachines. One of the Motorheads had lost a radiator cap somewhere down in the engine. Joseph and Joshua Pilgrim plugged the radiator hole, lifted the heavy machine in the air, flipped it upside down, and shook it until the cap tumbled out. The Motorheads looked at one another and smiled at the simple solution.

The boys' father walked over from the family wanigan base camp in town, opened a photo album, and described their homestead far off in the mountains. Mama and the young children were out there now. Papa Pilgrim said his boys could provide a daylong tour of the valley for fifty dollars a person.

The Motorheads had a debate. The political conservatives in the group thought fifty dollars each was too much and pushed for a group discount. The liberal majority said this ragged family needed the money. The conversation went on for some time because debate, unlike small-engine mechanics, was something these professionals were good at.

The next morning, Joseph and Joshua and another brother showed up on three small patched-together one-cylinder snowmachines. Each Pilgrim had a younger brother riding on back. Their sputtering little Tundras were half the size of the Motorheads' machines, and the Pilgrim boys wore light jackets and hats while the Motorheads were dressed like astronauts in one-piece snowsuits and helmets. But the Pilgrims snow-danced in circles as they led the Motorheads into the mountains on a blue, sun-glinting day. The trail was wide and groomed. The craggy summits were spectacular. They rode all the way to the scenic alpine headwall of the McCarthy Creek valley, where they could highmark like real motorheads on steep slopes below a glacier. The Pilgrims seemed able to ride as high as they wanted. The director of the state humanities council lost balance ascending and tumbled over backward, but he stood up laughing and his friends got some great pictures.

Later, when they got back to Anchorage, the Motorheads told stories about the country-Jesus family they'd discovered in the Wrangell Mountains. The whole family lived in a single cabin, crowding their sleeping bags into one big room at night. The little children could not stop staring at the group's one African American. They were all so cheerful, fed the snowmachiners a big meal, and played gospel music—"Hallelujah, I'm ready to go," they sang. They were living in the middle of a national park, but apparently this was not a problem in Alaska. It was one of those days that made everyone think: What a great crazy state we live in.

ON THE Motorheads' last night at the McCarthy Lodge, it was the visitors who did the singing. Every year the trip ended with the Motorhead Follies, celebrating the comedy of motorized touring unburdened by pretensions of competence. A dozen people from the community turned out, including Papa Pilgrim and Country Rose and a few of the older children, who had made their way down from the homestead. The big hit was a song about the Pilgrims to the tune of *The Beverly Hillbillies* theme. The Pilgrims didn't seem to know the original and gave the lyricists undeserved credit for their catchy melody.

Afterward some locals lit a bonfire, and several of the Motorheads drifted outside. Carl Bauman was pleased to see Papa come over. Bauman was a lawyer with a corporate firm in Anchorage and was rather more conservative than some of his friends on the trip (he was later appointed a state judge by Governor Sarah Palin). He had been the one pushing his friends, unsuccessfully, to seek a group discount for their day trip. But up at the homestead he'd been impressed by the family's resilience and music and their plight after the cabin fire. He admired the older sons' wilderness proficiency and good cheer. He was stirred by Papa's long and heartfelt prayer before they broke bread. On their return to the lodge that night, Bauman had gone around collecting a big tip for the Pilgrim boys. They talked about putting together a clothing drive when they got back to Anchorage.

"I do have a question," Bauman said by the fire. "You keep saying sixteen children. I count only fifteen."

"We always include our daughter, Hope," Pilgrim said. "Hope would have been our third child. She died at four months."

It took Bauman a few more questions to realize Pilgrim meant four months after conception. The visitor was moved that they counted the miscarriage of Hope when they added up their children.

"We buried her on the bend of a river in Texas," Pilgrim said. It was a story he'd recited to his family so many times that all except Country Rose had come to believe it was true. Rose remembered leaving the fetus—boy or girl, she never knew—in the freezer of a kindly couple who took them in after their truck broke down on a West Texas back road.

Bauman handed Pilgrim his card. He sensed the old backwoodsman had singled him out because he was shrewd enough to recognize a sympathetic worldview, despite superficial differences in education and affluence. They were both conservative fathers who understood the value of piety and the importance of family.

Later, though, Bauman wondered if Papa Pilgrim had singled him out that night because he knew he was going to need a lawyer.

6

The Rainbow Cross

F OR THE traveler approaching the Sangre de Cristo Mountains
across the high sagebrush desert of northern New Mexico, the
Mora River valley comes as a lush surprise. Foothill ridges of bare
rock and Ponderosa pine open suddenly into broad green panoramas
marked by clusters of cattle, isolated farmsteads, and big shady willows along the creeks and irrigation courses. In the town of Mora
itself, once an outpost of Old Mexico, families trace their roots back
centuries: Spanish was spoken here long before English-speaking
immigrants showed up. State highways crossing the valley turn at

Preacher Bob and family at the Rainbow Cross Ranch, New Mexico, 1986

ninety degrees to avoid old cemeteries and rotting adobe ruins. The
land rises through canyons to high peaks where snow lingers into
summer. The Sangre de Cristos are the southernmost extension of the
Rockies. The old Santa Fe Trail turned away here, marking the summits on early maps as "Impassable Mountains."

The range has a tradition of saints and mystics. The mountains
got their name, according to legend, from a seventeenth-century
missionary who asked God for one last sign before Pueblo Indians
martyred him. He looked up to see the summits bathed in sunset
alpenglow—the Blood of Christ. Scholars say the name is more likely
from the Penitentes, the cultish nineteenth-century society of poor
and isolated Hispanic mountain villagers whose Holy Week ceremo-
nies included flagellation with yucca whips, barefoot treks with heavy
crosses, and ritual crucifixion. Not far south of Mora is Hermit Peak,
where an Italian ascetic lived in a shallow cave atop a thousand-foot
cliff during the time of the American Civil War, subsisting on corn
meal and water gathered drip by drip from a rock seep. Giovanni
Maria Agostini was the son of a Piedmont noble who, it was said, traveled the world as a pilgrim with a heavy burden, the sin of killing his
cousin in a quarrel. He was said to have cured poor villagers of small-
pox with herbal potions and prayer. When they found him murdered
by renegades in a cave south of the mountain, a knife in his back, ad-
mirers erected a heavy wooden cross atop Hermit Peak in his memory.

One century later, another massive timber cross appeared in the
high country above the Mora River. It was the work of another pilgrim bearing a heavy burden, a bearded Jesus freak who rode the high
trails on horseback and lectured backpackers about salvation. He went
by the name of Preacher Bob, or Mountain Bob, or Holy Bob.

Down in the valley, people knew him and his young family as the
hippies who'd been struck by lightning.

☩

THE FAMILY drove down into Mora from time to time, looking for
hay or old truck parts. At first nobody knew where they lived. This
was not unusual. Land ownership and tenancy in the far reaches of
the local Mexican land grant tended to be deliberately vague. This
guardedness dated back to the Mexican War, when American volunteers taught a lesson to Mora's combative Hispanics by leveling
their town with a cannon. After the war, Anglo businessmen used
American courts to pry grazing and forest lands out of the hands of
the original families, who once owned vast parts of the nine-hundred-
thousand-acre land grant in common. Then, around the turn of the
century, the federal government expelled local grazers and tree cutters from the high mountains when it created the first generation of
national forests. For its complexity, opacity, and legacy of bitterness,
the history of land control in northern New Mexico makes Alaska's
modern disputes over conservation lands seem simple by comparison.

Another complicating wave of settlement arrived in the decade
before Preacher Bob, as hippies were drawn to the backwoods, most
famously around the artist colony of Taos. These were the mountains
supposedly home to the commune visited in the 1969 road movie
Easy Rider. Some of these newcomers lived flamboyantly, others took
quiet advantage of murky land titles, in either case causing stress
within traditional Hispanic and Indian settlements. In Mora, the seat
of the poorest county in New Mexico, many people assumed that the
hippie preacher was squatting in the national forest or on somebody
else's land.

One neighbor who knew exactly where the young family had settled was Editha Bartley, who owned a sawmill and a four-thousand-
acre cattle-and-guest ranch just over the ridge from their cabin.
Bartley had grown up in a prominent local Anglo family—her grandfather, a doctor, started a tuberculosis sanitarium in the Mora area.
Looking rather like Barbara Stanwyck in the old television series *The*

Big Valley, she continued after her husband's death to manage their ranch with the help of her son.

The hippie migration to the Sangre de Cristo Mountains had not gone well for the Bartleys. Their first neighbors in the high country beyond their back fence weren't exactly flower children. They looked like hippies, as Editha Bartley tells the story, but they were drug runners, cattle rustlers, and game poachers off the adjacent Santa Fe National Forest. Several dozen lived in a tent city and an early Spanish shepherd's cabin made of hand-hewn aspen logs. They called it a commune, but to Bartley it seemed more like a hideout.

The outlaws knew to stay on reasonably good terms with the Bartleys, who hired an ex–Green Beret to ride their north fence. Editha's son, John, rode up to the tent camp on horseback one time with the Vietnam War vet and glimpsed an arsenal that included two machine guns. One of the renegades was lying by a campfire, groaning, his leg wounded badly by an ax. His gangrene was being treated with marijuana, peyote, and alcohol. Eventually, he was rolled into a blanket and carried down the mountain to an emergency room, but it was too late. His friends carried him back and built a huge pyre in the meadow, and hundreds of hippies from all over the mountain range showed up for the funeral.

The party ended when several of the longhairs, caught poaching a deer, backed a forest ranger off the mountain at gunpoint. Three nights later, a posse of state police and federal marshals drove their horse trailers to the Bartleys' ranch and rode out at four a.m. to climb the ridge and descend into the outlaw camp at first light. They marched the backwoodsmen out of the mountains and arrested nine on various charges.

Compared to that, Bob and Kurina Rose Hale seemed a blessing, Editha Bartley said. At least at first. They showed up in 1979, a few years after the outlaws had been cleared out. In the high mountain meadow surrounded by spruce and fir, Bob Hale had built a crude log cabin for his young wife, still practically a teenager, and their two small children. It wasn't much—low ceilinged and dark, with rough-sawn boards for shelves—but there was a warmth to the place. At times, Editha Bartley would ride up to visit on her own, stopping for coffee and fresh strawberry muffins. Bob's ingenuity and energy impressed her. "We had so many problems with the bad hippies, he seemed like a gift of God himself," Editha Bartley said.

PREACHER BOB liked to tell how they came to the Sangre de Cristos, a story of heavenly signs and wonders. Soon after coming to know Jesus, while visiting friends in rural Raton, New Mexico, Bob felt a call to visit a dusty outhouse. Tucked in a corner of the ceiling, he discovered a note from somebody called Tin Man, looking for a family to caretake land in the mountains near Mora, south of Cimarron. The Hales ascended a rough Jeep road over rocky ledges, and at nine thousand feet all they found was a run-down lean-to shack. But Bob dug a hole four feet deep and declared that if God filled it with water by morning they would stay. He chose a low, wet spot to dig his hole.

Their daughter was about to turn four. Many years later, Elishaba sat down to write about her upbringing and recalled the struggle to survive that first winter.

As we huddled in the lean to, my father actually built our log cabin around us. I will never forget the picture of him driving long spikes into the logs as the snowstorm hurled huge snow-flakes all around us. At the end of each day, we would crawl into our little lean-to, lit with only a bare oil-burning lamp, where we snuggled up just to stay warm. I looked forward to cuddling with my daddy each night, as he felt so big, safe, and secure.

Tin Man and his friend Papa Bear claimed to be keeping an eye on the high-elevation forest for a local Hispanic elder. They turned out to be log rustlers, cutting and skidding old-growth trees off the land with a big white workhorse, brandishing guns and firing warning shots at the Hales' cabin to discourage interference. Elishaba remembered lying on the adobe floor of the cabin with her little brother as gunshots rang out, wondering who the "mean people" were. They came from the world below their mountain, was all that she knew. Her daddy sat defiantly at the window with his rifle, refusing to be intimidated. He had Mama check into the land records. That was how they discovered that the Hispanic elder didn't even own the land anymore. He had sold it to a movie star.

Jack Nicholson first came to the Taos area while filming *Easy Rider*. The movie's writer and director, Dennis Hopper, who also had a starring role, liked what he saw and returned to buy the Taos estate of the 1920s heiress and arts patron Mabel Dodge Luhan. Nicholson visited and wound up buying land on the other side of the range, backing the Santa Fe National Forest, from one of Mora's original Mexican land grant families. The 1977 land sale had been hushed up, not because of the buyer's celebrity but because the Hispanic community still frowned on selling land to outsiders. When the news finally trickled out, people were surprised the hippie couple had managed to get a ten-dollar-a-month lease to caretake the Hollywood star's land. Bob Hale claimed it was his eloquent letter about the family's subsistence pastoralism that won them the invitation to stay. He put an end to Tin Man's log rustling. The family became guardians of the ancient forest.

Then they were struck by lightning.

Bob Hale was turning more and more to the study of God's word. Rose, pregnant again, was responsible for running the primitive household—cooking on a woodstove, doing laundry by hand. When

Rose had visited Beverly Hills, her mother told her she was certainly getting to be "country." Papa was delighted by that line, and started calling Rose "Country" as a term of endearment.

He took charge of the family's spiritual well-being and made his daughter throw away her baby doll. The children took on more chores, learning to milk the cow and not spill it all on the walk back to the cabin. For a while, their days included time for organized home-schooling. Elizabeth—the name they started calling Butterfly after they got saved—loved her daddy's dramatic readings from a book of animal stories, particularly one about a bear and a wolverine. But before too long he discovered impure doctrines in the books. The reading lessons ended. He threw the books down the family's hand-dug septic hole in the woods. It was one of Elizabeth's jobs to carry the family's toilet bucket up the trail each morning and pour the contents into the hole. She was sad to watch those bright-colored books, the last vestiges of her formal education, subside day by day in the bottom sludge until they vanished.

After this, the only readings were out of the Bible. As a sign of their righteousness, their father erected a big cross above the ridge-pole of the cabin.

What happened next might have ended the career of many biblical prophets. The direct hit came during one of those black-cloud downpours that often boil through the summits of the Sangre de Cristos. David, their fourth child, was a baby: After they gave up calendars, Rose found, the easiest way to notch the passage of time was by newborns. The whole family was huddled inside the cabin, Papa and Mama and four tykes in two-year increments, praying as thunder ripped and exploded outside. The blast atomized the eighteen-inch barn spike that held the cross together. Rose's hand, resting on the hearth, flew into the air as a fireball rolled through the cabin. The next thing she knew, she was on the ceiling gazing down indifferently on her own unconscious body, as her husband ran for anointing oil in a torrent of prayer. The family had a houseguest that week—a troubled young man sent their way by a local Pentecostal preacher. He had just been complaining about the nonstop Jesus talk when the lightning hit. He ran out into the downpour and never came back.

Rose was revived, and once the storm had passed it was necessary to account for the cross lying in smithereens in the grass. Preacher Bob proved equal to the occasion. They had been punished for harboring an unbeliever, he declared. Thereafter, no unbeliever would ever be allowed in their home. They had the cross of their Lord Jesus to thank for absorbing the blast and saving their mama's life.

Still, bearing in mind their proximity to a mountaintop in one of the most thermally active regions of New Mexico, he erected the replacement cross a hundred yards away, across the meadow, where it could be seen from distant ridges.

Thus did the people of Mora first locate where Preacher Bob was living.

He called his mountain place the Rainbow Cross Ranch, for it came to pass that a rainbow touched down on the cross in the meadow just as another son, Moses, was being born. He had a photograph to prove it. His efforts to document a repeat of the miracle required running down the hill to line up subsequent rainbows. The photos nevertheless were touching affirmations of faith, like the rainbows vouchsafed to Noah after the flood, especially considering how hard Preacher Bob struggled to keep a cross on the mountain.

The second cross was also hit by lightning, and its replacement was knocked down by wind. At other times, the cross was felled by enemies when the family was away—neighbors, hunters, cattlemen, Hale was never sure—sometimes with chain saws and once with a lariat. Each new cross was bigger than the last. Finally, with help from his growing sons, he erected the biggest cross of all, more than twenty feet tall, sunk eight feet deep in concrete and riddled with 777 nails to discourage chain saw blades. The cross stands above Mora to this day.

✠

FROM THE Rainbow Cross, a rough Jeep trail led down the mountain to the world. This road was considered their access route, though it could also be described as the barrier that ensured their isolation. In her memories of growing up, Elishaba recalled the trials of getting home:

> The trail leading to our "sanctuary" was often filled with deep ruts and even deeper mud holes. From a little Spanish village, this "road" wound for several miles up the steep mountain hills. One place along the way we called the "Staircase," because the erosion of a hill had left the rock tiered in steps for us to drive up. The landscape was dotted with little fenced meadows, tiny shepherd's shacks and cool mountain streams. As we approached the cabin site, we would encounter tall, full pine trees, interspersed with white aspen and knurly oak. The road at times would turn into a bog, and because it was such a muddy mess, we would have to leave our truck and walk the rest of the way home. On the south side of our quickly constructed lean-to, was a thickly wooded hill; on the other side was a steep slope that ended in a vertical rock face that shot up towards the heavens. Our place was so high in the mountains that the spring and summer seasons were very short, and just a few thousand feet higher, the snow remained all year long. A trail leading up to the top of a snow-capped mountain went to a place that we called "The Wilderness." It was a vast area with acres and acres of open land, deep valleys, and thickly wooded forests that were frequented by large herds of elk.

Life on the mountain required constant work. The older Elizabeth got, the more was expected. Among her responsibilities was to care for her younger brothers—five of them by the time she was twelve. She recalled one family expedition, when they drove their truck down the mountain and spent a day filling feed sacks with little red winter apples.

It was time to make the all night run back up the mountain. Tired and wanting sleep I would find a corner in the back of our truck and curl for a nap. It was difficult to doze off between those incredible bumps, which were so severe that they would throw things flying from one side of the truck to the other. I seemed to grumble in my heart asking why I couldn't sleep like my brothers could. "Elizabeth, wake up, get Joseph up, get out there and put on the chains. There is no time for sleeping." It almost felt like I was having a nightmare, hearing my father yell, in the midst of an earthquake. So scrabbling around for a flashlight we crawled out into the cold dark night. It took a long time to untangle the muddy chains that were wrapped around the headlights, and secure them over the big dual tires in the rear; but it was finally accomplished. "Oh, now maybe I can get some sleep," I sighed, as I tried to find a place to put my muddy self.

The old truck sputtered and spit as she tried to negotiate those steep hills. "Oh Lord, help us make it up this hill please," I prayed in desperation and yet I felt somehow lazy; because I didn't want to budge, and if the truck stalled on a hill I would have to jump out quick to block the rear tires to keep the truck from careening back down the hill. Then it happened: "Oh no, the truck is going to die right in the middle of the hill!!!"

"Elizabeth, Joseph, get out quick, and put some rocks behind the tires," Papa said. While he sat there holding the brakes we secured the big truck with blocks. Then Pa cranked the engine over and over, but that didn't work so we finally came up with another solution. Joseph would sit on the front wheel well, hold the end of a gas line in the top of the carburetor while I stood on the running board holding up a gas can so the line could siphon enough gas out to keep the truck from dying. So off we went with Mama singing "Praise the Lord, hallelujah, I don't care what the Devil's gonna do." Papa tried to keep the truck on the road and bouncing off a big tree here and there while he peered over Joseph's shoulders. I was hanging on for dear life and trying not to drop the gas, when all of a sudden the truck starts sputtering again! "Joseph, keep that gas line in don't take it out." Papa's voice pierced my ears as he was shouting from right beside me. Joseph then began to cry, "I didn't mean to! It came out, I'm trying!" but the truck came to another halting stop. "Mother hold the brakes," Father commanded. It was emotionally hard as my Papa got out filled with anger, yelling at Joseph, blaming him as though it was his fault that it was taking us all night to get back home. My Pa was not able to accept the fact that it was his fault because he didn't plan the apple-harvesting trip any better. So everything felt hopeless and I could hear the children in the back waking up and crying.

The more Papa read the Bible, the more concerned he grew that the family was doing wrong. He would go on about how they would be thrown in the lake of fire, where people cry out and gnash their teeth and the burning never stops. He told them about a rich man who went to hell and could not buy so much as a small drop of water to ease the anguish of his tongue. It seemed Papa knew most of the Bible by heart. He painted verses on signs and quoted from Hebrews, where God says we must love our father who chastens us. He quoted from Timothy, about the disobedience to parents that will come as a sign of the last days. He said they could only understand the Lord through their own father. He taught that the children cannot know if they are among the saved—only God knows that, who knows all things—but they could confess their sins right away to their father and seek his forgiveness, and they could accumulate good works and follow the laws of God over the laws of man, and in this way they could hope someday to awaken, as their father had, to the joyful knowledge of their own righteousness.

Elizabeth took comfort from a dream in which she walked beside God unafraid, holding the tip of a giant finger that could easily have squished her. But when her father caught Elizabeth committing what he called a "forbidden sin"—lying or disobeying—it was an angry God who demanded discipline.

Once I lied about something for fear of getting in trouble, so my father had me get some willow branches off a tree. As he had done so many times before, he was going to use them to whip me. After that he had me go up into our little attic, which was musty, dirty, and mice infested. I was commanded to lie down in one spot and not to get up. For the next several days, he would call me to him throughout the day for another whipping and mama would bring me whatever leftovers there were from breakfast. I will never forget the long, long hours of torment as I lay there. I was a little girl with much energy and I could hardly sit in one place for very long. I became so hungry that I would lay there dreaming of the leftovers that mama would bring to me wondering what time of the day it was. Oh, the fear of those footsteps that sounded like Daddy coming up the ladder into the attic, as I knew punishment was on its way again. My heart would pound hoping just to see someone else, but "oh not this way again!"

As he beat me I would cry out for Jesus, but if I cried out too loud he would whip me on my head and the end of that willow switch would rap around my face leaving me with welts across my cheeks. I would then lay back down in relief that this one was over for a little while, but my little heart ached with hurt and confusion asking the question over and over again in my mind, "How can my Daddy love me and do this to me at the same time?" On the other hand it felt good, because my father would tell me that God is angry when we do wrong and if he didn't beat the devil out of me then I would go to hell. I had also learned that hell was a place where all the liars and rebellious people go. This left me with such a fear because I knew that I was full of evil and if my father really knew it he wouldn't have any hope for me.

This process continued, until one day we heard a car or a four-wheeler coming up the mountain. In a hurry not knowing whom it might be they told me to come down from the attic, fast. I learned two things, first was that my parents didn't want others to know about my discipline, and second that my father would put on a front with others that wasn't his real self when it was just the family at home.

VISITORS WERE rare. So were trips off the mountain. Therefore the children were excited when a small inheritance came the family's way from their grandmother in Texas, and Preacher Bob decided to take them out in the world.

He bought a used passenger bus and painted it with calls to love Jesus, and they set out on a tour of the Southwest. The gospel bus spilling with cute kids was received warmly wherever it stopped. But Preacher Bob had a hard doctrine all his own and quickly wore out his welcome in theological disputes with local church leaders. His talk about predestination reminded people of the Massachusetts Bay Calvinists. Frustrated and rejected, Preacher Bob turned for home, leaving one of his disputants a map of intricate detail, with a shining cross at the top, titled "Last Days Map to Rainbow Cross—A Refuge from the Storm that is certainly to come—In Jesus Name."

He returned to the mountain above Mora to study the Book of

Revelation and the stories of the flood and a government pamphlet about protecting yourself from nuclear radiation. He dug out a cliff cave beneath an overhanging rock. Here the family would wait out the tribulation as heirs to righteousness. In the meantime they could hide if persecutors came looking because the children were not in school. "Where there is no vision," Papa quoted, "the people perish." He added a heavy door with a tiny window. He bought a fallout meter and began caching buckets of food.

The children dug and toted rubble and waited for the annihilation of the world. It was a secret project. They learned to run like wild animals if they saw a stranger coming. They prayed that they would finish in time. One day an enormous rock emerged in the pit they were digging. They wrapped it with chains and cables, but it was too heavy to extract with a come-along jack. It was Elizabeth's job to loosen the dirt and rocks underneath with a pick and pass out buckets to her brothers. Just as she stepped out into the sunlight to rest, the cables slipped and the boulder crashed down. When her heart stopped pounding, Elizabeth took comfort from the close call, telling herself that God loved her enough to reach down and push her out of the slaughtering path of that evil rock.

Meanwhile, Papa reminded Mama about those cosmic visions singling him out as a prophet, years ago, in the mountains of South America, the ones he later rejected as temptations from the Devil. He was thinking that maybe they had come from God after all.

7

Hostile Territory

I N THE first daylight hours of February 11, 2003, three U.S. park rangers set out from town on snowmachines through the cold mountain shadows of the McCarthy Creek valley. Leading the party was Hunter Sharp, chief ranger for Wrangell–St. Elias National Park and Preserve. Their destination, thirteen miles away, was the Marvelous Millsite property owned by the Hale-Sunstar family, known locally as the Pilgrims.

According to the official case incident report, the rangers' purpose was "to evaluate the extent of resource damage done by the Hale-

Joshua Hale on the McCarthy Creek road, 2003

Sunstar family's bulldozer work on federal public lands, approximately locate public/private land boundaries within the drainage, and to determine the Hale-Sunstar family's level of hostility to our legal presence in the McCarthy Creek drainage." Park officials had begun referring to the family strictly by the names on their land deeds, as if to sweep away any cobwebby romanticism clinging already to their local reputation.

The valley was not well known to the rangers. Old equipment was scattered along the way, and they weren't sure which were rusting monuments from pre-park days and which had been left there by the Pilgrims. They stopped to examine a green army-surplus trailer with wheels. As they talked, they could hear snowmachines coming up the trail behind them. Three unidentified members of the Hale-Sunstar family appeared. The rangers asked if they'd like to pass on the trail. One of the youths shook his head. "All three individuals would not verbally reply when spoken to or questioned," the report said. "They would not speak to us. Their intentions were unclear."

The rangers had a camera and started to shoot video of their visitors. The Hale-Sunstar sons pulled out a camera of their own and shot video of the rangers. When the video shooting had died down, the rangers started up the valley again, with the Hale-Sunstars close behind.

"From this point forward, the Hale-Sunstar family members continually followed us, stopped when we stopped, maintained their silence, and periodically photographed us. They usually remained with their snowmobiles, and continued to stare at us. Again, we believed that this was an attempt to intimidate us." The report noted that each of the three shadowing sons was armed with a revolver or large hunting knife in makeshift holsters. It referred to the family's tactics as "passive-aggressive."

The rangers stopped near a ninety-year-old tunnel through a stone ridge and examined the ruins of an old bridge buttress. Most of Walt

Wigger's approaches had washed away completely, some bridges having consisted of nothing more than a pair of iron I beams spaced the width of a truck's axle.

At this point, one of the family snowmachines shot ahead and took up a high position "where he could have a visible advantage over us." Two additional snowmachines came down the creek—one driven by a lone teenager, the other by the senior member of the clan, Robert Allen Hale, with a teenage girl and a child who looked about eight years old on a sled behind. Waves from the rangers were not acknowledged. Hale disappeared, and the lone teenager joined the pursuit party. At further stops, the rangers offered to share lunch and attempted to discuss recent avalanche activity. The young men would not speak but were not overtly hostile. "Never, during the entire incident, did any Hale-Sunstar family member reach for, touch, or suggest any motion towards their weapon."

As they approached the Marvelous Millsite property, the rangers came upon two hand-painted signs posted on a tree. They could hear a dog barking up ahead. It was clear to the rangers they were still in the park's jurisdiction, well short of the mining cabins. Hunter Sharp described the scene later in a deposition: "The signs said PRIVATE PROPERTY NO TRESPASSING NPS and PRIVATE PROPERTY NO TRESPASS NPS NOT ALLOWED—BEWARE OF CABLES! These signs were located on Park land. We stopped and photographed the signs. As we photographed, the 4 individuals who had been following us took their snowmachines around us and placed one machine athwart the trail to prevent further travel."

THE NATIONAL Park Service has many missions, and some can seem contradictory: to protect park resources, for instance, but also to provide for public access and recreation. To handle its different responsibilities, the agency employs biologists and economists and historians and sociologists. Chief Ranger Hunter Sharp, a twenty-seven-year veteran of the service, was a cop. It was as a law enforcement officer that he considered the challenge posed by Papa Pilgrim.

Two years earlier, Sharp had received the Harry Yount Award for national ranger of the year. The award was named after an early leatherstocking in the nation's first park, Yellowstone, who started guarding against elk poachers in 1880 after the Civil War veteran general Phil Sheridan's cavalry gave up policing the geysers and rode off in pursuit of indigenous tribes. A government press release about Sharp's national award noted that his job in the Wrangells required overseeing rangers "whose lifestyle and duty requirements hearken back to earlier NPS days," protecting "wilderness glaciers, rivers, tundra, mountains and forest by aircraft, foot, boat and even dogsled."

The press release did not mention that Sharp—and his Wrangells predecessor Jim Hannah, another winner of the national award—spent much of their time on the job, like Yount in nineteenth-century Yellowstone, grappling with demands of local settlers, of whom the Pilgrim Family were only the most extreme case.

To many locals, the new parks were symbols of big government, not untrammeled nature. Defiance flared up in 1978 when President Jimmy Carter, facing a deadlocked Congress, used an executive order to set aside much of the Alaska parkland as national monuments. Congress finished the job two years later, and as the first park ranger in the area after that, Jim Hannah had it especially tough. A strapping Indiana native who once worked at Grand Canyon National Park, Hannah lived like an Alaskan with his family in a log cabin outside Chitina with no running water, but nobody considered him a local. He lost count of the flat tires he got from nails scattered in the ranger station driveway. During Hannah's tenure two remote Park Service cabins were burned to the ground. Sheep hunters poached rams from closed areas and issued press releases about it. A Fairbanks taxidermist promised a free mount for any hunter who succeeded in getting arrested. An outlaw faction of the state alpine club staged a "winter desecration climb" of Mount Wrangell, carrying a protest sign to the summit.

One night in the park's first year, an Alaska State Trooper called the park superintendent and reported that a ranger had been shot dead in a bar fight along the McCarthy Road. That could only have been Hannah—but it turned out the initial report was wrong. The shooting victim was one of the locals hired the previous summer as a seasonal assistant. That night at the Silver Lake Lodge, the ex-seasonal had argued with a musher from Wasilla about the relative merits of snowmachines versus dogs. The musher exited the lodge, returned with a pistol, and shot the man in the chest. The ex-parkie's twin brother grabbed a shotgun and blew away part of the killer's down coat, showering the bar with feathers. Hannah, whose recollections are preserved in an oral history with the University of Alaska, never forgot this story. He was relieved that the killing was not related to the man's park employment, but incidents like that made a law enforcement officer think twice about stepping into certain situations in this part of the world.

As career park rangers, Hannah and Sharp were proud of the agency's history of standing up to rapacious local interests and politicians who wanted to overhunt, sell off, or commercialize the public lands of the American West. But the park rangers had a hard time trying to interpret the special protections for landowners written into the landmark 1980 legislation. Local Alaskans were guaranteed the right to cut firewood, for example, even where the most common tree was the spindly, slow-growing black spruce. Hannah conceded that these privileged locals were few in number, but as the Copper River valley continued growing, he felt conflicts would only increase. Protecting subsistence hunting and fishing was arguably important to rural Native culture, Hannah would concede. But why should some schoolteacher who moves to Glennallen be instantly given the right, as a rural resident, to subsistence hunt for Dall sheep inside a national park?

Hannah's job, in the park's first decade, was further complicated by hostility from above, particularly from President Reagan's Interior secretary, James Watt, who in 1983 unleashed a mischievous land rush on ten thousand acres of black spruce bogs around Slana, on the north boundary of Wrangell–St. Elias National Park. To Hannah, this was hardly what the park needed: a new food-stamp community of subsistence hunters and tree cutters. It proved to be the last federal homesteading opportunity in American history, where Jefferson's agrarian ideal emitted its death gurgle in a mess of muddy muskeg trails and abandoned tar-paper shacks.

All of this obviously heaped difficulty on federal rangers like Hannah, whose job was otherwise to convince everyone that the pioneer moment in American history was over.

BY THE morning of Hunter Sharp's reconnaissance patrol up McCarthy Creek, many of these issues remained unsettled. But there was a new factor very much on the mind of Sharp and his federal superiors in 2003. The escalating confrontation at the Mother Lode was coming at the end of a decade of high-profile armed face-offs between government agents and militia-minded resisters in the American West.

Foremost in memory was the 1992 Ruby Ridge shootings in Idaho, where a siege had resulted in the death of a federal marshal and two members of an isolated, apocalypse-ready family. Later investigations blamed the deaths on miscommunication, mutual mistrust, and heedless escalation, all now in abundant supply along McCarthy Creek. Ruby Ridge was followed by the tense three-month showdown in eastern Montana between the FBI and the so-called Freemen. At least that one ended nonviolently. Then there was the case of the "mountain man" in Idaho who shot two Fish and Game wardens in the head after they caught him poaching bobcats. Law officers found it distressing that some people treated the fugitive executioner as a folk hero, especially after he broke out of prison and evaded capture for a year. There were also well-known incidents with religious overtones, most prominently the 1993 siege and attack on the Branch Davidian compound in Waco, Texas, an event that had particularly incensed McCarthy's pastor and newspaper editor, Rick Kenyon, who was now, in Sharp's view, encouraging the Hale-Sunstars, using them as allies of convenience in his effort to drive back the federal government.

Lessons had been learned. One was that government agents had to be careful about provoking armed resisters. It would be foolish to discount the potential for violence in an area where nearly everyone carried guns. Only a few months before, Kenyon had annoyed Sharp with a headline pointing out that attacks on park rangers nationally had gone up 950 percent in 2001. Most of those attacks were drug related along the Mexico border, as the story conceded, but Kenyon went on to speculate that this could be the explanation for the disturbing "military image" that park rangers had adopted for the Wrangells. The gunsmith turned editor seemed oblivious to the irony that the same issue included a story under his own byline discussing the best handgun to carry around McCarthy in case of bears.

Sharp considered himself a friendly law officer. He had written only a couple of tickets in his six years in the Wrangells. But he was not a big and burly officer like Hannah, and when pressed he sometimes found it necessary to compensate with an assertive toughness. He had attended the Federal Law Enforcement Training Center at Glynco, Georgia, where they taught not to let aggressive people get behind you or move too close. He was not at all comfortable with the way the young Hales tended to crowd in, guns at their sides.

Sharp was of course aware of the tragic history of the McCarthy mail-day murders in the park's first years. And just a few days before his winter patrol up McCarthy Creek, there had been yet another confrontation, this time at the footbridge, where voices were raised between a local and an Alaska State Trooper over the bollards. A few of the older Hales had been standing nearby, and soon another broadside was plastered on walls and trees around McCarthy—"Pilgrim Public Notice #3"—accusing the state trooper and a park ranger of harassment and assault. The barely suppressed fury directed at the officers was disconcerting.

> As they left, they passed us with smirks and pride. Congratulations, NPS and State Trooper, as you tried to turn McCarthy into a cement jungle where you think harassment and force is the rule and loving one another a dangerous moral. Such barbarous cursing and flagrant disregard for a person we had never seen before. . . . In our own outrage we do forgive, but do want you to know immediately what happened here to us because we work hard with our hands and mind our own business living a quiet life. Revenge is not ours, but understanding and compassion is. In Jesus Name we Say Amen! The Pilgrims.

Understanding and compassion, indeed—Sharp's understanding from the New Mexico State Police was that the Hale-Sunstar family had been considered an officer-safety threat during their twenty-three years in the mountains near Taos. Now, in Alaska, lawyers for the Interior and Justice departments had been passing memos back and forth for months, trying to decide how to handle McCarthy Creek. The federal prosecutor cited the remote location, difficult access, and possibility of armed resistance as reasons not to press criminal charges regarding the brazen bulldozing of federal land. The situation was too volatile. Instead, the government would prepare a civil lawsuit, seeking payment for damages to public resources. An expert from the NPS Environmental Response, Damage Assessment, and

Restoration Branch in Atlanta had already traveled to Alaska to start the investigation. "Every hour of manpower and resources needed to respond, assess and restore the damaged area will be included in this lawsuit," a park investigator wrote. "The numbers will be big." By spring 2003, according to the plan, the effort would require up to forty-three personnel, including a heavily armed Park Service equivalent of a SWAT team, who would be helicoptered in to protect the crime-scene biologists.

The first step was ground reconnaissance, hence the three-man February mission. Sharp remained professionally alert. How easy it would be, he thought, for someone to draw a bead on them from up high, or touch off an avalanche as the park rangers moved up the valley. As he scanned the silent mountains for clues to his fate, he said later, he realized how a cavalry scout might have felt in the days of the real frontier, traveling through hostile Indian country.

NOW IT seemed the park rangers had gone as far as they could up the valley. A Pilgrim snowmachine was blocking their path. Five other family members joined the teenager straddling the trail.

Sharp was certain they were still far from the private property. His training told him this was a situation that needed to be controlled. If Alaska State Troopers were here, he guessed, they would handcuff everyone and let the lawyers sort it out later. But that could quickly degenerate into pushing and shoving, with the family's video camera at the ready. One misstep and the Pilgrims' backers would have the Park Service on television news. On the other hand, if you showed people your back, they would be emboldened for the next confrontation. Either way, he could see events creeping toward another Ruby Ridge.

Sharp asked if the rangers could proceed just as far as the creek, where they would be able to turn their machines around in the open. Instead of answering, all six individuals turned their backs.

Sharp waited for one minute, then repeated his request, this time on videotape.

Unable to proceed, the rangers wrestled their machines around in the deep snow and started back.

Three Hale-Sunstar snowmachines shot past them. When they got farther down the valley, the rangers found that two ice bridges they had used to cross open water that morning were now gone. The ice had been cut away with a chain saw. It took forty minutes to cross the creek at a second site.

When he spoke later about that patrol up McCarthy Creek, Sharp said the prolonged river crossing had felt like a setup for an ambush.

"Maybe I'm feeling a little paranoid. I'm sorry," he said. He did not sound sorry.

THE PARK rangers' February 2003 patrol up McCarthy Creek was treated with derision in the next edition of the *Wrangell St. Elias News*.

The story was the first in Kenyon's paper to deal with the Pilgrims and the Park Service. It appeared under the pseudonym "McCarthy Annie." In the months ahead, Kenyon would closely guard the identity of the author. Laurie Rowland, one of his parishioners, was the young wife of a local heavy equipment operator, who homeschooled her children and gave music lessons and participated in community activities. Under her nom de plume, she was biting and sarcastic, and wrote moreover in first person plural, as if speaking for all the exasperated people of McCarthy.

The article was titled IN WHICH, NPS GETS A SPANKING—THIS STORY IS INCREDIBLE, BUT TRUE.

Over time, we locals have gotten to know the Pilgrims, and what we've seen, we like. As a family, they are God-fearing, peaceable, hard-working, sensible, and the most loving people we've ever known. Not only that, they are musical as well!

It has been with a growing sense of trepidation that our little community has witnessed NPS's hostility and virtual harassment of our neighbors over the mountain. The rangers have been careful, however, not to do anything overtly illegal or outrageous to the Pilgrims. This, you understand, would be unwise. That's why these latest events in the series have caused such uproar here in our sleepy, nearly deserted town.

The rangers showed up on the day of the patrol "looking for some dirt," McCarthy Annie wrote. The Pilgrims decided they should keep an eye on this "questionably motivated journey." So they stuck to the rangers like trained hounds. "When the rangers smiled nervously at them, the Pilgrims beamed joyfully, *confidently,* right back." She asserted that the family blocked the trail only inside their property line and that the rangers "turned tail and, with a last defeated glance over their shoulder, slunk down the mountain. I guess you can only push so much before folks start pushing back."

The reason the rangers were pushing the Pilgrims, Annie explained, was that the park resented the family's freedom and coveted their land. "You see, nothing galls those National Park types more than private inholdings, especially when the landowners decide not only to clear a runway and develop and build on their property, but to go and live there year round with their dogs, cows, goats, sheep, chickens, horses and all fifteen of their children."

McCarthy Annie's account included a startling allegation. As the boys stood nearby, they heard the rangers get reports from headquarters that the Pilgrims were planning to follow the rangers—information, she said, the parkies could have known only if they were monitoring a phone call that morning between the Pilgrims' wanigan in town and the homestead. She said one ranger looked involuntarily at the Pilgrims with a "guilt-edged face" as he tried to turn down the radio volume.

"I don't know about you, but whenever I think of government agents tapping citizens' phones, I get just slightly edgy," Annie wrote.

Kenyon seconded this allegation in his editorial. He reported that a park ranger denied any government wiretapping. Then he wrote: "We are forced to decide who to believe: our neighbors, who have never told us a lie—or a Ranger who is taught in Ranger School that it is OK to lie."

There was more to McCarthy Annie's story. The next morning, she wrote, the parkies found their trucks were missing. They had been parked beside the river on private land belonging to the Rowlands. Maintaining her third-person façade, she told how Keith Rowland towed the government trucks away because he was angry to learn that the park was monitoring local phones. The trucks were dragged a half mile to the McCarthy Road, with Rick Kenyon videotaping the process.

> Too bad they'd left the trucks in gear. The back tires now have less tread. . . . I hope they made it to Glennallen all right. I do worry about those worn tires.
>
> I guess between the Pilgrims and the Rowlands, the NPS got a spanking they'll, hopefully, not soon forget. And, maybe, just maybe, they'll someday mend their ways.
>
> But I'm not holding my breath.

THE ANCHORAGE headquarters of the Federal Bureau of Investigation is a brick bunker across the street from the downtown fine arts museum. On March 7, 2003, Special Agent Steven Payne received a visit from a bearded rural resident and seven of his children, including three adult sons. Robert Hale described his family's peaceful Christian subsistence lifestyle inside a national park and then reported that the National Park Service was tapping the telephones of most, if not all, of the residents of McCarthy.

"HALE portrayed the local NPS officers as arrogant, antagonistic individuals who view the local residents as squatters who have encroached on NPS land," Payne wrote.

Papa Pilgrim described two incidents in which overheard conversations suggested wiretapping. Payne explained the laws against wiretaps, and noted that the park might have a court order. Or, he said, it could be something as simple as a conversation overheard on a scanner.

"HALE's sons then advised that their family purchased the most advanced scanner available three years ago and conducted several experiments to determine if it could intercept the local radio/satellite phones, with negative results."

Pilgrim went on to recount in detail various harassments and transgressions by Park Service employees aimed at driving the Pilgrims off their land. He was particularly concerned by a rumor he traced to a park employee, accusing one of his children of carrying ammunition in a violin case.

> HALE was extremely concerned that NPS personnel would use this type of information to justify aggressive actions against his family, including "shooting my children" in a "Ruby Ridge" style siege. Immediately after each such comment by HALE, SA PAYNE reassured him that NPS officers were honorable people who would not engage in such conduct.
>
> HALE also indicated that his father, I. B. HALE, was an FBI agent from approximately 1938 to 1950. His father reportedly taught firearms at Quantico and was transferred to several other offices, including some brand new ones. I. B. HALE

reportedly resigned from the FBI to accept a position as the head of security for General Dynamics Corporation, rather than being transferred to open the FBI's new office in Butte, Montana.

The three-page, single-spaced FBI report, a model of buttoned-down agency decorum, recounts how Hale was urged to communicate openly with local park officials.

HALE and his children relaxed considerably during the interview, and at its conclusion he reluctantly indicated that he would write a letter to the NPS and that he would consider opening a dialogue with the local NPS officials. HALE appreciated SA PAYNE's assistance with this matter, and as a joint show of gratitude and to disprove the aforementioned rumor about ammunition being stored in a violin case, HALE and his children sang a folk song immediately prior to leaving the office.

Two weeks later, Special Agent Payne called Hale to follow up. Papa Pilgrim answered the phone "Hillbilly Heaven." Payne informed Hale that he had investigated the complaint and determined the Park Service had not conducted wiretaps on anyone in McCarthy. Payne said he had also obtained considerable information on mining claims, rights of way, and park permits, and he urged Hale to return to the FBI office at some point so he could share his findings. But the genial patriarch had changed his tone.

"HALE asked why he should meet with SA PAYNE, since the FBI and NPS are 'brother' agencies," Payne wrote. Papa Pilgrim said he was not particularly interested in the results of any investigation that relied on information from the park. He informed Payne that he had not written the suggested letter to the park, nor did he intend to open a dialogue with local park personnel. He declined Payne's repeated requests for a second private meeting.

"HALE indicated that he would contact SA PAYNE if he changed his mind and happened to be in Anchorage. HALE seemed aloof, argumentative and insincere throughout this contact."

Special Agent Payne then contacted Hunter Sharp, chief ranger for Wrangell–St. Elias National Park, and apprised him of the conversation.

8

Holy Bob and the Wild West

S OMETHING SEEMED amiss with the picturesque hippie family living in the mountains above Mora. It wasn't just how they drove around town in their brightly painted Jesus Jeep with born-again exhortations on the hood, on never-ending scavenger hunts for spare parts, the children ducking their eyes if anyone came along. It was how they wouldn't let anybody get close. After a decade in the Sangre de Cristos, the look in Bob Hale's eyes had changed, according to nearby rancher Editha Bartley. Calls were made to child welfare and the state police. Something just wasn't right about those cute little

The Hale family, New Mexico, 1992

blond boys and girls, and those teenage sons riding horses through the canyons with rifles and fence cutters.

A few people got to know the family just a bit. Karen Brown had bought a piece of high-country land next to Jack Nicholson's place back in 1983 and visited for a week or two every year to work on a little cabin. She and her husband were intrigued at first by the young family with their notched-log home, a hand-dug well, an icehouse, and an outdoor bathtub set up on stones and cement above a firebox. The Hales hunted and gardened and got by on a little cash from breeding Great Pyrenees. Plenty of hippies dreamed of living in the mountains, but few made a real go of it.

But the more Karen Brown saw of Preacher Bob on her trips up from Albuquerque, the less she cared for her neighbor. His wife and children sat silently in his presence, speaking only when prodded to confirm something he'd said. Bob Hale seemed to think of himself as a kind of modern-day Noah, preparing to repopulate the world after its sinful demise. He smirked and painted a sign that he placed down the Jeep trail, NOAH'S LITTLE ARK, to sell his dogs and sheep and goats. Bob would peel away her two little girls and tell them how worried he was that they would go to hell like their parents. Karen Brown got him to stop by insisting on equal time alone with his children.

Some people found the father colorful and harmless. Lloyd Parham, an insurance agent in nearby Las Vegas, New Mexico, recalled that Hale kept a macaw on his shoulder and wore moccasins of buckskin tanned with animal brains. Parham's home became a regular town stop for the Hale family, providing the kids' first tastes of pizza and strawberry shortcake—"They were ravenous"—and notarized statements for birth certificates that were essential to obtain the food stamps that helped sustain the pioneer dream. The Hales came down the mountain in an old ton-and-a-half truck with a house built on back, complete with a woodstove and a section partitioned for a mule. "The people at the office got a big kick out of 'em," Parham recalled.

The family never lacked for charitable donations, especially bags of used clothing from churches. Karen Brown found the younger children sleeping on the cabin floor atop piles of used clothes. One winter, when the sheep were starving and had lost their wool, the animals were wrapped in donated sweaters and shirts as the children led them in search of grass.

Years later, Papa Pilgrim blamed his troubles in New Mexico on cultural misunderstandings with the clannish local Hispanics. One land-grant descendant he got to know well was an outlier—a young Mora businessman leaving the Catholic Church and drawn to the persuasive flow of Scripture from Preacher Bob. "I thought, wow, this fellow has spent some time studying the word of God," Jacob Pacheco recalled. He and his wife rode up on horses to visit. The children all ran barefoot and the family got by on next to nothing—"right out of a romance novel," Pacheco said. "He would cure the kids with horse antibiotics. If that didn't work, it was because you had sin in your life." Their friendship broke up after Hale wrote to say he had discovered through prayer that Pacheco's wife—who had disputed some of Hale's Bible interpretations—was demonic.

One day in the summer of 1987, the Hales' trip down the canyon to town was stopped by a new fence. A family from Santa Fe had bought a piece of the old land grant for a country home. Scott Vail walked down to the creek to meet this rustic clan and agreed to put in gates so they could travel as they always had. Bob Hale thanked him profusely, holding his cowboy hat over his heart in a silent prayer that went on so long Vail started to regret his offer.

After that, if someone needed to reach the Hales, Scott's wife, Carolyn, would hang a white sheet from an adobe wall that could be seen with binoculars from up high. She was impressed by how the family could dismount by getting their horses to lie down. If hikers ever got lost in the national forest, she said, Bob or his sons were the ones who could track them down. The children moved so silently through the woods they could show up at the Vails' door at night without stirring the dogs to bark. The youngest ones, longhaired, wide-eyed, and barefoot, pulled at her heart.

That first year, the Hales came down for Christmas Eve. They sang carols, and the children played with some of the Vail family toys, though the antique doll collection had to be put away because Bob called them false idols. The oldest Hale daughter, eleven-year-old Elizabeth, disappeared for two hours upstairs in a hot bubble bath. Kurina Rose impressed Carolyn for trying so hard to live "the lifestyle of the original followers of Yahweh." Bob, with those hypnotic eyes, was harder to handle, she said. Bob and Carolyn argued over certain Bible verses. Carolyn, it turned out, had taught theology at Loyola University. Though the barefoot children continued to come by for snacks, Bob kept his distance from the Vails' place after that.

By the 1990s, change was coming fast in the mountains—more Texan summer homes, more backpackers in the federal Pecos Wilderness, more reports of strange encounters with armed hillbillies.

Hikers reported gunshots and vandalized cars. There were suspicions of illegal hunting and cattle rustling and reports of cabin break-ins where tools were taken and perfectly good electrical appliances left behind. Petitions circulated. State social service agencies, game wardens, and brand inspectors began asking questions. Carolyn Vail noticed hay disappearing from her barn, and discovered that the smallest Hale children were able to sneak into her house at night, through a tunnel built for the dogs, to steal food from the kitchen. She never complained, but others did. The state police and county sheriff were frustrated: There was never enough evidence to begin developing a court case—or even to compel a queasy-making trip up the old Jeep trail and through the family's crude gate in the aspens.

One neighbor, the caretaker for a big mountain ranch north of Nicholson's land, stood up to the man she called Holy Bob. Ana Martinez got annoyed when people talked about Bob Hale like he was some legendary desperado. She claimed expertise in local outlaw folklore: Her great-great-grandfather had been a jailer in Las Vegas, New Mexico, and gave Billy the Kid chewing tobacco when he passed through on his way to Lincoln, where he killed those two deputies and escaped. "People made up Billy the Kid," she said. "Billy the Kid was a murderer. He wasn't good. But people remember him, and Holy Bob wanted to be someone people remembered like that."

She was a tall, wide-beamed woman with a salty demeanor and the faint barb of a Spanish accent. Her job was to watch out for fires, timber theft, illegal grazing, and broken wire fences, and she kept running into Holy Bob and his sons riding across the property with wire-cutting pliers in their pockets. She called him a "holy terror."

"This place was the Wild West when I got here, let me tell you. I had to sit up at night with a shotgun. I had four bears going through the place and also Holy Bob. That family would steal from your freezer or your shed, a little at a time so you wouldn't notice. A bridle. A shovel. If you had chickens, you didn't have eggs in the morning. They would steal the horses that were pregnant and send the animal back down the mountain without the colt. Every time you caught him red-handed, it was the Lord this, the Lord that. He would come to preach at somebody's house and take advantage if they were elderly people and stay for days. The old folks' kids had to come and make him leave."

Hale asked for access down through her property. It would be a third escape route, she figured. She said no way. Then she stood mutely when he tried to draw her into an explanation of how her co-operation would serve God. "He needed conversation to play the game. I don't conversate," she said. He rode away when she pulled out a camera.

The family ran off a logging crew cutting Ponderosa pines in the mountains—the kids passively blocking the logging trucks and stealing batteries from the skidders at night. A scary confrontation developed, Martinez recalled, with the Hales holding rifles and the Mexican loggers holding machetes. The logging company had a legitimate contract but there were no serious consequences, she said, because they had hired illegal immigrants and nobody could show up in court.

But the logging confrontation was much discussed around Mora, and in December 1995 a community meeting about Preacher Bob and his family was convened in Editha Bartley's living room. Hispanic residents in nearby LeDoux had sent a petition to landowner "John Nicholson" asking that the Hales be barred from moving onto the lower part of his ranch near town, citing physical and verbal threats to anyone who came across the family in the Pecos Wilderness. "They do not respect property rights," the villagers wrote. "We believe them to be a menace that will disrupt our community."

The Bartleys, meanwhile, had sent a letter asking that Nicholson revoke the family's right to use the upper place as well. The ranching neighbors, once charmed by the family's innocence, now contended the Hales had overgrazed Nicholson's place with their sheep, goats, and burros, and were leaving gates open and cutting fences to graze them on the Bartleys' land as well. The family was suspected in the disappearance of cattle and the poaching of game, the Bartleys wrote. "None of their children have ever been to school, their living conditions are squalid, and they all are aggressive—we now consider them dangerous," they wrote. "We regret we have to send such bad news, but we don't break the laws of the land and we don't like when our neighbors do."

The Bartley house was full for the December meeting, not just with neighbors and Hales but also with representatives from the state police, the state Game and Fish department, the livestock brand inspection board, and the Forest Service. As eleven hungry Hale children helped themselves to cookies, everyone was polite, explaining the laws and regulations. Bob Hale was especially sorry about so many misunderstandings and the false and slanderous accusations made by people not in attendance. There were all these vague suspicions, he said, but when you looked at anything specific you could see the explanation. A storm had blown a tree down across the fence, letting their livestock stray. Those branded horses in their pen had been found by his sons in the wild, injured—they were being nursed back to health so they could be safely returned. Sometimes the young men might seem unfriendly to hikers, but that's because so many people came into the forest to steal Christmas trees.

The charm offensive worked. Editha Bartley wrote a letter to Hale, carefully spelling out an understanding about fences and such. Then she sent a follow-up letter to Jack Nicholson's agent, saying the family could stay:

> The lifestyle the Hales have chosen obviously works well for them. They have a big happy family and we have no criticism— they should live the way they have chosen. Until now our very limited communication with them led us to believe our property was involved in various law-breaking activities. We now realize we have no proof of this. . . . To quote Bob Hale: "As we work together for a loving and peaceful community all of us shall put these things behind, encouraging our friends to do the same, and move onward to love our neighbor as we love ourselves." Very well said!

Ana Martinez had stirred restlessly in the Bartley home, fuming as Holy Bob addressed the government officials and well-meaning local residents. "He made a fool out of them," she said.

9

God vs. the Park Service

I T WAS once a point of local pride that no government ranger ever slept overnight in McCarthy. For the first few years of Wrangell–St. Elias National Park, staff made diplomatic visits, as if to an independent principality, but kept them short. Over time, however, this strict policy eased in face of the elements and the local custom of hospitality. The first rangers to sleep over arrived one dusk in a winter storm, wet and shivering, and even then had to be talked out of riding their snowmachines another two hours in the dark to reach their trucks. Eventually, the Park Service bought a cabin to house its traveling employees.

▲

Left to right: Elishaba, Moses, and Joshua on the way to Hillbilly Heaven, August 2003

By the start of 2003, when the three park rangers made their reconnaissance run up McCarthy Creek, the government had finally decided to base a full-time ranger in the biggest national park's only town.

They had somebody in mind with just the right mix of local credibility, backbone, easygoing nature, and federal work experience. He was a young man with a neatly groomed beard and wire-rim glasses who lived with his girlfriend in a tidy cabin two woodsy blocks from the McCarthy Lodge. The only problem with hiring Stephens Harper was that he lived right next door to the Pilgrim Family's camp in town.

Stephens Harper remembered running into the Pilgrims for the first time at the mail shack by the airstrip. In their Davy Crockett fur hats and prairie dresses, they were buttonholing locals to ask where they lived and how they got their land. People grumbled at the time about the family's presumption—it seemed the complete opposite of the painstaking process by which Harper himself had been vetted, interviewed, and admitted to McCarthy three years earlier.

At that point in Harper's life, a decade of rootless seasonal work around Alaska—part-time park ranger in summer, remote lodge caretaker in winter—had drawn to an end, along with his first marriage. He had looked for a place to put down roots and begin again. He was intrigued seeing McCarthy on a map, a wilderness town at the toe of a glacier. After a visit to look around, he focused on a log cabin built by a longtime resident, a local seamstress and dog musher, who had been one of the few survivors of the murders back in 1983. One of her dogs had been in heat that morning so she hadn't waited by the runway with her friends. She moved away afterward, saying the place never felt the same, but she had kept her cabin.

Careful about who took her place, she had already turned down a number of prospective buyers. Stephens Harper seemed to have the right values, but in light of past events she had concerns about a single, bearded, bespectacled young man fleeing a broken marriage who would choose to spend his winters in one of the most isolated communities in Alaska—a pretty fair description of the mail-day killer, Lou Hastings. To his credit, Harper found these concerns reasonable. He agreed to fly out on the mail plane in winter, stay at her cabin for two weeks, and visit a dozen people whose names she wrote down. When her McCarthy neighbors reported back that Harper seemed all right, he was allowed to buy her cabin.

In the summer of 2002, Harper was away working as a seasonal ranger at Katmai National Park when he got a letter from his renter saying a big family had moved in right next door. Their cow was blocking the path to the outhouse. Harper knew it had to be the Pilgrims. He recalled that Walt Wigger had parked his wanigan trailer in a clearing near Harper's house. Wigger told the Pilgrims they could use the wanigan when they came to town on mail-plane days once he removed the old dynamite stored inside. The family didn't wait, taking over the wanigan as their in-town base camp. What happened with the dynamite, they never said.

The cow was gone when Harper returned home in the fall. His new neighbors had moved themselves and their livestock up to the Mother Lode. Harper settled in with his girlfriend, Tamara, a Peace Corps veteran with a master's degree in resource conservation. That winter, they traveled in South America. But when they returned in March 2003 to get ready for Harper's new full-time job with the Park Service, they discovered rusty trucks parked around the wanigan, a bus that had been pulled across the river, horses, goats, stacks of recycled construction materials, and a swarm of busy Pilgrims.

Elishaba and her brothers were friendly. Harper introduced himself to their father, who described his family's joy at completing their first year in McCarthy. The two spoke pleasantly regarding plans for the material strewn in front of Harper's cabin. Papa Pilgrim assured him that by mid-April they would be hauling everything by bulldozer and sled up the road to their land. Then Pilgrim asked Harper what he did for a living. Harper said he was going to be a ranger for the park.

Pilgrim turned on the spot and disappeared into the wanigan. Moments later he returned, with a small daughter at his elbow, and launched into an angry tirade about government snooping.

Within days, the Pilgrims had posted notices around town accusing the Park Service of planting a spy next to their camp.

Harper realized it was not going to be easy to separate his new job and his home life because the Pilgrims were going to be part of both—morning, noon, and night.

COMPASSIONATE NEIGHBORS were the last thing Papa Pilgrim expected when they moved deep into the Alaska wilderness. The citizens of McCarthy were not their friends, Papa told his family. The way the community pulled together in times of need, helped one another out, and wanted to get to know the Pilgrim children better—these things might seem like good Christian behavior, but in fact they were dangerous temptations. He warned his children against becoming man pleasers. They needed to turn their attention inward again toward God. His old fighting instincts were aroused. Once he finished bulldozing open the road along McCarthy Creek, he said, his family would see how nosy and angry and unsupportive the people in McCarthy really were.

The government had certainly responded according to plan. The Park Service was aghast, the family under a state of siege, the children inspired and indignant. Papa's dramatic unmasking of a police spy on their doorstep helped raise the level of tension. Any lone impulse to mutinous dissent could be more easily suppressed during wartime. When Elishaba suggested God might be opening a door through Stephens Harper, Papa accused her of selling the family out.

But news that the Pilgrims had started using the old Green Butte Road to travel back and forth from the Mother Lode had not riled people around McCarthy, not even those who might have considered themselves environmentalists. The family struck some neighbors as passing strange and grandiose, their defiance of the Park Service oddly petulant for a cabin full of avowed pacifists. But the use of a bulldozer to clear a grown-over mining trail did not register locally as a flagrant environmental crime.

For some people, in fact, Papa Pilgrim was now a local hero. And Pilgrim didn't seem to mind his new stature one bit.

On the morning of April 11, 2003, a community meeting was convened at the lodge to talk about the McCarthy Road, the footbridge, and the latest bollard extraction. Joining via teleconference were state transportation officials and the local state senator, an Athabaskan woman from the Yukon River village of Rampart, whose sparsely populated legislative district, extending north to the Arctic Circle and west to the Yukon and Kuskokwim River deltas, was the largest in the United States. State officials agreed not to replace the bollards at the footbridge.

Two park rangers were in McCarthy and listened quietly at the lodge. After it was over, they walked around town and stapled up a public notice at the lodge and on a tree by the trail leading out of town:

> No motorized vehicles are permitted to use the illegal roads bulldozed on federal lands located in the McCarthy Creek Drainage, connecting the state land around the town of McCarthy with the Marvelous Millsite private property. This notice does not apply to the use of snowmachines on adequate snow cover.

The government notice hit McCarthy like an artillery shell. The decision to close a historic road threatened to undo two decades of peaceful coexistence with the park. Maybe it was true that no one had used the road in recent years—but no one before the Pilgrims had needed to. In a few days, the family planned to bring a bulldozer down from the Mother Lode to get supplies. There was no other way to haul so much material—lumber, insulation, hay for livestock. The sudden road closure seemed cold and heartless. Park critics called it a government blockade.

And why had the two rangers skulked through town, not telling anyone what they were up to? The notices were torn down and burned.

Two days later, Stephens Harper was roused from bed on a Saturday morning. Peering out the cabin door in his underwear, with Tamara watching curiously from behind, he saw two neighbors: Keith Rowland, with a rifle over his shoulder, and Rick Kenyon, brandishing a microphone. They told him they were about to take their four-wheelers up the McCarthy Creek road to go rabbit hunting, in violation of the road closure—did he want to arrest them?

Harper told them to seek their redress of grievances elsewhere: His job didn't start for another week and they were trespassing.

McCarthy Annie retold the incident in the next issue of the *Wrangell St. Elias News*. The cover photo showed Bethlehem and Lamb perched endearingly on a set of bull-moose antlers, with the title THE PILGRIMS—NEIGHBORS, FRIENDS.

The story did not name Harper except as a local "parkie" whose voice was a "low, menacing growl."

Curious thing, how that door kept slamming shut. Hopefully he'll get it fixed, or I'm afraid that, after a while, the good folks here in McCarthy may begin to think him an unpleasant sort of guy. . . . Desperately, the parkies tried to calm the situation, protesting to one caller, "We didn't mean for the notice to be aimed at your community. It was really just meant for the Pilgrims!" Well, fellas, this was the wrong thing to say, because if there's one thing that will unify a small, close-knit community in a hurry, it's this: Big, Bad, Powerful Government Men singling out a peaceable, law-abiding family with lots of adorable, defenseless children, and doing illegal and mean things to try to force them off their land.

The national park's road closure boiled into a full town meeting a few days later.

The park superintendent, Gary Candelaria, showed up with Hunter Sharp and Marshall Neeck to explain the decision. Candelaria was not especially well liked in McCarthy. Critics found him inflexible. Even locals sympathetic to the park's goals had not warmed to this superintendent during his four years at the Copper Center headquarters near Glennallen. A few previous park bosses had fared better, showing more of a common touch. They had been hunters or fishermen who considered the Alaska assignment a storybook job. Candelaria had been a surprising choice. Officious and slightly pudgy, he was nearing the end of a government career that had concentrated in smaller park units: Saratoga National Historical Park, Ozark National Scenic Riverways, Fort Laramie National Historic Site. When Candelaria arrived to take over the system's biggest national park, the government's press release described him as an aspiring bookbinder and an amateur historian.

It was the latter interest, perhaps, that led Candelaria to conclude he had come to Wrangell–St. Elias National Park at a crucial moment in American history. He knew this would win him no popularity contests. But from now on, Alaskans were going to need permits just like other Americans to do certain things on federal land. He arrived in McCarthy that April day in 2003 ready to argue the point.

More than a dozen McCarthy residents were waiting in the lodge dining room. Some were eager to challenge the federal overlords, some merely curious. The Pilgrims refused to participate. The children stood across the street from the McCarthy Lodge with

Papa, holding protest signs before their horse and wagon. One sign said IF GOD IS FOR US, WHO CAN BE AGAINST US? Another, held by the blue-eyed four-year-old named Lamb, said PLEASE LET ME GO HOME TO MAMA. There was defiance, too: A sign on a bulldozer read MCCARTHY CREEK TRAIL RIDES.

The Kenyons and Rowlands led the argument. They demanded to know how the Green Butte Road up McCarthy Creek could be declared illegal, since it had been used for much of the century. Candelaria said the road had been erased by time and nature. The new road, rebuilt illegally, wandered off the original route.

For more than two hours, temperatures rose in the lodge as the sides hammered back and forth. Kenyon had been researching the issue in fine detail. The discussion turned on technicalities involving legal access rights under two laws: the 1980 Alaska conservation act and a Civil War–era law regarding historic trails known as Revised Statute 2477. The Pilgrim supporters said the family had just been doing road maintenance on a legal historic route. Candelaria said access to inholding properties required a permit. No one had ever sought a permit for the Green Butte Road and the Mother Lode.

Every time the park officials looked into the street, they saw the Pilgrims standing in front of the bulldozer. Candelaria finally pointed out the window and said, "Do you know who created your problem? Those folks created your problem." The crowd hooted in protest, Kenyon wrote later.

McCarthy Annie, in her more pungent account, said the parkies showed up for the community meeting "with their trademark park green bulletproof vests, and packing Sig-Sauer handguns and pepper spray." She said the park rangers added insult to injury when they called the McCarthy residents "inholders." It was another way of asserting control, she said—"Let me tell you, Control is the name of their game!"

But, she said, the local folk had a measure of sweet revenge when the meeting broke up and a protest parade of vehicles started up the Pilgrims' road: "After all, we mountain folks know our history and law. . . . When you're on the right side, there's no need to hide, apologize, or give in." And there was no question who else was on their side—she pointed out that another of the Pilgrims' protest signs said GOD IS BIGGER THAN THE NPS. WATCH OUT, HE'S GETTING MAD!

AFTER THAT, no one in McCarthy could avoid getting drawn into the Pilgrim drama. Not even the flinty homesteading elder of the area, Jim Edwards, who had stayed away from the protest meeting at the lodge. He could never hear much of what people said on such occasions, for one thing, having spent most of his life around bulldozers and airplane engines. More important, he had no wish to take sides in a contest over who was tougher, God or the Park Service. He had always preferred to engage Nature in the Wrangell Mountains directly, without interference from either of those meddlesome outside parties.

But one morning, as spring gave way to summer, Papa Pilgrim showed up at Jim Edwards's door, clutching his cowboy hat to his chest, with two small children clinging to his coat. He had come to ask a favor.

A bemused indifference toward the religious ferments of his neighbors had served Edwards well in McCarthy for fifty years. He had never been a churchgoer, not even after his wife, Maxine, was killed in the mail-day murders. His personal religion remained pretty much the same as the day he first flew a small plane into the country as a twenty-four-year-old and saw the Kennicott Glacier spilling off the mountains. You could call it nature worship, he said: the trees, the animals, the summits migrating all the way from South America. It about killed him to cut down two perfectly healthy spruce on his homestead so he could see through to a television satellite.

On the other hand, he held no great affection for the Park Service. He remembered how things were before. Despite promises in the

1980 Alaska conservation act, the park had pretty much confiscated Edwards's part-time placer gold operation on Dan Creek. They told him they didn't have one thousand dollars to buy him out but could spend unlimited funds flying helicopters across the Nizina River valley to inspect his operation and explain the latest regulations.

Edwards was a soft-spoken man with the shambling demeanor of an accountant, though his diffidence was misleading—he had a ropy strength, stubborn opinions, and unstoppable energy. He had ties as strong as anyone's to McCarthy's mining past. His gold claim had once belonged to a tough old Croat named Martin Radovan, a holdover prospector from the Kennecott days. Edwards had befriended Radovan in the 1950s and one summer led a geologist's crew out on the face of a cliff above the Chitistone River to examine a Radovan claim known as the Binocular Prospect because not even European mountain climbers hired by Kennecott Copper had been able to reach its turquoise stains. Radovan got there, however, and told people he might have found the greatest bonanza of all. Edwards led the team along a ledge several thousand feet up, nudging scree with their toes to make steps. In places the ledge was ten inches wide. Where the rock bulged, they crawled on hands and knees. A hanging glacier hundreds of feet over their heads dropped blocks of ice that whistled like bombs. The survey crew got close enough to see the cotton mattress atop a boulder where the old prospector bivouacked, but rocks buzzing past the geologist's head convinced him to turn back without actually reaching the pay streak. Radovan finally sold his interest in the claims to investors and continued working for the new owners into his eighties. After he died, a mining company helicoptered in, looked it over, and turned the claims over to the new park. Radovan's lifelong dream of a mountain of solid copper blipped off the screen as a corporate tax write-off.

Radovan's placer gold claim disappeared next, a few decades later, when Jim Edwards, using it mainly as a hobby, surrendered it to the government. Now there was hardly any mining left in the park. The man at his door, Papa Pilgrim, the new owner of the Mother Lode Mine, was not even a hobby miner. It wasn't clear to Edwards what exactly he planned to do with his hole in the mountain.

Pilgrim said the family's goats had escaped from the old mill-site property and were scattered somewhere in the high country. Edwards knew the Mother Lode valley well, having led packhorses up McCarthy Creek for a prospecting crew in territorial days—a hell of a difficult trip, he recalled, given how the road was grown over before Wigger cleared it again.

Edwards always tried to think the best of people. Sometimes he lived to regret it. But he figured family cohesion like the Pilgrims' was to be admired in this day and age. And he was hardly one to hold the newcomer's bulldozing against him. Before Papa Pilgrim steered that Caterpillar D5 down from the Mother Lode, Edwards had been famous locally for the most audacious bulldozer ride in the history of the Wrangells.

Back in the winter of 1961, when there was still no road to McCarthy, Edwards left Chitina for home on a D4 cable-blade dozer. He crossed the frozen Copper River and rumbled along the old tracks, finding just enough room to move between the iron rails. He crept across wobbling trestles, built detours around washouts, dynamited broken rails, and at one point hiked back to Chitina and flew to Anchorage to get a replacement front axle, approaching each new obstacle as calmly as a mathematician working his way across a chalkboard. Finally he crossed the Kennicott River, pulled up at his house, and presented Maxine, his wife, with her pale-green 1949 Chevy Deluxe sedan. He had pulled the car all the way to McCarthy on a sled behind his bulldozer. He had come sixty miles and it took him thirty days.

In his seventies, Edwards was still flying his kit-built plane off the grass strip he'd cleared on his homestead. He told the abjectly grateful Pilgrim he would fly up McCarthy Creek and have a look around.

The escaped goats were easy to find. Edwards landed at the Mother Lode and described their location high on a flank of the Green Butte. He was warmly thanked, and invited back for a visit any time. The next time he flew there, he brought a guest, a hardy young German who had bicycled thousands of miles to Alaska. The visit to Hillbilly Heaven seemed to go well. Elishaba served fresh bread, and Pilgrim regaled them with stories. But when they got back to Edwards's place that night, the German friend surprised him. He'd found the afternoon disturbing.

"That Elishaba really hates her father," the German said.

THROUGH THE summer, the McCarthy Creek situation deteriorated. The U.S. Justice Department formally notified the Hale family of plans to seek an injunction against further bulldozer work in the park. A Park Service team was assembled to complete a summer assessment of the bulldozed road and prepare damage estimates. A second team would finally survey the Marvelous Millsite and other related Mother Lode properties to establish where the family's clearing activities had violated park boundaries. All steps necessary to assure the teams' safety would be taken, including dispatch of an armed Special Event Tactical Team.

People started to worry. Nearly everyone in town, regardless of their comfort level with the Pilgrims, felt deployment of a half dozen flak-jacketed government riflemen was more likely to escalate matters than to calm them. The more vehement government critics fastened onto this resort to arms with a mix of horror and relish. E-mails began to fly from remote Alaska to national property-rights and other conservative mailing lists, describing how the "NPS is hunting this family like a wolfpack stalks a pregnant elk."

"Bear in mind that these folks are pacifists, very akin to the Mennonite faith," Rick Kenyon wrote in one e-mail alert. "We plan to evacuate the children from the property and send observers up to the property, but beyond that, we need help. What should we do? We feel like the Wrangell/St. Elias National Park has become 'occupied territory' and is being ruled by a dictator."

The Alaska regional director of the National Park Service, Rob Arnberger, called Kenyon to try to clear the air. Arnberger's exasperation was plain in a subsequent e-mail to several colleagues, reporting on the conversation: "[Kenyon] stated he felt the 'NPS was coming in to do its work and kill some kids.' I expressed my deep disgust with this kind of irresponsible comment as direct evidence of his intentions to inflame the process and that his assertions of fairness in representing the issue was a fallacy and fabrication. We both severed the call with a quick commitment to look for ways to better communications."

In midsummer, the park set out once again to close the last remaining tunnel entrance to the Mother Lode mine. It was an old ventilation tunnel that led from park land into forty miles of catacombs, where temperatures remained a few degrees above freezing year-round. The Pilgrims had chiseled their way in through the ice that blocked the entrance. A ranger flew out by helicopter and found a hand-lettered sign on the tunnel door: THIS ENTRANCE IS CLOSED TO ALL PUBLIC AND "PARK" OFFICIALS—LIABILITY LAWS ARE NOW IN EFFECT WITH THE NEW OWNERSHIP! WORKERS ARE INSIDE AT THIS TIME—AND THIS ENTRANCE IS PATROLLED DAILY—VIOLATERS WILL BE PERSECUTED TO THE FULL EXTENT OF THE LAW! "PILGRIM" FAMILY.

The ranger replaced the Pilgrims' sign with his own—a skull-and-crossbones above a list of generic underground dangers: rotten structures, deadly mine openings, lethal gas and lack of oxygen, dangerous animals, unsafe ladders, cave-ins and decayed timbers, unstable explosives, deep pools of water. He padlocked the door. Two weeks later, tipped off about paying customers headed to Hillbilly Heaven, three park rangers returned to the mountain and spent a night staked out with binoculars. They watched Joseph climb to the tunnel. When they scrambled over they found the lock broken by a pickax and ticketed Pilgrim's oldest son.

Then in August they sent an undercover agent posing as a tourist to book a horse ride to the Bonanza Mine. The rocky trail, a full day's hike on foot above the Kennecott ruins, climbs past abandoned timber tram towers and around ravines and rocky turrets that give the ridge a look of deep relief in the shadows of a long summer sunset. The trail leaves the state-owned roads around McCarthy and enters the park. At the end of the trip, Joshua was cited for operating in the park without a commercial permit.

Federal court dates in Anchorage were set for the Pilgrim brothers later in the year. Kenyon complained that the potential fines could ruin the family. Carl Bauman, the conservative Motorhead lawyer, agreed to represent Joseph and Joshua for whatever money Kenyon could get by passing a hat.

A crew of federal surveyors flew to Hillbilly Heaven, but the park backed down on sending a team of armed guards. The surveyors cleared a swath of trees around the Pilgrim perimeter, which turned out to be pretty much where the park expected. The Pilgrims had indeed been clearing park land, but from the air, the rectangular perimeter in the forest was a more jarring sight than the homestead itself. The logging was a tool of rough frontier justice. A line was drawn through the wilderness, and the Pilgrims had been told not to cross it.

The property line ran through the middle of the Pilgrims' kitchen.

WITH AIRPLANES and horses their only options for going home, the Pilgrims spent more time around town that summer. It was their second summer in McCarthy, and locals were starting to feel less charitable. One day the horses got loose and scattered across the runway. Natalie Bay, a formidable Australian who owned Wrangell Mountain Air with her pilot husband and managed the complicated logistics for dozens of backpacking and hunting parties every summer, lashed into Papa. It was bad enough that the horses left piles of manure by the community's drinking water spring, and that the family's horse-drawn wagon, competing for Kennicott tourists with the air service shuttle van, had now evolved into a rasping dune-buggy taxi. Cute little Pilgrim children were posted by the footbridge to direct tourists to their own "Jelly Bean" rig. Natalie had even heard reports of the children trying to solicit footbridge-crossing fees. She had put up with all this, in part because she appreciated having the Pilgrim girls around to play with her own young daughter. But endangering the pilots was over the line. She went up to the airstrip with a rifle and threatened to shoot the horses.

Pilgrim apologized. It wasn't long after, though, that he ignored Natalie's wishes one afternoon and snuck her daughter away to play with his girls in the wanigan. Then he tried to prevent Natalie from going inside to retrieve her. "There's nothing you can do about it," Pilgrim told her, blocking her way. He was wrong, it turned out. But the rest of the afternoon several Pilgrim boys followed Natalie and her daughter around town, taking videos.

At the Hardware Store, where the summer college program was again under way, Ben Shaine worried that the escalating antagonism might leave permanent scars in the community. Kenyon was blaming every problem not on the Pilgrims but on the Park Service blockade. It was brilliant political theater. Shaine marveled at Pilgrim's performance art the day Papa stopped by the Hardware Store and monopolized an open house, drawing the college students about him with his tales of bush living. The occasion left Shaine's daughter, Gaia, indignant. She had graduated from college back east and had come home for the summer to guide whitewater rafting trips. Gaia found it insulting to hear the Pilgrims, in only their second summer in the Wrangells, refer to McCarthy as "our town." They didn't understand that the town had always gotten along by common law and respect for neighbors. By forcing the park to get nasty about rules, she felt, they were changing the place in ways that would last even after the family's wilderness experiment failed and they moved on.

Neil Darish at the McCarthy Lodge continued to serve as the family's go-between with the park. But even he began to wonder whether the description of "colorful" was quite adequate. Pilgrim rejected his suggestion that the family manufacture copper wall hangings of salmon as a cottage industry, saying it would be idolatry to fashion the image of a living being. Pilgrim's source was Deuteronomy, in which Moses extended the commandment against graven images to cover specifically the likeness of any male or female, or beast on the earth, or winged fowl or fish or anything that creepeth on the ground. When they lived in Fairbanks and drove through the highway town of North Pole, Pilgrim made the children look away as they passed the Christmas factory with the giant Santa Claus.

All that was fine with Darish, though he shared the estimable Ayn Rand's atheism—even charming in its eccentricity. But Pilgrim's attitude about law enforcement was another matter. The police never just come over and celebrate your birthday with you, he told Darish. They justify their lies with their higher purpose. He had grown up around law enforcement, he said. There's nothing you can tell an officer like Stephens Harper that can help you. They're only out to get you.

SOMEHOW IN the midst of the commotion surrounding his new park job that summer, Stephens Harper and Tamara Egans got married. Tamara's parents flew to McCarthy in July 2003, and Kelly Bay took everyone on a flight over the vast ethereal emptiness of the largest subarctic ice field in the world. They landed on a river bar and Bay read the essential words off a fluttering three-by-five card and took off promptly because the wind was picking up.

Back in McCarthy, the newlyweds had to cross a neighbor's yard to reach their cabin. The meadow out their front window was blocked by the dreary dark brown wanigan, along with old vehicles and oil drums, stacks of storm windows, pallets, batteries, saddles, and other tack hung in a shed built of tree poles.

Tamara had planted a little garden, and one morning she found the Pilgrims' goats finishing off the tender seedlings. Stephens told Joseph that if he saw the goats in his garden again he was going to shoot them. This was no longer park business, in his view. This was his hearth and bride. He checked with a state trooper acquaintance as to whether Alaska's law regarding defense of life and property, generally invoked when grizzly bears were shot out of season, could be applied to domestic goats. The trooper recommended trying anti-bear pepper spray first.

Harper was surprised a few days later when Elishaba came over with new seedlings to help replant the garden. It felt like she was trying to clean up the mess. When she asked them to say nothing to her papa about her visit, he felt a flicker of sympathy. He felt it again a few days later, as he was threading his way through the junk piles in the Pilgrims' camp—it was, after all, his legal access—and Joseph, following behind, picked up a hammer. When Harper turned around and stopped him with a practiced lawman's stare, Joseph set the hammer down and blushed.

Harper did some more legal research. This part of town looked like vacant woods. The old schoolhouse and other nearby buildings had burned or collapsed, the poplars and cottonwoods grown back. But all of it was platted town lots, and Harper found that Wigger never owned land there. The wanigan had been left on an overgrown lot owned by an elderly lady in Anchorage, an original McCarthy kid whose father had been the local U.S. commissioner. Wigger apparently assured the Pilgrims they could claim the land by adverse possession since his little trailer cabin had sat there for so long. This legal advice proved unreliable. The owner, contacted by Harper, said she wanted the Pilgrims off her land.

The Pilgrims checked the survey corners themselves and moved everything into the platted road right-of-way. Unable to haul the material to Hillbilly Heaven because of the park blockade, they had now used it to block Harper's legal access completely. Harper felt like he had been drawn into some eye-for-an-eye battle out of the Old Testament.

On the night they finished making their piles, the family lined up at the Harpers' property line and sang "Mind Your Own Business." They hung up blue tarps and surplus parachutes in the poplars to screen the view of their wanigan. Then they moved a twenty-kilowatt generator with no muffler to the edge of the property and ran it all night so that Stephens and Tamara had to sleep with ear plugs.

IN AUGUST 2003, the team of government specialists assembled at the park's May Creek outpost across the Nizina from town.

The post consisted of a remote cabin purchased by the park, and wall tents set in military fashion around a mowed-grass parade ground. It was used by firefighters and would provide a helicopter base camp for the next two weeks. The assessment team had been whittled to nineteen, including three cultural resource specialists, a plant ecologist, and rangers to keep the Pilgrims outside the work perimeter. Stephens Harper would carry a video camera, to record the work and any confrontation that might develop at Hillbilly Heaven.

In Rick Kenyon's newspaper, McCarthy Annie described what came next. First she set the garden-like scene into which the government machinery came crashing: a little old-fashioned cabin, a curl of woodsmoke, a "chuckling stream" and "wildflowers on the breeze." Sounds of singing, children playing, doing chores, the faithful old dog. Amid forbidding peaks, this little piece of paradise that Country Rose called home.

She tried not to let her mind dwell on how vulnerable she was—a woman alone on the mountain, with half a dozen of her youngest children to care for.

Far from help. Far from Pilgrim and her sturdy, capable older sons.

With a suddenness that made her head jerk up, the heavy wooden door flew open. An excited voice called out, "Mama! The helicopter! I can hear it coming! Hurry, come on!"

Alarmed, Country Rose left her bread bowl and scooted out the door.

The rangers were "warlike apparitions." Little Psalms offered them a plate of cookies, "as trusting eyes the hue of faded bluebells searched earnestly for approval." She was pushed roughly away, the paper's correspondent wrote.

The Park Service saw things differently. The Pilgrims shoved up against the single ranger guard, trying to provoke something. One afternoon, Marshall Neeck was fending off the three oldest boys on the trail. At a signal they split, running in several directions into the trees toward the assessment team. Neeck retreated to join the others and they circled up, not sure what the Pilgrims, crashing unseen in the woods, would do next. They called in the helicopter and retreated for the day.

Stephens Harper was able to reach Tamara on the phone each night after they flew back to May Creek. She reported that the Pilgrims still in town had put up protest signs in front of the blue tarps. The generator with no muffler was running again. They played loud recordings of old-time spirituals and pointed the headlights of two trucks right at Tamara's cabin. It sounded to Harper like the Branch Davidian siege, except with the religious crazies on the outside.

On the night she finally moved out, she looked out the window and saw teenaged Moses in a nearby tree, watching her. Hanging from a limb below was the butchered and skinned carcass of one of the Pilgrims' goats.

10

The Pilgrim's Progress

T HE OLDER Pilgrim children were raised to believe they shared a special destiny. The younger siblings grew up in the hopeful belief that their older brothers and sisters knew what they were doing.

In the mountains of New Mexico, they had access to only two books. One was the Bible, of course—the King James Version, preferably, but other translations as well, some of them underlined and carefully annotated in Papa's small fine print. The other was a book with pictures, written by a Puritan preacher who lived in England in the seventeenth century.

▲

Bible lessons in the Sangre de Cristo Mountains

The Pilgrim's Progress is considered one of the great books of the Western canon, never out of print since it was published in 1678. To modern scholars, it is a landmark in the development of English fiction and allegory, an imaginative historical and religious novelty, a window into the literal-minded piety and harsh Calvinist theology of another age. For many modern evangelicals, it remains a relevant testament to faith and a warning against errancy. In the immanent landscape of the Sangre de Cristos, however, it was much more. The centuries-old story was encyclopedia and atlas, the textbook describing how the world worked, the treatise explaining why few ever make it all the way down the perilous path to salvation and a father's love.

The family took comfort from John Bunyan's classic. On special occasions, Papa read parts aloud. The children studied the geography of the straight and narrow path to the Celestial City as closely as the canyon road leading up the Staircase to home. They, too, skirted the quicksands and the By-Path Meadow, refreshed themselves in the River of the Water of Life. They had built their own Wicket Gate, like the one the hero Christian passes through—in their case, poles of aspen sunk in concrete on the Jeep road to the Rainbow Cross. They struggled as Christian did to leave earthly burdens of sin behind, to match his single-minded quest. To be sure, the adventure stories of Christian's battles with fiends and giants had unusual appeal for children growing up without exposure to television, movies, or other books. Yet these were inescapably moral battles, as were the hero's encounters with dissemblers and tempters such as Obstinate, Timorous, and Mr. Ready-to-halt. The lessons shone with clairvoyant Truth once explained in consuming detail by their learned father, for whom sleepy little Mora posed worldly dangers comparable to the seductions of the market town known as Vanity Fair.

The children also learned stories from the Bible, of course. But they did not know these as well as other devout families might imagine. Papa's lessons tended to bring together essential passages from separate chapters and books, making connections he alone had discovered in his long hours of study, a distillation process that sometimes deprived the original stories of their narrative power, not to mention their moral context.

Family readings of *The Pilgrim's Progress* were special occasions. When a black thunderstorm would force them into the cabin, they would make popcorn and gather around. Papa's renditions were expressive and dramatic, and it was agony for any child to be excluded as punishment. Papa liked to toy with his captive audience, cutting off Bunyan's tale at some cliff-hanging moment. It was tantalizing the way, in later years, he refused to read the end, never sharing the part where Christian finally reaches the Celestial City, never dispelling for the younger children that cloud of gloomy Puritan uncertainty.

The saved do not let doubt or temptation or worldly wickedness lure them from the path—that much of the book's message was clear. If the children strayed, Papa was near to guide them back with a loving correction. This was the duty of a father. Sometimes the correction involved an explanation or a lecture. Sometimes it was the quick whip of a switch across the palm, followed by a reading from Scripture. These corrections could be private or they could go on for hours with the family assembled to witness. If it grew late and one of the younger children nodded off, a small slap brought her back.

When someone committed a forbidden sin such as lying or disobeying, the discipline was commensurate. Some corrections were blunt and direct. He used a braided leather thong, and sometimes just his fists. All the children had known bruises and welts, bloody noses, and swollen lips inflicted in front of the others. There had been a few broken bones. "Correction is grievous to him that forsaketh the way," as Proverbs says. Papa was trained as a boxer, and his children could be grateful for his mercy in not inflicting the kind of pain he was capable of. This is what they learned to pray for, what Papa called his "mercy"—the moments when God's angry heart would be moved to forgiveness.

One of the worst corrections was to be put on silence. It was like being excommunicated. The offender could not be spoken to. A child might get no food except bread and water, or be made to eat outside the New Mexico cabin. He would sit out in the rain or snow. Or sleep outdoors for seven nights. Mama had to take crying babies away, and the older children learned to sit silently while he read the Bible to himself.

Papa corrected Mama all the time. It was an ongoing project, he explained, to save her from going to hell. In the early years, when she had been happy as an old-fashioned frontier mom, leaving spiritual matters to her husband seemed an easy concession. But it turned out that she had conceded everything. Any activity might figure into their relation with the Lord. It was a rare day that had no major drama, no signs and wonders and revelations from on high.

Living in rural New Mexico had actually been Mama's idea. When they found the land owned by Jack Nicholson, it had not really been Papa's eloquence that secured their position as caretakers, but rather a call from Mama to Beverly Hills, where her mother's movie-producer husband was a friend of the movie actor's agent. But now Rose had become an unhappy servant. She had to prepare Papa special meals, with fresh food the others never tasted. She had to remember to call him "Lord," for it was through the father that God spoke to a family. As their eldest daughter grew into her teens and Papa turned more to her for help and company, he had to devote even more time to guiding Mama away from jealousy and rebellion.

Jerusalem was the second daughter, born fourteen years after her sister. One of her earliest memories was a day when the children were kicked out of the New Mexico cabin. She could not bear the screams so she peeked in the kitchen window and saw her mother getting beaten with a broomstick. This was horrible to behold, but Papa explained and explained until they all understood how the correction would help Mama get her heart right with God. If Mama persisted in challenging him, he would hold her hair and scream in her face until she was in tears. Only when Mama got to shaking hard and couldn't stop, like she was having some kind of nervous breakdown, did Papa back off.

In this world, God's law was more important than man's. The boys learned to butcher a deer and sweep the spot clean in fifteen minutes so no trace of blood was visible. In fact, it's pretty much against man's law to be a true Christian family, Papa said, because so many things in the Bible are illegal. The state uses the word "abuse," but doesn't Proverbs say that a father who spares the rod hates his child? If you brought some matter before the judgment of a state court instead of God's eternal judgment, the choice to do so was already your defeat. The state would entice children to speak against their own parents and then send them off to jails and foster homes. It would turn them all from righteousness and drive them from the land.

AT CHRISTMAS they feasted in the Sangre de Cristos and enacted their own manger scenes in the snow, with sheep and cows and every other year a new babe to wrap in swaddling clothes. As Hosanna, Job, and Noah were born and Papa got deeper into his preparations for the tribulation, he began to use the name "Elishaba" for Elizabeth, his oldest daughter. It was the original Hebrew version of her name from Exodus, he said, the name of the loyal wife of Aaron, the brother of Moses. He called her "Elishaba" when he put her on a pedestal as an example to her mother. When he interrogated her in anger, however, he went back to "Elizabeth" and the old name jabbed her like a stick.

Elishaba did not grow up resenting her father's discipline or the absence of books. She understood his rule was hard, but so was the secret sin in her heart. The corrections from her father were her best hope. Every time she came out of a discipline, she would work harder to do right and please him. It made her angry when her siblings did not do what their father wanted. As she grew older, sometimes the intensity of this desire to please made her confused and forgetful. She stumbled and broke things and the punishments got worse. Still she did not question them.

What did seem hard and unfair was being so cut off from other families. Her father's attitude toward the world surely did not need to be so harsh. At times the natural longings of adolescence edged her dangerously toward rebellion. She wanted a friend. She hated that the world called her family weird. Why would God say in the Bible that they couldn't have people in their house? On the rare occasion a visitor came up the mountain, the girls hid in the cabin and the older brothers stood beside Papa to bar the door. When they drove to town the girls had to duck down in back, so no one would see them and try to snatch them away.

Elishaba later recalled how it hurt to hear false rumors being spread. "I began to feel like a wild animal, prone to run every time I saw a person. . . . It made me draw back from people, and try to find some sort of happiness in being the rugged, tuff, and hard working, dirty little mountain girl I was."

She found comfort in the high country. By the time Elishaba was thirteen, she was being sent off with a black powder rifle to guard the sheep against wild beasts.

Rising up early in the morning when it was my turn, I would get my leather shepherd bag which held my Bible, refried beans wrapped in a tortilla, and fire starting kit. Strapping it over one shoulder, with my staff in the other hand and a brother in tow, we would head for the sheepfold. The sheep were very happy to see me, especially my own little lamb (or "baabaa" as we called the ones that were our special lambs). "Baaa come on baby let's go," I said. After feeding the little lamb, I opened the sheepfold, raising my staff to count the sheep as they rushed out to find grass and kicking their little hoofs. Shepherding became more and more of a challenge as we took turns taking the sheep out on the mountains and down in the valleys to find them fresh green grass to graze. We could take them just about anywhere on the neighboring properties because they could easily crawl under the bob-wire fences. I felt a bit scared when I took the sheep down in the valleys on to other people's properties not knowing what might happen. Anytime I heard the sound of a vehicle I began to rush the sheep into the deep woods to hide, as I was afraid they would see us. It was hard to get those sheep to move as fast as I wanted them to, so at times in frustration and fear I would yell at my brothers telling them to hurry, "Papa is going to be mad if we don't hide these sheep now, please help me or I'm going to tell Papa on you!"

The children were trained to report misbehavior and to listen for prideful or rebellious words. Failure to report others was grounds for punishment. Timely information could win their papa's smiles. He seemed to go out of his way to make the children jealous of one another. Elishaba's brothers and sisters came to resent her bossiness. They offered no support when Papa was angry and his impatience rained down on her. Like the time she helped him run an old-timer's cattle across the property and up into the high summer meadows. Riding bareback, she could hardly hold on as the family's red mare leaped through thickets of fallen trees to nip at strays. Her father was mad about how stubborn the stupid cows were and took it out on her. The day was long and when they finally made it to the top and her father turned to look at his little girl—bloody with cuts, clothes torn, matted hair and hungry and face streaked with tears—she saw that he was sorry. On occasions like these he would admit he was wrong, ask forgiveness, shed tears of remorse. The Bible teaches to forgive so the children learned to reach out and hope the harshness would cease. It was not safe to speak among themselves about their desire for his mercy, however.

They were attuned to nature but not to all of nature's secrets. Human sexual relations, for instance, were an unfathomed wilderness—the Impassable Mountains from the old maps of the Santa Fe Trail. As the children began moving into puberty, the family continued to sleep all together in two large beds. Then in 1994, when Papa returned from a trip with Elishaba and Jerusalem to visit his twin brother in Texas, seventeen-year-old Joseph confided that some of the siblings had been experimenting on their own bodies and with one another in the big bed they all shared.

This admission kindled Papa's wrath. To lust themselves was an abomination. He ordered the boys to take all their meals outdoors, for the Lord said you shall not eat with an adulterer. They slept on the floor in an upright sitting position. In the trees by the cabin, where no mountain hiker might spot them, Papa turned a barrel on its side. One at a time, the five oldest boys hung over the whipping barrel. Papa showed them the seriousness of lusting with a long leather bullwhip until the welts drew blood. Their mother, whom he blamed for these sins, held their hands to feel what they were feeling. If they screamed too loud, she had to thrust a handkerchief in their mouths. When it was her turn, she was allowed to keep her clothes on. The lashing of the boys was repeated twice a day for weeks. Then the punishment stopped. Then it resumed.

The boys were not particularly surprised at how the corrections turned on and off for more than a year. The way Papa's rage came and went seemed a natural phenomenon, like the gathering of black clouds that brought lightning to the peaks of the Sangre de Cristos. It would be many years before they learned the real reason their bloody whippings came and went was that Papa had been teaching Elishaba about God's mercy.

✠

THEIR NUMBER one prayer was that they would all ascend to the Kingdom together. Elishaba grew up confident she would meet Jesus soon. Each dawn, in fact, might be the day where future and present became one. By the time she turned sixteen, however, she started to worry because she had always counted on heading to the hereafter while she was still young and pretty. What if Jesus didn't come until she was old?

She knew she was pretty because her papa told her so. He used to call her his "little sleeping buddy." She would sing to him a song about never being discouraged. She would bathe beside him in the outdoor tub, and rub his feet till her hands hurt. She would not be discouraged and would devote herself to hard work and pure thought and diligent service until that day when tearful prayers would be answered.

She felt bitterly rejected when she did something wrong and was not allowed to sleep beside him. It had never been easy to confess her failings, because his discipline could be so harsh. She felt sorry for herself to be deprived of the love that a father feels for his child. To be banished from his side, silenced, cast out of the house. To be beaten and denied mercy. Fed nothing but a bowl of cold boiled oats and sent out to drive a posthole digger into hard ground, chop wood, haul water from the well, milk the cows, clean the stalls, carry buckets into the woods. Asking herself if her father really loved her. Weeping as she worked, remembering how Jesus himself cried out, "My God, why hast thou forsaken me?"

Did God answer by touching her heart with fear? Elishaba had nowhere else to turn. Her mother had never been close. There was only Papa and his instruction on the modesty and shame that a girl should feel. Yet on the day she turned fourteen and he asked if she was ready to know about relations between a man and a woman, she sensed a fear inside herself. He had invited her along to town in the Jesus Jeep to look for hay, and made her sit in the middle seat beside him. On the way back he turned onto a detour that tunneled picturesquely through big willow trees. Something was not right in her papa's spirit when he asked that question. She told him she did not want to know, and he drove home. She put him off again at sixteen. Then when she turned eighteen, he told her she was now the proper age before man as before God.

One night as they bathed together in their long underwear, he rubbed her in places that gave her new feelings. He instructed her not to dress in dry clothes but just to put on her robe and get in the back of the pickup truck where he sometimes slept, and she saw he had a purpose in uncovering her nakedness—the intent to make her feel the need to respond to him in a physical way. She could hardly bear the shame and guilt this laid upon her heart. But he insisted that this was right before God, that God had sent him dreams and confirmations about it ever since she was a baby girl in the desert. All young women went through this, he said.

It would be many years before she could speak of that first night in the back of the pickup, or how, a few days later, he followed her into the woods and forced her to the ground and tore off her clothes and began pawing her like an animal. It was so disgusting that she pushed him off and ran away. After that, he changed and treated her really sweet. Until one day she thought about those new feelings and felt guilty and confessed it to Papa. He told her it was a sin to touch herself and lust her own body, for that was something that was only right between a father and a daughter.

Then came the dark weeks when her brothers were getting whipped bloody over the barrel. Papa told her she was the one who could deliver them mercy. It was so confusing that he could be so angry at his family and want nothing to do with them—that he would tell them they were going to hell for answering the cravings of their flesh—but then would take them back again overnight if only she would satisfy his own animal-like desires. It did not seem right when Papa said it was her fault that the corrections continued, and yet it was agony to see her brothers beaten so, and her mama, too. She would sacrifice almost anything to make it stop.

After this, Elishaba became the exalted one in the household. She was the one Papa consulted on family matters. She was no longer allowed to sleep with the other girls. She called him Lord.

Whenever she was outside chopping firewood, she was aware of her father in the cabin window, watching her.

But she began to argue with him more. She told herself if she could get him to say he was wrong about small everyday things, he would see that he might be wrong about how he was treating her. As a consequence, she began to receive harsher correction than anyone else.

Papa went to elaborate lengths to hide the new relationship from the family. He kept her close at his side when they traveled. He would get her alone in the back of the pickup, and ask her what was wrong and why she didn't appreciate the beautiful thing they had together. He pointed out the small signs God sent to encourage her.

One time in the high wilderness, he sent her in search of two lost donkeys and told her to watch as well for a seven-point elk horn. He had seen the horn in a dream as a sign that God blessed their being together. She crept through the woods, terrified the antler would suddenly appear. It never did. The next day Joseph rode into camp with an elk horn he'd found. It had only six points, but Papa showed them where he said a seventh had broken off. Elishaba saw bitterly that he was making it up. She was too afraid to say anything—though whether it was fear of her earthly or heavenly father, she could not have said.

She cried when she was with him and reminded him it was important to the Lord that she remain a virgin. He told her she was still a virgin because he was always careful not to penetrate fully, careful to spill his seed outside. Everything would turn out fine, he said, if she prayed for a perfect husband to be waiting in the Kingdom of God, a virgin like her without sin.

But it didn't sound to Elishaba like he wanted to let her go even in the Kingdom. Because Papa reminded her of the family's prayer that they will all live together or die together with the coming of the Lord. When his time came, he said, even if the others were not called, he prayed that she would be ready to come along.

THE YEARS passed in the mountains of New Mexico. Papa had started drinking again. He learned he had diabetes, and his moods rose and fell. And then, after a rebellion among the neighbors was quelled by Papa's eloquence during the community meeting at the Bartley ranch, an old idea of moving to Alaska came back.

Mama and Papa had talked of moving north as long ago as the early 1980s, when they heard it was still possible to homestead in Alaska for free—perhaps picking up on publicity at the time surrounding Interior secretary James Watt's land disposal in the Wrangells. They had studied maps to see if they could make the journey on horseback, following the spine of the Canadian Rockies. But life with toddlers in the Alaska wilderness could be dangerous, they reasoned, if a bear came along and all they had was a muzzle-loading black powder rifle. They decided to wait until the children were older.

By 1996, their New Mexico mountains were feeling crowded and so, to be sure, was their cabin. Then a tall, tough-talking Texan showed up to build a summer home. Bill Leonard had bought an open parklike expanse of land in the valley above the Vails'. On the mountain farther up, he'd been told, there lived a big family headed by some ex-hippie from Texas who was "crazier than a shithouse rat." Leonard was no fan of the government—"They'll piss on your boot and tell you it's raining"—but he had worked for federal law enforcement himself and had connections back home. The name "Bob Hale" rang a bell, and he made some calls to check. His contacts told him that after John Connally became governor in 1962, the Texas Rangers summoned Bobby Hale and told him to get out of Texas.

It's a story that Hale's family would later deny. Certainly it's true that, before too many more years, Bob Hale would be coming and going from Texas again. But Leonard did know the story of John Connally's daughter before the family came down the mountain.

"Here comes this old boy in some gosh-almighty wagon full of kids and goats, and they stop in my stream to wash their dishes. I ask him, 'Are you Bob Hale?' and he says, 'No, I'm not.' I told him I know who you are and I don't have a problem with it. Just don't mess with me, and I won't mess with you. But if you try to pull anything around here I'll goddamn kill you."

It must have been a shock to have his past closing in. The family started leaving the mountain more frequently. When he toned down the religious talk, Papa noticed, people responded more favorably to his clan. They went to several black-powder festivals, mountain-man reenactments where the Hales' buckskin attire didn't stand out. At a bluegrass festival in Santa Fe, musicians were taken with the way the children picked up old-time stringed instruments and sawed away unself-consciously. The musicians showed the children some basics, and the kids practiced on thirdhand instruments. The family made a very appealing presentation, Bob Hale decided proudly.

They traveled with three ravens taken from a nest and raised as pets: Shadrach, Meshach, and Abednego, named for the three servants of God rescued from the fiery furnace of Nebuchadnezzar. They visited cities as far away as Lubbock and Amarillo, where their colorful-looking truck would invariably break down and the family would perform in public to raise funds for repairs. Sometimes they didn't even need the music: The ragged blond children deployed on street corners with PLEASE HELP signs seemed to be all it took for God to direct contributions their way.

Then Papa's twin brother, Uncle Billy, showed up and start nosing around.

Other kin had been cut off for years. Rose's mother, Betty Freeman, recalled the last words she heard over the phone from her daughter: "He is my lord and master, and if you want to talk to me you have to go through him." Papa remained in touch only with Billy, a respected veterinarian in Fort Worth. In 1993, however, Bobby visited Texas to give his brother a gift of *The Pilgrim's Progress* and Billy caught a religious fever. His wife, Patsy, came home one day to find her clothes and belongings and other devil's playthings burned in a backyard pyre. "Bobby was always the dominant twin," said Patsy, whose children blamed their uncle for the destruction of their family. "He had ways of doing things with people that no one else could do." Billy gave up his veterinary practice and left to become an itinerant preacher in the Great Plains, occasionally ascending the Jeep trail from Mora to visit his twin.

Billy's final visit came in early 1997. Bobby, Rose, and the children were all camped high in the Pecos Wilderness with their sheep. Billy saw what was going on—as he later told Patsy—though what he saw remained between the brothers. Elishaba thought maybe Uncle Billy had come to rescue her, but the next thing she knew he'd been banished. Papa ordered Joseph and Joshua to take their uncle to a high promontory in the national forest and leave him alone in the unfamiliar mountains at dusk. Billy hid under a boulder for the night, finally making his way to a rural barn for safety. They never saw him again. He traveled to Central America to evangelize, and died in Nicaragua, probably from complications of diabetes.

That same summer, a case involving the state police and Preacher Bob's first nonfamily disciples brought the Alaska decision to a head.

Short on hay during a summer drought, the Hales moved their live-stock to southern New Mexico to graze on open range in the Gila River country near Silver City. They lived semi-nomadically in a twenty-two-foot teepee, where Rose gave birth to another daughter, Psalms. They attracted the sympathetic attention of a local couple with an eleven-year-old daughter. The young mother became infatuated with the family's lifestyle and holy mission, and soon ran off with her daughter to join them. The angry husband summoned the state police, who staked out the arroyos and searched the national forest by helicopter. The runaway wife was sought on a charge of custodial interference, though a flyer distributed by the husband trumpeted a much bigger concern:

> We fear that this is a satanic cult. . . . The mother, Elizabeth, does not have legal custody of the child, and we are afraid that she is being drugged. This cult could be part of a larger group, that could lead up to the level of movie star involvement, or even higher! We have evidence that could indicate a possible "Jon Benet Ramsey" type situation evolving.

Papa was happier than anyone could remember, persecuted and on the run with disciples. He renamed his followers Naomi and Ruth. Rose and the youngest children hid with their guests in the end-of-the-world cave in the cliffs. Meanwhile, a private posse ransacked the Rainbow Cross cabin. The chase continued for months as the family drove around in their fleet of hillbilly vehicles, drawing their New Mexico acquaintances into the drama. Carolyn Vail warned Elishaba over the phone that a deputy was watching the canyon with binoculars. Bill Leonard, the tough-talking Texan, declined a sheriff's request that he go up and look for Hale, recalling his pledge to live and let live. Joseph escaped the police by darting out the back door of their accountant friend's house in Las Vegas, New Mexico. Through it all, the legend of Preacher Bob and his family grew: Supposedly they had slipped over the high-country trails into the headwaters of the Pecos River and found temporary shelter in an Indian village. In fact, they had left the area altogether, hiding out in Idaho.

In the end, mother and child left of their own accord, husband and wife were reconciled, and no charges were filed against the "cult leader." But the commotion made it hard to ignore God's reminders of Alaska. They bought a small bus in Wyoming. The seller's business, painted on the side, was Alaska Sled Dog Tours.

Preacher Bob's children were more excited than they dared express about the talk of moving. It would be their passage out of Egypt, their Conestoga wagon across the plains, their journey through the Delectable Mountains to the Celestial City. With innocent pioneer fervor, Elishaba prayed for a chance to start over. She imagined a simpler world where it would be possible to have friends and a father who was happy.

There were details to attend to. The older children needed driver's licenses, which meant digging out birth certificates. Elishaba was mortified to discover that she would be known on her license as Butterfly Sunstar. Attention turned to fixing their vehicles. They pulled the seats out of the small Alaska bus and rebuilt it as a camper. They outfitted the two trucks with hand-built shacks on back, finding new windows at the little cabin of their neighbor Karen Brown. Brown was furious to discover her windows missing. Long annoyed by the pious verses Bob Hale posted on signs around his place, she marched down to where the trucks were parked and used a nail to scratch across her glass: THOU SHALT NOT STEAL.

They could not bring everything on this first expedition. They would crowd into the Alaska bus. After a winter scouting possibilities in Fairbanks, they would return to New Mexico to gather up their other vehicles and two decades' worth of squirreled-away material.

They cut the horses loose to forage and be rescued by neighbors. The maroon Jesus Jeep was abandoned next to the cabin, to be cannibalized for parts by cowboys.

In the Eighth Month of 1998, Bob Hale and his family left the Sangre de Cristo Mountains and headed for Alaska. He had started calling himself Pilgrim. The small bus with the family of fourteen bounced across the mountain meadow, past the tall timber cross defended with 777 teeth, down past the aspens, and out through the crude Wicket Gate, where a last Bible lesson remains to this day written in the footing of concrete: TO LOVE HIM YOU MUST OBEY HIM.

Part Two

The Farthest-Out Place

These all died in faith, not having received the promises, but having seen them afar off, and were persuaded of them, and embraced them, and confessed that they were strangers and pilgrims on the earth.

—Hebrews 11:13

11

Hillbilly Heaven

N OT LONG after the Pilgrims reached McCarthy in early
2002, I started hearing stories. I had friends in the Wrangells
and a long-standing journalist's interest in the place. Moreover, given
events of the preceding decade, the words "Ruby Ridge" could not
be brandished in rural America without someone in the media taking notice. I finally made some phone calls in June 2003 and wrote a
front-page story in the *Anchorage Daily News* about Papa Pilgrim and
his bulldozer.

▲

Papa Pilgrim and daughters in the kitchen at Hillbilly Heaven

"We could see down the road that they were trying to set up some kind of Ruby Ridge type thing," Pilgrim told me helpfully in our first phone conversation. He recounted a rumor, supposedly spread by park employees, about the Pilgrim children hiding ammunition in a fiddle case, like Chicago mobsters. "We prayed and the Lord just told us to stay away from them."

Phones were a recent innovation in McCarthy, where noisy gasoline generators and solar cells still provided the only electricity. Years before, on my first visit to McCarthy, after flying for hours in a small plane as dawn filled the mountains, the place had seemed cruelly isolated from the world. It was the morning after the murders in 1983, and vinyl body bags still lay beside the snowy airstrip. McCarthy was so cut off that when I departed to make my newspaper deadline, homesteader Jim Edwards asked me to get word to his son back in Anchorage that his mother was among the dead. Despite that grim introduction, I found myself going back again and again, at a time when getting in touch required a letter on the weekly mail plane, a bush message over the Christian radio station in Glennallen, or a bone-rattling drive. Now the Pilgrims had a microwave line at the Mother Lode camp that connected through a cell phone tower on Sourdough Peak to a satellite uplink in McCarthy. They also had a landline at the wanigan in town, where I reached Pilgrim.

He was guarded at first, saying he wasn't used to talking to reporters. He said others had approached them in their time in New Mexico, struck by his family's pleasing countenance and musical abilities. He had always turned them away.

When I mentioned my wife and I had a cabin a few miles from McCarthy, he perked up.

"So you're a neighbor," he said.

He told me he hadn't seen his own wife and small children in weeks. They were up at the homestead. Since a knee operation, he was no longer able to ride a horse. The family had no more money to pay for airplane charters. They had never been separated like this, he said, and it was tearing them apart emotionally.

"We really enjoy our Christian life together," he said. "We're not a political family at all. We knew this land was in the middle of a national park, but to us that just meant our neighbors would be few and far between."

We discussed community attitudes in McCarthy. Each of us tried to be ingratiating. He told me about the shepherd's life in New Mexico. I described our cabin and Sally's fiddle playing. We agreed that bluegrass and gospel and New England folk music traditions shared certain fine American qualities.

After this first story, I said, I would surely be writing more about conflicts between the national park and the community. Sally and I were planning a trip out to our cabin later that summer, in August— would it be all right if I came up to the Mother Lode?

He thought about it a minute. He decided I should see the historic road to Hillbilly Heaven for myself.

"Come on by, neighbor," he said. "You'll see we're just modest simple folks, not some strange religion."

MY DUBIOUS claim to being Papa Pilgrim's neighbor I owed to Sally, whose attachment to McCarthy was older than mine and even more improbable, given her career in environmental politics protecting Alaska's national parks from encroachment by mankind and womankind.

Recently, while going through old boxes of Sally's things, I found some hidden-away journals from her first years in Alaska. I had never fully realized, in the time we had together, the strength of her early infatuation with McCarthy—the mesmerizing daily focus of cabin living, the long drives out from Anchorage to play music and visit friends, all the sweet resolutions to make herself into a woman strong enough to live on her own in the Wrangells someday. It helped explain how a

Sierra Club lobbyist came to own five acres and nine foundation posts inside a national park. The year after we were married, we built the cabin above the Nizina River canyon. It was our hopeful pioneer moment. Sally chose not to punch in a short road or open up the view by knocking down more than two or three spruce trees. She wanted to camouflage her presence and be a good inholder.

When we returned to our cabin out the McCarthy Road in August 2003, on my way to meet the Pilgrims face-to-face, the worn spiral guestbook told us how long we'd been away. Our son, Ethan, had been a newborn our last visit. Now he was turning nine—Sally had brought a chocolate birthday cake from home. Our thirteen-year-old daughter, Emily, had only faint memories of the cabin's interior: playroom-pink fiberglass insulation under a clear plastic epidermis. The gangly willow wood was closing back in, the access footpath even narrower than the summer we hand-carried our lumber to the building site—the Bored Feet Trail, we called it then. We were both a little disappointed to realize we had taken our nibble out of the continent's last wilderness for nothing more ennobling than a recreational getaway.

There were reasons we hadn't come more often—the distance, our careers, the demands of raising two kids in another hand-built cabin far away on the coast, where we hauled children and groceries home in winter a half-mile on a sled. And now, above all, there was Sally's advanced-stage ovarian cancer, which by that summer, three years out from her diagnosis, had begun another slow march. She was trying a new drug that would have left her too weak even for this long-hoped-for family trip—except that her blood platelet count fell so low she had been forced to skip a chemo cycle altogether. Not good news, really. But it left a small window of energy for the Wrangells trip and a chance to lead the life we once imagined.

After a day of gentle biking and a night of birthday cake and drumming rain, I said good-bye and headed to the end of the road to meet the Pilgrim Family.

Across the clanging metal footbridge in town, I met up first with Marc Lester, a watchful and shrewd photographer from my newpaper. Someone else was waiting at the McCarthy Lodge as well: Ray Kreig, an Anchorage property-rights advocate with a long list of grievances against the National Park Service in other parts of Alaska. I was surprised to learn Kreig and his wife, Lee Ann, had been invited along to see the disputed route for themselves, and apparently to serve as media minders.

Papa Pilgrim showed up in the puddled street outside the lodge. He wore a denim shirt, a dusty gray quilted jacket against the morning chill, and a broad-brimmed Western hat of dark felt under which white hair spilled to his collarbone. He looked lean inside the puffy jacket, a little used-up for someone only sixty-two. His eyes, set in leathery webs of worry, were a crystalline blue-gray. A wavy silver beard, untouched by scissors but adoringly brushed, trailed away like a waterfall.

Seven of his older children, smiling with quiet intensity, assembled in wings at his sides.

"I wish I could ride up there with you all," Pilgrim said in a soft Texas drawl, his beard shifting emphatically. "But I can't get up on a horse no more with my knee. Since they closed that road on us last spring, I haven't been home but four days. It's been a hardship on us, not being together as a family. But you can see we're not beat to the ground."

He would join us that night, he said. A local pilot would fly him up the valley.

My senses hummed as we followed the Pilgrims through the woods to their town camp, where their gear was still stockpiled on the town site right-of-way in pointed rebuke to park policies. The wanigan's porch was crowded with tools, washbasins, jars of salmon, a guitar case. A handmade bird feeder hung from a rafter. Nearby, a canvas wall tent was carpeted with old sleeping bags. Goats and kittens and big furry dogs—a Great Pyrenees and a Newfoundland— wandered in the mud and around horse piles and puddles made iridescent by workaday hydrocarbons. The bark of several cottonwoods had been chewed down to fleshy wood. A long-skirted daughter approached with a string of horses and joined her brothers in preparing for our ride, collecting bridles and saddles and replacing a hind shoe on a sleek brown horse.

Pilgrim was telling us how the Mother Lode property line passed right through their cookstove.

"Two-thirds of our cabin was not on our property at all. We all were devastated. Walt Wigger stands in a very liable position on this. His reason for telling us wrong was just based on his own greed and own evil purposes. I said we would move the cabin, but the park rangers flew Wigger up to our place and he put a lock on that bulldozer. So we can't do anything about it. Then park ranger Stephens Harper did a survey of this property here. What happened was really ironic. *His outhouse* wasn't even on his own property. You could really see God's hand."

The park team was still helicoptering back and forth to his place every day, looking over the old road for damage. "There's thirteen highly qualified people up there wandering around, almost doing nothing," he said. "They've spent *hundreds of thousands* of dollars hassling the Pilgrims. Just to try to run us out of the national park." He veered away to a gentler theme. "We're really just a simple family, who never lived anywhere but in the mountains. We brought what the epitome of a wilderness family really is in Alaska. We consider this, McCarthy here, the last part of real Alaska. You got to admit— McCarthy is pretty down home."

I watched the sons and daughters at work, wondering what their lives could be like. Many fundamentalist Christians spoke of living apart from the world, but few had gone so far.

Pilgrim was sending three of his offspring to guide us up the contested trail: Joshua and Moses, sons numbers two and four, ages twenty-three and eighteen, and Elishaba, eldest daughter and first-born child, now twenty-seven. "Most people leave home by that age," Papa Pilgrim said with a twinkle. "There's a reason why ours don't, and you'll pick up on it."

He doffed his hat and said a blessing, asking the Lord to watch over our travels. We closed our eyes, all except Marc, who stepped back to take pictures, and Moses, who stared curiously into the lens.

GOD SAID in Leviticus never to round the corners of thy head nor mar the corners of thy beard. This was why the Pilgrim boys wore hair to their shoulders, Joshua explained matter-of-factly. I was surprised how relaxed and talkative our guides proved to be, once we were mounted and plodding along the sloppy road by the creek. Joshua described the challenges of traveling the valley road in a wagon pulled by two Percheron workhorses. The creek was too high for the wagon to cross after these rains, he said. He had a youthful downy beard and an easy one-handed manner in the saddle, wearing a broken-down black Western hat and green Carhartt jacket. He was the family's expert horseman, their farrier, in charge of the trail rides for tourists that helped pay for the upkeep of the horses they were accumulating.

"The park says we need a permit if we take people in the back-country," he said. Applying for a permit meant getting insurance and cooperating with the government, both of which were apparently out of the question. Joshua was still sore about the undercover ranger who had tricked him several weeks ago by requesting a trip up to the Bonanza Mine. "He was talking about all those boodles of money they're going to spend, and trying to entice me, so why shouldn't I?"

The sky above the steep-sided valley was turning with clouds after the night's rain. The muddy trail narrowed onto hard gravel. We rode out by the river and made the first of a dozen crossings. In baseball cap and borrowed slick-yellow rain pants, awkwardly lifting my hiking boots as the silty gray glacier water splashed the horse's belly, I recalled the horseback drowning of the Irish prospector James McCarthy. I was grateful to feel the sure-footedness of my steed on the loose underwater cobbles. Approaching a steep rocky climb on the far bank, I considered how to urge both of us forward, but without encouragement the horse rocketed powerfully from the water and over the berm. I relaxed, sensing someone competent was in charge.

The valley swung to the north and opened up. Occasionally we could see ahead to cloud-sheathed mountains that were white year-round. Twin rock tunnels left no question that a road had once been blasted through here. Elsewhere, though, the roadwork looked new, marked by piles of freshly felled trees and, on gravel bars, cuts where Papa's Cat had sculpted a lip of rocks or detoured around a stream meander, conforming to current geology rather than any historic survey. The swiftly eroding valley toyed with my sense of timeless nature: The landscape was newer than the civilization.

The road climbed high on the left to avoid a steep cut bank, then descended to some flats, where we could see how willows and poplars had rushed in thick after the biblical floods of 1980. In plants, as in people, the country favored pioneer species, able to move quickly and throw down shallow roots.

We stopped by a small dump truck with pale-green paint peeling off the rusted cab. The truck was surrounded by small spruce trees, as though imprisoned by a sorcerer's spell. Ray Kreig rode up to say the truck had been used as recently as 1973, proving in his view that the Pilgrims were only doing maintenance, thirty years later.

The truck had been left by Gary Green, a local bush pilot. I'd known Gary since my first visit to McCarthy at the time of the murders, when he had been the pilot who warned the mail plane away. He came to McCarthy originally to hunt for gold and learned to fly when he worked for sheep-hunting guides. These days his flying customers were mostly national park visitors—backpackers and flightseers and the occasional hunter in the preserve, where one could still hunt for sport. But he missed the way things were before the Park Service domesticated the mountains with their aerial patrols and ridge-top radio repeaters. The scenery was still there, he said, but the wilderness feeling was gone. His pale green dump truck would be a rusting junker anywhere else, but here by the creek it was a museum piece.

"You see how minor the damage is along this road," Ray Kreig was saying. "The park did FAR MORE DAMAGE when they clear-cut the survey line around the Pilgrims' property last month."

Kreig was a big man—big bones, big head. Under a purple rain sombrero, he dwarfed the horse that carried him. He was helping turn Papa Pilgrim's fight into a national cause. A self-employed engineer, he got started in national park issues at Kantishna, the turn-of-the-century gold-mining district that in 1980 was absorbed—"engulfed," in his words—by Denali National Park and Preserve. He had a cutting and effective way of pointing out how the park set up visitor displays about Kantishna mining history once it had finished driving the last few placer miners out of business. He ran a website that collected accounts of alleged Park Service perfidy, editorializing heavily in capital letters, and in person hammered away with the same bold-faced urgency.

"The Park Service is waging a HEARTLESS AND FANATICAL war of intimidation against the Pilgrims with this investigation," he said, riding on. "I ask you, is the reaction of the government a measured, reasonable reaction, or is it gross overkill? It's punishment, pure and simple, for trying to use their access rights."

When Rick Kenyon began looking for reinforcements, it made sense that he would hear about Kantishna and find Ray Kreig. Now

Kreig was enlisting support from national property-rights groups to get supplies past the "blockade" to Hillbilly Heaven. A top mining lawyer in Anchorage had agreed to take on the Pilgrims' cause, and talks were under way with the Pacific Legal Foundation, a conservative nonprofit law firm from the lower forty-eight that envisioned these facts developing into a U.S. Supreme Court case.

On the other side, environmental groups were urging the Park Service not to back down. They worried about the political pressure that might be brought to bear, from President George W. Bush and his libertarian-leaning Interior secretary, Gale Norton of Colorado (who once worked for a legal firm linked to the Pacific Legal Foundation), down through Alaska's all-Republican congressional delegation and Governor Frank Murkowski, to the development-minded state legislature. Environmentalists could foresee any number of similar situations around Alaska, with latter-day Daniel Boones in the seat of D5 Cats ready to blade open the widest interpretation possible of the Alaska conservation act's unique inholder protections.

"Instead of a SCORCHED EARTH EXTERMINATION POLICY, they should let these people thrive. The Pilgrims can provide a great service to visitors," Kreig said. "Does the park really want to see a Hundred Year War out here?"

"Why won't the family talk to the park rangers?" I asked. "Couldn't this have been avoided?"

"You're dealing with an INNOCENT FAMILY that has never had to deal with the government before," Kreig said. "They think that to ask for a permit is to give in. But we're working on that."

BY AND by, the horses halted in thick grass. We climbed down gratefully to stretch and eat some lunch. The Pilgrim boys ate popcorn. Elishaba hooked one hiking boot in a stirrup, lifted the other across her horse's neck, and leaned back in the saddle to nap. She clutched her battered white cowboy hat to her chest like a security blanket.

We stopped again at my request when we came to a little tin-roofed log cabin that had been home to the last man in the valley before the Pilgrims.

Loy Green was a trumpet player and a painter of oil landscapes tending toward the surrealist: mountains with pyramids floating in the sky. Sally knew him pretty well and had hung a pyramid-free landscape on a wall in our bedroom. Long-faced, lean, with mussed hair and a few buttons left open, Loy had been the model for the hermit in Ben Shaine's novel, listening to Mahler symphonies on his small cassette deck. The Wrangells gave him space, he used to say, to think about nature and God. His woodsy Transcendentalism did not prevent him, however, from rigging a shotgun trap in his cabin, aimed at taking out the grizzly who tore into a plywood wall every time he went off to McCarthy.

Loy's environmentalism was old-school and pre-park. After living through the 1970s in abandoned Green Butte mining cabins, he got help from current and former Santa Cruz students to tear down a collapsing bunkhouse kitchen and move the milled logs across the creek. The logs were reassembled on his unpatented mining claim, which Loy defiantly named "Copper View." The cabin-rebuilding project, during the land freeze in the last few years before the park, had been surreptitious and unsanctioned. But Loy's place looked so venerable the Park Service never caught on until much later.

Access had been a challenge for Loy, as it was for the Pilgrims. Before the big flood, his system involved two sputtering dirt bikes and an aluminum canoe cut and welded into a pair of half canoes. Leaving town, Loy would ride one motorcycle to the first ford, then cross the river in a half canoe hooked to a cable angled downstream so that the current, sweeping him along, delivered him to the far side. (A second cable angled back for the return trip.) He would continue on a second dirt bike hidden in the bushes, and at the next river crossing deploy the other half of his canoe in a similar fashion. From there he could walk the rest of the way home. When alders had grown in too thick over the old road, he built a one-man airplane from a kit. This system worked flawlessly except when a nagging carburetor problem caused the engine to quit. Most of his crashes were minor, and he only had to replace the entire plane once, after a forced landing in the trees. Loy trod so lightly on the land—his shotgun bear trap notwithstanding—that the park granted him a lifetime cabin permit after he surrendered his worthless mining claim.

We climbed through a dead electric-wire fence and peered inside at the wreckage left by bears. A few years earlier, Loy's friends had eased him out of his McCarthy Creek cabin and into a state Pioneer Home after he showed growing signs of Alzheimer's. When the Pilgrims came upon the abandoned cabin, Papa praised God and cleared out the rifles and dishes. Loy's unsalvageable belongings were now piled outside in the weather. In a decade or two, the tin-roofed cabin would be flattened, rotting and rusting away in the brush, as grown-over and indiscernible as Loy's memories of living in the antediluvian valley.

When we started riding again, I pushed my horse to catch up with Elishaba's. I asked if her name was really Butterfly. I had seen it on a Park Service complaint.

"When I was born, that was what they named me," she said with a shy smile. "They were hippies back then I guess. These days it depends who I'm talking to. Elishaba is from the Bible. My grandma calls me Elizabeth. The little ones call me Eba."

She spoke with a Texas drawl developed, I supposed, from living in isolation with her father. She wore a flowered blouse with a bandana around her neck, a gray hooded sweatshirt beneath a denim vest, and a riding skirt. Under her cowboy hat she had long brown hair and dark bushy eyebrows, and the pink-cheeked outdoor prettiness of the Pilgrim girls, round-faced where their brothers tended more to Hollywood-cut cheekbones. Everyone always commented on the kids' good looks.

"Nobody calls me Butterfly no more," she said. "Nobody but the park, I guess."

She loved to ride and hunt and work outdoors. But the five siblings who came along after her had all been brothers, Elishaba explained, so it fell on her to take care of the young ones. Each of the children had special duties in the family, she said. Some were assigned by Papa, and some just came naturally to their personalities. She had prayed hard for a sister, she admitted.

Elishaba looked around pensively as she rode along the creek. I asked if she ever thought of going away to do something else.

"Why would I leave?" She seemed annoyed by the question, but not surprised. "I love taking care of the children here and living how we do."

I pulled out a reporter's pad and scribbled something indecipherable as the horse jostled me back and forth. She was not finished.

"People can't understand us, the way they rush around in their busy lives these days. We just have a different way of looking at things out here. I know my life here has been blessed by the Lord. I'm really lucky. It's all I could ever want."

What about grandparents? Did they ever travel to see their relatives?

"Papa's parents are dead. His daddy was with the FBI. He was the best shot in the world, but he never had to kill anybody, because he was so good at his job."

She had mentioned a grandmother who called her Elizabeth.

"She lives in Los Angeles. We used to visit, but we don't see her no more. Her heart has been turned against us."

What happened?

"She doesn't understand what we're doing here. She thinks we're all crazy, living off alone the way we do. Her world is just so different, just money and material things." Elishaba grew more animated. "I feel sorry for her. I really do. I wish she could see us and understand who we really are."

A dog barked up ahead. Elishaba heeled over and paused at the head of the line. "Hallelujah, Jesus!" she called as loud as she could. A child's voice called back, "Hallelujah!"

A few minutes later, the forest opened to bare dirt ground and the cabin lay ahead. Small children were spilling onto the porch. The place looked neatly picked up, with an air of industriousness—the fenced-in garden and outbuildings a contrast to the neo-Appalachian desperation of their place in town. There was a flurry of dismounting, hand shaking, lowering of bags, and surrendering of reins. Then I stepped onto the cabin porch for a greeting from Country Rose, the matriarch of the Mother Lode, a sad-eyed woman in a long skirt, smiling, but with her arms clasped behind her back.

"We Pilgrim girls don't shake hands," she said.

"WHEN MAN got down off the horse, things changed for the world," Papa Pilgrim said as we sat around the big country kitchen. His words came slow and were heavily cadenced. "Somehow we thought Alaska would be some old wooden hotels and dirt roads. Our vision was trappers and people living an old-fashioned type of real life. It's the way everybody used to be. All of us should be interested in keeping that lifestyle and not *destroy* it. The park would have *so much* to benefit from a relationship with a family like ours, working together to inspire people who come here."

With the sun slipping behind Bonanza Ridge and the valley turning cold, even in August, Pilgrim warmed himself by a wood-burning cookstove where apple pies bubbled. The room exuded comfort, with cast-iron pans on the walls, open shelves heavy with jars, a big slab of a wooden table. Overhead a few bare lightbulbs ran off a generator somewhere out of earshot.

Two solemn little girls, Psalms and Lamb, balanced on their father's knees. The rest of the family sat without a murmur at the kitchen table behind me, or further back in the careworn living room. All attention and energy in the cabin was focused on Papa. If the children were hungry, they weren't saying.

I had lived in enough Alaska cabins to be able to consider this one's architectural demerits. The walls were thin for such a cold valley, mere two-by-fours clad with paneling. The place had been built for summer mining. The barrel stove, a converted oil drum, could probably pump out heat like a sauna, but would require a tremendous supply of fast-burning spruce. The main room was furnished with two threadbare sofas and had plenty of open space for spreading out sleeping bags. In winter, I imagined, the outermost orbit from the stove would be the least desirable. In a small back room was a pile of sleeping gear, and on a shelf a Bible, a hymnal, and a fax machine. There were no toys or other books.

Pilgrim recounted the story of the fire that took their other cabin, garbling the time sequence as he swung effortlessly from gripping tale to plaintive conclusion: His reason for opening the road was to bring in emergency building supplies. It was God's own desire.

"I believe God is moving in our lives all the time," he said. "It's the basis of our hope."

He recited the Pilgrim Family story, smiling a bit at the colorful parts. He told of meeting Country Rose at a hot spring and the Lord's promise of twenty-one children. He talked about New Mexico and how their numbers grew, how he held each baby up to divine the child's name. Then God sent them to Alaska, truly a land that provided for its people. The moose they hunted. Salmon in the Copper River. And the state's Permanent Fund dividends. "We got on it and they okayed it, and we couldn't believe it. Thirty thousand dollars. That was more money than we'd ever had in our life."

I asked about their family backgrounds. His father was indeed an FBI man, he said—"practically the right-hand agent for J. Edgar Hoover." Pilgrim also claimed his father had been a famous all-American athlete. I imagined these must be wild exaggerations, which seemed curious coming from a self-proclaimed ascetic and defier of federal authority, and resolved to check when I got back to my office. His own children did not engage in competitive sports. The only grandparent still alive was Country Rose's mother. They were not in touch, Pilgrim said. She did not agree with how they had chosen to live. She did not understand the great togetherness of the family, nor would she accept his authority as the patriarch. "But that's what God said. The father is the head. There's no question about it." The children have never left and have no desire to leave, he said. "No one ever goes anywhere alone. This is a godly principle, too, for He sent his disciples out by twos. He required a witness. And I can honestly say my children do not know what hatred and bitterness is."

Elishaba was pulling out the apple pies and came over to stroke her father's forehead. His long white hair was thin on top. He told us about his diabetes and heart trouble and reminded us about the bad knee. He wore a buckskin holster on his belt in which he carried nitroglycerin tablets for a heart attack, matches, and a heavily underlined Bible.

When I asked about the bulldozer, he considered the newspaper's audience.

"I had *no idea* the hornet's nest I was stirring up. We just did what Walter Wigger told us to do—go down that road and get your materials. I am as much an environmentalist as anyone could ever be. We wanted to get to the farthest-out place where we could live. We *wanted* a place you couldn't get to with a road. But once I was here, I realized that in order for me to love my children, I have to be a provider.

That was God's word to me. Everyone in town kept asking us, are you going to use the road? I kept saying no. Neil and Rick had told us you have a real good road as a 2477. It took me so long to memorize those numbers. Two, four, seven, seven."

The innocent hillbilly sighed at the perplexity brought on by that obscure government statute and a simple act of love.

"My family are not discouraged in any kind of way," he said. "We're almost more concerned for the people in McCarthy. It's really become evident that their very existence is threatened. The park wants this to be like another Yosemite, where you got to stay on the boardwalk and if you get off you'll be arrested. They say they're doing it to protect the land. Their purpose is to run people off."

It was getting dark and I felt rude for holding up supper. I spoke up at last, and though there had been no rustle of family impatience an immediate movement of children erupted as the simple provender came forth, kettles of potato chowder and loaves of fresh bread and bowls of salad from the garden. Before reseating ourselves we stood in a circle as Pilgrim closed his eyes, gave thanks for our safe arrival, and asked the Lord's guidance toward a just resolution in the matter of Revised Statute 2477.

THE NEXT day at noon, the Pilgrim Family were assembled beside the gravel airstrip as we bounced past in Gary Green's accelerating Cessna. They were smiling and waving—the whole big and woefully needy clan in their farthest-out place.

As guests of the Pilgrims, Marc and I had been pampered in a little outbuilding for tourists, which they called the Happy Cabin, with actual beds, framed pictures, and wildflower bouquets. The contrast only underscored the squalor and strangeness of the family's everyday existence: the absence of printed matter, the young adults' refusal to leave, that rule about traveling around in twos, the back-to-nature children who had never seen a naked body. The silent unanimity of purpose had put me on guard. The older Pilgrim offspring, thoughtful and articulate on their own, had hardly spoken once we got in the cabin. The only mirror was small, with smoky glass and a cross painted in the middle—to discourage vanity, I was told. You'd have a hard time getting anyone to sign up for a cult this rigorous. But in the farthest-out place, it seemed, you could raise up children to do almost anything.

Airborne, the plane banked in the narrow valley. Gary Green, in a sharply creased cowboy hat, aimed us back at the homestead. Marc squeezed off some last photos and I looked up for visible remains of the Mother Lode above. All I saw was two thousand feet of bare rock, a sheer slope that dumped avalanches regularly into the creek next to Hillbilly Heaven. A retired geologist who lived in McCarthy had warned Papa about this hazard, but he was dismissed, along with his natural science.

Below, Ray and Lee Ann Kreig stood in the family's midst and waved. They'd stayed behind to talk strategy with Papa.

OUR VISIT that morning to the site of the national park's forensic investigation had felt secondary and anticlimactic—a few men and women poking at shrubs with clipboards, a dour ranger standing in the trail to keep the family at a distance.

The morning did give me a chance to peel away the two eldest sons, Joseph and Joshua, asking them to show me a controversial planting of oats near the cabin. It had turned out to be in the national park.

"The only thing we did was this, which to my mind wasn't very bad. It's just not natural, is all," Joseph said.

What about never applying for a permit to do work on the road, I asked—was that a naïve oversight, too?

Joseph, who was bigger than his brother and more full-bearded but somehow softer in manner, looked abashed. He said it was too bad they went about it in a way that got everyone stirred up, but Joshua jumped in.

"Once we admit we need a permit, that's something they can take away from us," Joshua said, echoing his father. "We learned by being here we have a real good case for a 2477. We don't want to apply for a permit not so much for us as for the sake of the entire Alaska community. Because if they win on us, they'll roll it over everyone behind us."

Their mother had been skittish, but when I managed to get Country Rose alone she tried to persuade me that their way of life was a rare thing worth defending.

"These children aren't under some kind of spell," she said. "They know where they're going. People come away from meeting them with a feeling of joy and amazement in the kind of confidence they have. You asked about my mother. She once told me we will just see what happens when they all turn eighteen. Kick 'em out the door—that's the attitude of the world. Then she had to tuck her tail and hide, because they didn't want to go nowhere."

Raising such questions directly with Pilgrim had proved more difficult. Had I been intimidated by whatever was smoldering behind his gentle pacifism? It would have made a great story to be banished into the wilderness for impertinence. But during the evening it had seemed more important not to put him on the defensive, to keep him talking. Like any good politician, Papa dangled access as a reward that could be withdrawn.

They played their bluegrass gospel for us after supper, and then as the guitars and fiddles were put away, I plunked down beside Pilgrim on a sofa—possibly the one Jonathan had been born on, I thought squeamishly—and asked how he liked owning his own copper mine. Here was a topic to which the good politician warmed easily. They had gone in with flashlights, he said, their beams disappearing in the darkness. The surviving support columns were made of pure copper. The minerals in the tailings, the malachites and azurites, sounded like tribes from the Bible.

"It's like a miniature Carlsbad Cavern, made by hand," he said.

I asked what the access tunnels were like. Did the family feel claustrophobic going into the mountain?

"My children don't even know what that means, so they're not afraid of it," he said.

I found this response a little unsettling—as if one could wish away some basic human reflex by suppressing knowledge of it. But it brought me indirectly to a bigger physiological concern. Did he consider his children free to marry and start families of their own?

He faltered. I noticed several older Pilgrims look up sharply.

"If someone believes what we believe, and is willing to come join us, they would surely be welcome," he said.

What about the future? I asked. His children seemed to have all the skills necessary to live out here in the wilds. But what did he foresee them doing twenty years from now?

This answer was easier. They didn't need to look that far ahead, he said. "We truly believe the Lord's return is coming before my death," he said.

I pulled the notepad from my hip pocket to write down what he'd said.

"I never did trust talking to a reporter," Pilgrim said, watching my hand. "There was a reporter once who wrote a story about my father. It was a terrible thing he did. He just told one lie after another. I wouldn't be talking to you now, but for this thing the park is doing. And you being a neighbor."

I said I'd do my best to tell the truth. But I scribbled a note to check when I got home whether someone had ever written a scandalous story about an FBI man named I. B. Hale.

✛

THE JOURNEY back to the Internet took several days. Once there, I discovered Pilgrim was telling the truth about his famous father, the national football championship, and the law enforcement career. I checked further, and found there had indeed been a story that took a different angle. It was written by one of the most famous investigative reporters in the country.

I called my editor and mentioned Seymour Hersh and John F. Kennedy. I told him the Papa Pilgrim story was turning out more complicated than expected. He agreed to give me more time.

After another week or so, I called Pilgrim on the phone at Hillbilly Heaven with new questions.

The first time I called, he denied everything. It was wrong to write about the past, he said, because it would just confuse the people of Alaska.

"If you write those lies about my father and my past, people will think, 'Well, no wonder they ran off into the wilderness.' We're here because it has to do with my new life with the Lord. It doesn't have to do with running from my past."

The next time I called, he said those were stories he had never even told some of his own family. Now he had been forced to reveal everything. They had all sat up until one that morning, going through the events of the past before they appeared in the newspaper, "with many tears and explanations."

He appealed for sympathy. Then he got tough. Why would I tear at his family this way, when they had trusted me?

"You promised us, and very encouragingly so, you wanted to be fair. You know we draw a lot of jealousy. People are always looking for something bad. You're giving them bullets for their guns and I'm going to pay for it. People are going to reject us just because of that.

Sports cars and golf, that's not who I am. They don't understand the kind of spiritual changes a person can go through. I'm going to be living under the shadow of Jack Nicholson and John Connally and I. B. Hale."

The next time I called, Elishaba answered. She was a different person.

"We were very honest with you," she said angrily. "These stories you're talking about, that's not who we are. And if you don't know that, then you're stupid."

Her father got on the phone. I asked the questions I had to ask, told him what more I had learned—really just the surface of things in New Mexico and Texas, as I would find out later. I said I wanted to hear his side of the story. Impatiently, he disputed his neighbors' complaints from the Sangre de Cristos, but as he talked about Texas, an old sorrow crept into his voice, almost a sob. When he was a teenager he'd lived through his own Romeo and Juliet story. It changed his life forever.

"Mommy and Daddy didn't have answers, for the first time in my life. It really scared me," he said. "I realized nobody had the answers. That's when I became a pilgrim."

I called once again after my stories about the long strange journey of Papa Pilgrim appeared in the newspaper. When I said my name, the line clicked dead.

12

Flight of the Angels

"**W**INTER IS near and the situation is becoming dire," declared a Web alert in the second week of October 2003, as the volunteer airlift to Hillbilly Heaven got under way in McCarthy. Hay bales and windows and insulation were stacked by the Kennicott River. Food, clothing, and money flowed in from around the state and the lower forty-eight. Pilots arrived from Glennallen and Anchorage to combat the government blockade and stand up for the Pilgrims' rights.

Chuck Cushman, the longtime leader of the American Land

▲

Hauling supplies from the Hillbilly Heaven airstrip

Rights Association, came to Alaska and declared the Pilgrims to be the new poster children for the national property-rights movement. Financial donations were filtered through Rick Kenyon's church. Laurie Rowland, the wife of the local heavy equipment operator, called the pilots angels of mercy in the *Wrangell St. Elias News,* where she had shed the sarcasm and secret pen name of McCarthy Annie. She was now in charge of ground logistics for the airlift. She quoted a ninety-year-old widow from Oregon who contributed money to fight the government and was glad her veteran husband never lived to see the day—"Would Hitler have done any worse?"

The air above McCarthy Creek buzzed with small airplanes and earnest historical analogies. Hitler, jackboots, Ruby Ridge, and Waco came easily to the tongue. Pilgrim, phoning in to a local talk show on the Glennallen radio station, was true to his Texas roots: "If you don't wake up, you're going to end up with seventeen dead Pilgrims out here. They want to starve us out, like the Alamo." But Cushman's national website provided the metaphor of the day: the Berlin Airlift of 1948, when Harry Truman sent planes to West Berlin after the Soviet Iron Curtain closed road and rail access. "For many months America and other countries joined to keep a starving city alive and supplied with food, fuel and other materials," said the website, which was actually being run from Anchorage by Ray Kreig. "So now it is time for the citizens of America and especially Alaska to rise up again against a top down command and control heavy handed bureaucracy, the National Park Service, and keep the Pilgrim Family and their animals from being starved out in the Wrangell–St. Elias National Park and Preserve. As in Berlin, heavily armed Park Service personnel dressed like a S.W.A.T. team are preventing access for the Pilgrims." First it was the Pilgrims, the website warned, then it would be everyone else in Alaska, as the environmentalists continued plotting to impose their "Green Iron Curtain of Exclusion."

My stories about Papa Pilgrim seemed to stoke the antigovernment fervor. The articles, which along with Marc Lester's arresting photos filled nine pages in the *Anchorage Daily News* over two days, had made the Pilgrim Family a subject of general supermarket conversations around Alaska. Their war with the park was getting national coverage, including a front-page story in the *Washington Post*.

I worked hard to balance the politics with descriptions of the park's iron-fist response and Rick Kenyon's assertion that the Pilgrims' coming to McCarthy was "a match truly made in heaven." But the portrayal of Hillbilly Heaven's claustrophobia, the description of Pilgrim's efforts to take environmental laws into his own hands, and even a cursory account of Robert Hale's complicated beginnings and his winding trail through Texas and New Mexico had not added up to an endearing portrait. Our newspaper ran a full page of letters to the editor. A few commended the family's effort to live by what one writer called ancient "Christian-Israelite values." Many more readers raised alarms on behalf of the isolated kids and accused Pilgrim of running a welfare scam built around Alaska Permanent Fund dividends.

For true believers, though, the series was just one more example of issue manipulation by the liberal media.

Things actually seemed to be turning out pretty well for the outcast of the Sangre de Cristos. Sixty ten-minute angel flights from McCarthy over the course of a few weeks shunted supplies to the family's citadel at the Mother Lode. The cabin's attic was now stuffed with a multiyear supply of toilet paper. A shed by the airstrip had filled with vacuum-sealed buckets of Y2K provisions that survivalists, having safely reached the new millennium, were happy to donate to a new cause.

Kenyon was given space to respond in the *Anchorage Daily News*, where he bemoaned the government's "willing allies in the press." He told a story of how two Pilgrim boys put out a fire at the church that summer and then on their own accord rebuilt the damaged church themselves. The family, he said, "epitomizes gentleness, strength born of faith, and a respect for all about them." An e-mail alert circulated by Cushman asserted that the press was being spoon-fed "character assassination" material by the Park Service. It wasn't true—whatever the park knew about the family past, they wouldn't tell me anything. I called up Cushman, who ran the national property-rights organization out of his home in Battle Ground, Washington. He was cheerfully combative. He told me that emphasizing the strangeness of the family's dress and way of life made it easier for the government to go after them. "Well, America was settled by people who were persecuted," he reminded me.

THERE WAS a story in McCarthy of a tourist who spotted some younger Pilgrim children up at Kennicott and told them they looked like a line of little penguins. A blank look from the youngest prompted a question to each child up the line. None of them had any idea what a penguin was.

Alaska's homeschooling laws are the most lax in the nation. In New Mexico, the family at least had to fake participation in an organized correspondence program. Alaska does not require children to be part of any approved program. Parents have complete authority.

When the *Anchorage Daily News* stories about the family appeared, the children could do no more than look at the pictures. Papa Pilgrim gathered them around and read the newspaper out loud. He paused from time to time to ask rhetorically why the newspaper would tell such lies about them.

Joseph chimed in that it sounded like the reporter had just written down whatever the family told him.

Alone among the children, Joseph would sometimes speak up in an earnest and naïve way, as if his first few years as Nava Sunstar, before the Lord touched their family and changed his name, had left a mark of waywardness. Papa dealt with this by mocking and marginalizing his twenty-six-year-old son, calling Joseph "the family two-year-old." When the newspaper people came, he had sent the more reliable Elishaba and Joshua to serve as trail guides.

Papa ignored Joseph now and continued reading. He was incensed by a quote in the story from Rose's mother in Los Angeles, who had called the family a brainwashed cult. How ironic, he said, because it's the NPS that's the tree-worshipping cult. The reporter didn't have to pass along such a bitter comment, he said. It showed where his heart was.

Joseph tried to respond lightly: "Maybe we are brainwashed. How would we know?"

Papa exploded. It was nothing to make light of, he said. He forced Joseph to apologize. The oldest Pilgrim son never forgot that moment, surprised at such an overreaction—he thought it was a pretty good joke. How, indeed, would anyone know?

THE AIRLIFT—a beautiful act of love, in Pilgrim's words to an Associated Press reporter—nearly produced a martyr. The landing gear on a Cessna 180 buckled when it hit the Hillbilly Heaven airstrip, causing a strut to dig in the gravel and the plane to pivot and flip—a crash known to pilots as a "ground loop." The angel of mercy, a fifty-two-year-old real estate developer from Anchorage named Kurt Stenehjem, walked away from the wreck and was welcomed into the Pilgrim fold. Stenehjem spent a week at the Mother Lode, and upon his return to civilization published a story, "An Angel Falls to Heaven," in the *Wrangell St. Elias News*. He said it would be the first chapter of an inside-view book about the family.

His account of the family of "Civil War throwbacks" was unambivalent in its support of the property-rights cause and its depictions of the father's "southern country charm" and the kids' maturity and empathy. Beyond that, the chapter published in Kenyon's paper focused on two topics: the tedious cargo details of Stenehjem's mercy flights, and an equally detailed critique of my stories in the *Anchor-*

age Daily News, which had introduced Stenehjem to the Pilgrims and their struggle.

He opened his piece disdainfully: "I don't have the habit of reading the newspaper. I used to, but I've lost my stomach for it." He went on to say he was sucked into reading the big story about this family of cowboy characters—"I sat down, hooked. . . . The fact that the local paper didn't like them assured me these people were all right and I searched for a way I might find to help them." He described how his own insightful deconstruction of the stories had taught naïve Papa Pilgrim to recognize the "verbal land mines" strewn by the liberal media to demonize the family and discredit their cause. When the story said Pilgrim made the down payment for his land with a pocket full of hundred-dollar bills from the state's Permanent Fund Dividend, the reporter was trying "to fan the flames of jealousy among other PFD recipients." When mentioning the biblical names of the children, their closely guarded virginity, or how Papa followed the word of God, the writer was clearly trying to make them sound dangerously eccentric.

> Papa was shocked. He had read the article without realizing the hot buttons that would be pushed for many people over the many points the reporter was raising. "A hundred years ago everyone lived like this," [he said]. "We know the world is different now but we never imagined these things would provoke people to hate us."

Stenehjem never said much to me about what really happened during his week at the Mother Lode. The family later told me the pilot had been cast out for trying to woo Elishaba. They said the airplane accident happened when Stenehjem tried a fancy landing to impress Pilgrim's eldest daughter. Elishaba conceded it was hard not to wonder about the young-looking visitor suddenly in their midst. Papa noticed her making eye contact and when they were alone socked her because of it. Stenehjem eventually told a magazine reporter that he noticed strange things: The Pilgrim children were ordered not to peer into his laptop computer, and Papa had led a prayer saying "Lord, if they come at us with guns, we pray that they would have a bullet for each one of us." Stenehjem failed to mention such odd details in his published account that fall, however, which served as one more laudatory testimonial to the last American pioneers.

THE WRANGELL–ST. ELIAS National Park superintendent, Gary Candelaria, was in a cheerful mood the day I stopped by the new visitor center at Copper Center. He had distributed an angry letter to curious visitors during the summer, defending his actions and accusing the Pilgrims of breaking the law "openly, deliberately, repeatedly." SUPERINTENDENT DEFAMES INHOLDERS was the headline on Rick Kenyon's rebuttal. But the superintendent did not seem racked with regret about the publicity and the escalating confrontation on his watch. If anything, he embraced the opportunity to clarify lines of authority in a period of historical transition.

Candelaria would eventually receive a prestigious national award for defending park resources against local political pressures, and in our interview he happily enumerated the trespasses of the Pilgrims. The speech went on for some time.

"The thing is," he concluded, "we have a pretty good record when people come to us and have a need and follow the rules. The Pilgrims might not have gotten everything they wanted, but all this trouble could have been avoided. If this were Yellowstone, would there be a question?"

Indeed, it was hard to imagine someone driving a bulldozer through a national park in the lower forty-eight and not suffering consequences. But wasn't Alaska supposed to be different?

"It does mean we have to take a light touch," the superintendent said. "But the thing about the park is it's here forever. Right now, people say, 'I used to do things this way and didn't have to bother with a permit.' In another twenty years, people will say, 'My mother never used to need a permit.' Over time, you remove that mind-set. You have more people who never had anything to lose in the first place. Like the Hale family. I know, we still have people in the Shenandoah Valley arguing that 'my great-great-grandfather lost his farm' when the Park Service came in there. But things change. Times change."

THE PILGRIMS' most avid angels weren't ready to concede Candelaria's point, however. Their fundamentalism was not necessarily the religious kind. They longed for a return to fundamental American virtues supposedly prevalent at the time of the continent's settling. Government was stripping these freedoms away. Alaska was a last redoubt.

There were signs of this bigger agenda when Papa Pilgrim, pressed by his new handlers to work with the system long enough to establish a legal case, finally applied for an "emergency" access permit from the park. He said they needed to haul in equipment by bulldozer before the deep winter snows. The small planes had not been able to carry all the building supplies they needed. The family submitted an eight-page handwritten letter, in which Pilgrim said they had been prepared to take care of themselves until the iron curtain came crashing down.

As a wilderness family from day one we exemplify "traditional and customary way." The road itself expresses the historic and personability of a road that pioneered this country, "The Last Frontier," a land of extremes, hardship and dangers, blood, tears and laughter of its peoples—To wipe out its people and access, would not only make it virtually unenjoyable for 99.9% of this country's people, but would as in the case of "Cades Cove" rid the wilderness of such beauty and flavor of love, that its true nature and meaning would be lost.

It was telling that Pilgrim invoked the name of Cades Cove. The story of that vanished Appalachian community was a prominent grievance in the decades-long battle waged by Cushman and Kreig and their allies against the "broken promises, abuse, and misconduct" of the National Park Service. Theirs was an important front in the broader counterrevolution centered in the American West, known at various times as the "Wise Use" movement and the "Sagebrush Rebellion," aimed at beating back the rise of environmentalism as a national political force.

The people of Cades Cove, Tennessee, were uprooted during the Great Depression to make way for the Great Smoky Mountains National Park. Then, having swept aside the old rural way of life, park officials became alarmed as brush choked the farm fields and the depopulated valley lost its rustic appeal. Federal funds were spent to reconstitute a museum-version farming landscape that is now a major park attraction. In spring, they say, observant tourists may notice jonquils and roses blooming in the midst of empty meadows, a last trace of the old homesteads.

And so the stories went, in a string of cases in which property-rights groups accused the National Park Service and other agencies of corrupting "America's Best Idea." The government protected treasured vistas by clearing out ranchers and family farmers who were there first—to say nothing of Native American tribes. It was a tragic view of America, where the rural landscape seemed unstable, doomed to change. Either the countryside was to be paved over for shopping malls and tract homes or rolled back in the name of conservation to its primordial presettled state. (It must be said that development of new shopping malls was not seen as the bigger problem to most of these private-property rebels, land speculation having always been the very pulse of America's westward expansion.)

In any event, and unfortunately for Cushman and his fellow Sagebrush Rebels, their rural-rights movement had never found much national traction. The federal inholders were few, they lived in distant valleys, they could too easily be dismissed as tools of big resource corporations or greedy right-wing nuts. The media reflex had been to treat the National Park Service deferentially. And no galvanizing romantic injustice had given the movement a public face.

Until now.

The Park Service had spent twenty years since the passage of the Alaska conservation act treading lightly on local sensitivities in the forty-ninth state. That agreeable attitude had clearly reached its limits in the Pilgrim case. The park's advice to the family on how to obtain an emergency access permit was at first vague—the system for such things was still being worked out—but grew more insistent, and more onerous, with each new exchange. The park declared that "emergencies" under federal regulations had to be unanticipated. The approach of winter in Alaska was, by contrast, entirely foreseeable, something other inholders dealt with, and not a basis for emergency action.

Government biologists had put out a net in McCarthy Creek and found some Dolly Varden trout in the glacial water. Given that each of the Pilgrims' trips would require at least a dozen crossings of this fishy stream, an environmental study would be necessary before even a temporary access route could be approved. The Pilgrims would not be forced to pay for the study themselves, but even an expedited study would mean a sixty-day delay. Officials also suggested contacting the Army Corps of Engineers and the state Department of Natural Resources for additional permits.

The Pilgrims did not follow through. Instead, on November 2, 2003, the Pacific Legal Foundation sued for access in federal court.

✠

WHILE THE Wrangell Mountain airlift continued that fall, my phone rang with calls from individuals and officials who had read the *Anchorage Daily News* stories and wanted to talk about their own brushes with the family.

In Fairbanks, where the family had commenced their footloose period in Alaska, a Catholic charity had found them to be aggressively helpful in the local soup kitchen. The charity loaded them down with winter gear, but after frequent resupply requests finally had to turn them away, sensing they might be selling the gear they'd been given. At that point, I was told, the family swarmed, some of them distracting the warehouse employees, others walking off with sleeping bags and hand tools.

A state Fish and Wildlife protection officer on the Kenai Peninsula had ticketed Joshua for illegally shooting two Dall sheep along the Resurrection Pass Trail. Eight children at the scene wept pitiably as Papa Pilgrim described their poverty and begged for mercy. When the trooper wouldn't relent, Pilgrim turned red and told him he was going to hell. The family was all sweetness again by the time they got to court, with the smallest children perched charmingly on the courtroom railings, but Joshua was convicted anyway.

In the conservative small town of Anchor Point, a senior citizens' thrift store instituted a policy limiting individuals to one bag of clothing per visit because of the Pilgrims. The family had a local reputation, two volunteers said, for deploying their underclothed children "like gypsies" to arouse sympathy. "This isn't another Ruby Ridge, as those people thought they had a cause," the thrift store's bookkeeper wrote in a letter to the paper. "The Pilgrims just want everything handed to them and will take advantage of every situation that comes up and they are not always sweetness and kindness. There is a lot of anger there. Just beware."

There was far more than I could print in the newspaper—not without repeating myself and seeming to pile on unfairly, especially given the political overtones around the state and the stony silence from Hillbilly Heaven.

A small-time gypo logger in Anchor Point had hired the Pilgrims and then got in a fight over pay. The dispute resulted in numerous calls to the state troopers and one of the Pilgrims' trucks getting buried in gravel by the logger's backhoe. A story about the fracas in a local weekly paper drew an angry rebuttal letter signed by Elishaba:

> We in no wise pointed no weapons at no one's head. . . . You cut off the whole story that we told you, just to make us out to sound bad. . . . He grabbed my papa by the beard, and drug him across the room. My little brothers and sisters crying, Buz! Buz!—please don't hurt PAPA!! He hitting my little brother and stomping on my sister's toes. . . . He with a big Golden ring on his finger, broke PAPA's nose in two!

Like other callers, the logger told me he'd gone to the local child protection office to report the family. He described walking in on the daughters as they bathed their naked father. He said the state office chased him away for slandering such fine Christians. (The state agency, citing its usual policy of confidentiality, would tell me nothing.)

"They know how to ride this Welcome Wagon. They have it down pat," the logger said.

Every new story had a weird twist. The Pilgrims had lived for a short while in a gravel pit near Homer on the coast. They'd helped a local commercial fisherman repair a wooden boat that had been run onto the rocks. A swarm of Pilgrims replaced the keel, and in exchange the fisherman agreed to take four of the older sons along as deckhands on a commercial halibut trip. They were in the Barren

Islands, hours from Homer, when four additional children climbed out of the hold. The skipper was angry to have his boat overloaded with stowaways, but the weather was flat calm and they made it back to Homer with twelve thousand pounds of fish.

Pilgrim was a Texas plainsman but maritime living and the bounty of the sea must have looked pretty good at that point. The family climbed in a flat-bottomed boat they'd hauled down from Fairbanks, where they'd traded for it with thoughts of living along the Yukon River. It was a riverboat not meant for sailing on the sea. They headed out of the harbor with eight passengers to look at remote waterfront property. On the mudflats at the head of the bay, they were stranded for half a day when the area's immense tide sucked out. Floating again, they made their way to a cove with land for sale, tied their boat off a rocky point, and returned at the next low tide to find the skiff dangling from a cliff, its stern submerged, their contents drifting away. They hit a big northwest swell in a snowstorm coming back and were bailing fast until they found refuge behind an anchored oil tanker. That was it—the Pilgrims left Homer and moved inland.

I tracked down the lawyer who represented them in the dispute with the gypo logger. He gave them a place to stay in a subdivision he owned in Soldotna, a town north of Homer. The lawyer and his wife came from Mennonite backgrounds and had been moved by sympathy and charity. They soon found themselves in the awkward position of enforcing strict covenants against all the new homes in the subdivision while overlooking the growing piles of junk around the original homestead house they'd loaned the Pilgrims. There were many happy gatherings with food and music, the lawyer told me. But no attention was paid to the future of the children, several of whom he thought brilliant. He attributed this to Papa's belief that they were living in the end days. After many months, the couple began to push more firmly to arrange formal schooling. Pilgrim left without warning, calling to inform the lawyer he was no longer welcome in their family's life. They hadn't been in touch since.

Then there were really dark and troubling allegations. A woman who knew Pilgrim when he first arrived in Fairbanks called to tell me he beat his children and physically "corrected" Country Rose when she failed to call him "My Lord." Papa told others to call him Abraham, and went about with a live raven on his shoulder. She also alleged Pilgrim had tried grooming her for some future role and brainwashed her husband. He took her small son away and made her kneel and ask forgiveness to get him back. "That was the worst feeling in the world, having his hand on my head," she said. A Christian woman in Ninilchik who took the family in said Pilgrim would show up at her home smelling of alcohol—"a little wine for my diabetes," he explained. Whispering in bed, the littlest Pilgrims asked the woman's children if their older sister slept at night with their father.

There were allegations of thievery, and repeated rumors that one of the daughters had been pregnant. It got to be overwhelming. Much of what I was hearing was "off the record" or not for attribution, which meant it was deemed unusable by my newspaper's strict sourcing standards. Or it was potentially slanderous and difficult to substantiate. My editors pressed me to move on to other subjects. Pilgrim still wouldn't come to the phone—though he was now speaking to other journalists, and even to television cameras.

I reported some of the new anecdotes and allegations, but in stories balanced by endorsements from their political supporters.

"They're wonderful, loving people who I find to have a high degree of integrity," Kenyon insisted.

I asked Cushman about all the complaints.

"We keep tracing down these things and finding there wasn't much to them," he said.

Laurie Rowland had been explicit on the subject during the summer, talking to a reporter from the conservative website WorldNetDaily:

They had to prove themselves to us. When we first saw them we were wondering who are these people. They looked so different. Do they have an agenda? Are they trying to prove something? Are they a cult? We couldn't figure them out at first, and we wanted to be 100 percent sure of them. But we got to know them, and we found out they're OK right down the line, straight up, nothing cultish about them. Nothing strange. That's what we were worried about, and these people had to prove to us who they were just by living their lives in front of us.

PILGRIM DID finally take my call. He was frosty, but also concerned that I had published a story without talking to him. When I asked about the thrift shops, he had elaborate explanations. They had a vanload of gear stolen in Fairbanks, by someone they had trusted. "We worked really, really hard in Anchor Point. Folding and hanging clothes, hauling out the trash. We donated more to them than we ever took." He said his friend, the store's bookkeeper, would vouch for him. I told him about the letter she'd written, warning people to beware.

Then I started into the harder things. I said I'd been told the family had a contingency plan in which everyone would commit suicide when he died.

"Oh my goodness," he said. "That's not what I'm talking about at all. It's a prayer for a blessing. *We ask you, Lord, to make our way safe together or let us die for you together.*"

Angry now, he refused to respond to other allegations. There was no more ingratiating chatter about traditional music and cabin living. At last, I locked horns with the Papa Pilgrim other people described.

"If you wanted to treat us fairly, you would have to go into the details of the national parks and their past abuse, as well as the details of a mistake a man makes when he's seventeen."

He pushed back hard. They had gotten in only one-quarter of the supplies they needed. The hay and lumber were impossible to transport without a bulldozer. The park would never back down now, after I wrote that the Pilgrims were bad people. Pilots were risking their lives because of the park—and because of things I'd written.

"Just one mistake and someone could be dead. Before God, you'll have to answer for that."

He dragged other details from my stories before a heavenly tribunal. He threatened lawsuits against the Catholic church in Fairbanks and against the *Anchorage Daily News*. He started after the "rumors and gossip" I'd reported from New Mexico. He described extenuating circumstances that, had I known them, would have explained his actions. How could I have let myself be so misled? he wanted to know.

"If you can't read character better than that, you're in the wrong business," he said.

He was turning the stories inside out, finding vulnerable spots, exposing small uncertainties, worming his way in. I should have taken another week before rushing to print. Had I misunderstood, misjudged him, jumped to a conclusion? Should I have made another call to triple-check some accusation?

Was this what it felt like to be trapped in a cult?

"Those things the troopers told you. They never once came up to my place. Did you ask them for the police report? You never checked after false stories," he said. "There's no way you can prove that I done wrong. Jesus said, 'If I've done wrong, prove it. If I didn't, why did you hit me?'"

I told him the main issue had always been access through the park. That was why I'd come to McCarthy Creek. It was a political story. "Both sides make some good arguments," I said, lamely toeing a professional line.

"That's what you told us—you were there to write about the road. What you told us was the opposite of what you did," he said. "I can't believe I did this to my family, in the name of love and trust. The whole article looks like you were hired by the Park Service. It's really obvious. I understand why. We all saw where your wife works for the Sierra Club and just won a big environmental award."

"My wife is dying of cancer," I hissed. "She had nothing to do with this."

Pilgrim fell silent.

I was horrified by my own words. To wield Sally's illness as a weapon was unthinkable. My whole career, I had kept her separate from my work, avoiding any story in which she had a direct professional interest. It was my own little religion. She hadn't worked on national park issues in many years. In fact, she hadn't worked at all since she'd been sick. If Papa Pilgrim only knew—her affection for McCarthy had contributed as much as anything to my interest in his story.

Though Sally had indeed muttered, after the first stories ran, that she worried the Pilgrims would figure out the location of Neighbor Tom's cabin and burn it down.

I waited. Despite my horror, I had to suppress a fatuous pride at delivering a blow powerful enough to stop Papa Pilgrim in mid-harangue.

When he spoke, his drawl was slower. He said his family would pray for my wife. Then he gently ended the call.

13

The Pilgrim Family
Minstrels

P APA PILGRIM'S surprising rise from recluse to celebrity would
continue after that fall's political mobilization and airlift. The
following spring, musical as well as political fame beckoned outside
Alaska. Pilgrim said he could see God's hand in how the whole story
was unfolding.

First, though, there had been a winter of hardship to endure, and

▲

Music in the cabin for visitors

trials both physical and legal. Despite dozens of small-plane flights in the fall of 2003, little new construction had been accomplished at Hillbilly Heaven. The family was still penned in the single mining cabin with thin plywood walls. Some children slept in an uninsulated storage shed, or in wall tents by the wanigan in town. They had new buckets of dried food and grains, but hunting went badly and the outdoor pole where they hung their frozen meat was nearly bare. And now the extended hunting season for local subsistence families inside the park had closed.

Back in New Mexico, a closed hunting season would have struck the family as more of an irritant than a serious imposition on their diet. If God did not want them to eat meat, He would not send animals their way. Lately, however, the older children had been trying to follow the laws against poaching. They were hoping to establish better relations with their neighbors. They felt better about themselves, too—Elishaba, a crack shot, had packed home a legal Dall sheep with her sisters and two little brothers from a summit above the Mile High Cliffs, happy not to have to hide what she was doing.

Then one morning Papa was riding to town with his daughters and encountered a huge bull moose with a remarkable spread of antlers punching steps along the snowmachine trail.

The bull turned away and floundered toward the trees. Something caused Papa to pull out his rifle and drop the bull before there could be any argument. Elishaba sensed it was his way of showing the kids who was still in charge. She sat there stunned, counting up the problems this suddenly created: a huge trophy moose, shot in violation of more state and federal laws than she could count, lying in the open on bloody snow in a national park, with only her sisters and small children on hand. Papa refused to let them gut the animal, insisting they continue to McCarthy and take care of the meat on the way home. Using shovels they always carried to maintain ice bridges, the children swarmed the job in Pilgrim style, burying the moose in snow and erasing signs of blood. They drove snowmachines back and forth across the spot to obscure it.

By the time they got back from town and dug into the snow, the animal was still warm and the meat had gone bad. They cut it up with a chain saw and sledded the quarters home for dog meat.

Papa hid away the massive antlers. He would have to wait for another legal hunting season before showing them off.

JOSEPH AND Joshua were in Anchorage. The week before Christmas, they drove in with Mama and stayed at Ray Kreig's house and reported to federal court. A magistrate fined Joshua one thousand dollars for taking the undercover agent on a horseback ride into the park. The case against Joseph for breaking the lock on the mine tunnel was trickier. The government produced witnesses and experts, and other park officials watched to see how the question of legal access in Alaska through an underground shaft might get sorted out. There was no quick decision when the prosecution rested.

Carl Bauman, the Motorhead lawyer representing the boys, was being pressed by his firm to wrap up the pro bono work. But the family's legal needs were growing more and more complicated, as they contested certain handshake portions of the sales agreement with Walt Wigger. The old miner had completely soured on the Pilgrims and was attempting to reclaim his wanigan and bulldozer. The sons produced a secret tape recording of Wigger making promises.

"They were naïve in a sharp way," Bauman recalled. "They could live with a little ambiguity, if you will."

The family's big headline case, the Pacific Legal Foundation lawsuit, was not going well. The park was winning. A federal judge had ruled that the guarantee of "adequate and feasible" access to inholdings in Alaska was subject to "reasonable regulation" by the park. He said the 1980 Alaska conservation act spelled out this balancing act explicitly.

The bottom line was that the Pilgrims could not ignore the fact that their road ran through a national park. They had to get a permit, and if the government's rules seemed too stringent, the family could come back to court seeking relief. The federal judge, Ralph Beistline of Fairbanks, added that the family's emergency didn't seem so dire, considering all the help they'd received: "Many Alaskans who choose a wilderness lifestyle routinely experience similar hardships, without the benefit of a large scale airlift of goods." He lectured both sides about their "showmanship and emotionalism."

By the time the judge ruled, winter lay deep in the valley. At that time of year, a pale sun would appear for only an hour or two a day. Many chores got done by moonlight. The Park Service had decided the family could have temporary access by bulldozer—but only during winter, when the creek was frozen and the ground protected by snow. The family refused to sign off. They put their faith in an appeal. They wanted a summer road. Winter travel was too dangerous, they said.

As if to emphasize the point, a massive avalanche let go from Green Butte that winter with Joshua and David squarely in its path.

The boys had been snowmachining down the valley in a heavy wet snowfall. David was driving, with Joshua holding a towline on a pair of old downhill skis. Two of them on the machine would have bogged down in the fresh snow. Even as it was, David got stuck. They were by the creek, digging at the machine with shovels. The snow was falling in big, thick flakes, and they could see nothing in the gray darkness but they could hear the long roll of thunder. It was a familiar sound in this valley, though there was no telling where this avalanche was coming down. Suddenly an enormous wind struck them, thick with powder and crusty snow and leaves from the decimated woods. They crouched behind the machine, gasping for air as the whirlwind engulfed them, their hearts bursting with repentance, as they waited for the crush of snow to end their lives.

Then there was silence. After crashing through the trees, the wall of snow had stopped several hundred yards short of where the brothers waited. But they had felt the breath of God.

IN THE cabin's tight quarters that winter, the fighting between Elishaba and Papa was getting worse. Elishaba's brothers pressed her to give up her bitterness toward their father. She was making life impossible for everyone. Papa punished her, when his diabetes and leg pains got worse, by choosing Jerusalem to accompany him during another hospital stay in Anchorage. Papa had warned Elishaba that her younger sister could always take her place—that Elishaba could be reduced to servitude in the family. He had stirred Elishaba's jealousy this way from the time Jerusalem was born.

Elishaba was left behind to work with her brothers at the portable sawmill in McCarthy. She had so many emotions as she worked, she couldn't keep them straight—relief being away from her father, dread on behalf of her fifteen-year-old sister, and envy over the trip to town.

Country Rose went along to the hospital as well. The family was thus spread all over the landscape when, on the seventeenth day of the Third Month, Abraham caught his finger in the generator at Hillbilly Heaven.

The last joint of the nine-year-old's middle finger was stripped clean off. The children looked all over the shed but couldn't find the fleshy tip until someone thought to check inside Abraham's work glove. David, left in charge of the homestead, put Abraham on the back of a snowmachine and rushed him down the valley, the finger fragment in a bag of snow. They were flown to Anchorage where their parents waited. But the doctors at Providence Hospital seemed cold and unfriendly. They were less concerned about Abraham's finger than about lateral welts they discovered on his back.

Papa called the homestead and told the children there to run into the woods and hide because social workers might be on their way. He slipped into Abraham's hospital room and forgave his son for the theft of candy that had made his whipping necessary. These were the times he had often warned about, Papa said, when the family had to stick together. The state troopers were summoned to the hospital. Each family member was interviewed separately, but everyone told the same story about Abraham falling down some stairs at the homestead.

Meanwhile, Country Rose found a doctor in Portland, Oregon, who agreed to try to reattach the fingertip. Abraham was allowed to leave and was medevaced to the Pacific Northwest. Papa went along on the plane to care for his son. Jerusalem followed on a commercial flight to take care of Papa.

It turned out to be too late for Abraham's finger. But as they camped in Abraham's room in the Portland hospital, they had a visitor. Chuck Cushman, the beefy, white-bearded property-rights advocate who had helped organize the Wrangells airlift, lived right across the Columbia River in southern Washington.

And that was how the Lord revealed His plan in their dark hour, Papa Pilgrim told an audience a few days later when he took the microphone on stage.

It turned out that Cushman, the political activist known by the nickname "Rent-a-Riot," was also a musician. He played autoharp in a bluegrass-style band. He took Papa and Jerusalem to an open-mike concert and encouraged them to perform. He was astounded to watch their bashful country manner blossom into stage charisma before an audience. Pilgrim turned out to be a sly showman. Jerusalem was a mandolin prodigy. Their tunes were so well received that night, and the next when they played at another show, that Cushman proposed a real concert to raise funds for their return trip north.

The onstage authenticity of Cushman's land-rights icons could not have been more pleasing. He moved Pilgrim into his home and arranged for more of the family to head south and join the band. He called a friend with ties to a local recording studio. Like many others before and after him, Cushman was moved to help this family that seemed a little troubled and lost in the world. But he was excited, too, to think this could be the missing piece at last—the romantic family whose struggle against the National Park Service would become a national rallying cause.

Folksy and acerbic, Cushman had once sold insurance in Los Angeles. But he was the son of a seasonal park ranger, and he often told audiences that he was inspired to start the National Park Inholders Association in 1978 by memories of how his father was blackmailed into selling the family's inholding cabin to keep his job in Yosemite. Expanding his mission to include miners, ranchers, and Forest Service cabin owners, Cushman traveled the country to advise local groups—usually for a fee—on the perils of new proposals for parks, wildlife refuges, or "scenic river" designations that could interfere with their property rights. On one such barnstorming tour of Alaska in 1979, on the eve of the Alaska conservation act vote, he had flown into McCarthy. Rick Kenyon would later describe that visit as his own moment of political awakening. The jingoistic spirit of those times, and the infighting that hobbled the anti-environmentalist opposition, was nicely evoked by the names of the four groups that sponsored Cushman's trip but couldn't combine into a single organization: the Real Alaskan Coalition, Alaskans for Alaska, Alaskans United, and Alaskans Unite.

Cushman's stump speech invoked the values of salt-of-the-earth rural Americans whose bucolic real estate dreams were threatened by affluent urban elites seeking new playgrounds. Even his critics conceded Cushman helped force the Park Service to rethink a high-handed preference for secret land acquisitions and condemnations. But they accused him of a divisive, shoot-from-the-hip style that tore communities apart and relied on exaggeration—equating, for instance, park policies to genocide in the Balkans. When I spoke with

Cushman, he chuckled about the Rent-a-Riot nickname, saying he often used it himself. "In my world, controversy is a friend," he said. "If I can create enough controversy, I can move a bureaucracy."

American roots music, though, could move public opinion. And as the Pilgrims' music caught on, there was also good news back in Alaska on the legal and political fronts. The federal courts agreed to hear an appeal of Judge Beistline's decision. Then the federal magistrate ruled narrowly in the Mother Lode mineshaft case, imposing a mere three-hundred-dollar fine on Joseph for breaking the government's padlock and lecturing the Park Service about being a better neighbor. The day after his sentencing, Joseph went to a meeting in the eastern Alaska crossroads of Delta Junction and was asked to serve as district delegate to the state Republican Party convention in May.

Papa Pilgrim's allies were being rewarded and his enemies vanquished. After five years of butting heads with local critics, park superintendent Gary Candelaria was moving on to Harpers Ferry, West Virginia. The new NPS Alaska regional director told staff they needed to come up with better access rules to accommodate well-meaning park inholders. Internet traffic was flooding the "War in the Wrangells" website put up by Kreig's organization, the Alaska Land Rights Coalition. Kurt Stenehjem, the fallen airlift angel turned correspondent, wrote a story for Rick Kenyon's paper about Cades Cove. Neil Darish at the McCarthy Lodge won attention for a levelheaded opinion piece in the *Anchorage Daily News* that called for preserving McCarthy's "remote wilderness culture" in light of new thinking around the world regarding ways to engage indigenous communities in conservation. Darish argued that part of the appeal of Alaska's national parks was the lingering opportunity for self-reliant living, which sometimes included "driving funky vehicles somewhere unpopulated" over old roads and trails.

Summoned south by Papa, family members loaded their instruments and sleeping bags in the back of one such funky vehicle, a seatless, windowless panel van usually parked by the Kennicott River. Hosanna, David, Joshua, Lamb, and Elishaba were turned back at the Canada border because of a badly cracked windshield. But help from a Christian family in Delta Junction got them back on the road. They made it to Portland in time for the concert.

They were a hit. The family went on local radio and then played another concert, and then gave six more performances, all of them small-theater sellouts. They developed a following of other large Christian families, high schoolers, and traditional music fans fascinated by the loving and untainted family out of the Alaska wilderness: the father with his wry sparkle, the smiling musicians, the yodeling, the youngest children clogging wildly in their loud tap shoes. People said it was like discovering the Carter Family back in 1927 in rural Virginia. They played the indigenous folk music of America, vernacular hymns born in the populist religious ferment that swept the Jacksonian frontier and took root in the Appalachians. A singer in a popular Portland acoustic quartet helped organize the shows and told a reporter, "It was tempting as a musician to want to offer them a tip, but we would just bite our lips because we didn't want to contaminate them."

A recording studio executive came to one of their shows and opened his doors, so they went in and recorded a compact disc. They called themselves the Pilgrim Family Minstrels, a name that Papa said picked up on the idea of musical "ministry," of being instruments of God. The CD featured original and traditional gospel tunes of struggle and reward. Elishaba sang solo on one of them, "Pilgrim's Daughter":

I am a pilgrim's daughter on the way to Heaven's home
Gonna hold his hand forever, only one way to go . . .

Papa called the CD *Put My Name Down* and dedicated it to his brother, "Pilgrim Billy," who "passed over the Jordan River to Glory" while recording was under way. A reviewer for the *Anchorage Daily News,* waving off their "hillbilly get-ups and well-publicized legal scraps," called their music "pure as a mountain brook."

With successful concerts and glowing reviews, Cushman talked of bringing the family back to the Pacific Northwest for an extended tour. The English writer Pete McCarthy had once predicted "brighter lights than McCarthy can offer" for the family band, and the time did seem nearly at hand.

There was a moment, though, during their stay at Cushman's house, when the property-rights activist caught himself wondering about his pure-as-a-mountain-brook poster family. He shared some sheet music with the children, not really expecting they would be able to read the music. But it was worse than that—they couldn't read the lyrics.

BY LATE May, the Pilgrims were back in Alaska, arriving in force at the sports arena in Soldotna for Joseph's debut in state politics. It was the Republican Party's 2004 state convention, and the Pilgrim Family were the featured entertainment.

They showed up in a van they'd been given in Washington State—one with windows and actual seats. On the side they'd painted PILGRIM FAMILY MINSTRELS TOUR VAN 2004, and on the back, HONK IF YOU LOVE JESUS—WE DO! Papa Pilgrim spoke approvingly to a reporter about the Republican platform, saying it appeared to take a "godly approach." The family's homespun manner offered a welcome distraction from the internal warfare tearing at the Alaska Republicans that election year, over ethics charges leveled against the party's paid chairman by its rising young star, a former mayor of Wasilla.

Coming off their recent successes, it should have been the performance that established the Pilgrims as darlings of the state's political conservatives. The family's down-home values, their religiosity, and their battle against federal landlords all seemed elements of a powerful brand for Alaska Republicanism. But when the big moment came and the Pilgrim Family Minstrels played their gospel tunes, the response from delegates was surprisingly muted. Crevasses were opening in Alaska's dominant political party at the start of Sarah Palin's era. Despite the growing influence of Christian churches in the state's majority party, libertarian Alaska actually ranks low among states in measures of religious piety and church attendance. Some conservatives, especially in the more secular, oil-and-construction business sphere of the party, found the Pilgrims distasteful—probable welfare cheats, creepy in their isolation, newcomers exploiting the state's beloved Permanent Fund Dividend program.

One attendee who was especially uncomfortable about the performance was Dallas Massie. In his day job, Massie was an investigator for the Alaska State Troopers. Several months earlier, he had been called to Providence Hospital to examine the welts on Abraham Hale's back. It didn't appear to Massie that the boy had fallen down some stairs. But the family's story had been consistent, and the state couldn't hold them when they took off for Portland. In Soldotna, he found the music entertaining, but every time his eyes fell on Papa Pilgrim his heart sank. He watched the way the father kept his kids lined up, awaiting his commands, huddled apart from everyone else at the convention. Massie knew something was not right.

The Pilgrims had come to Soldotna hoping for a timely boost from the Republicans. Governor Frank Murkowski seemed a natural for their cause, steeped in the old antagonisms of Alaska conservation politics. For twenty-two years as a U.S. senator, he had fulminated that the 1980 conservation act was like "waking up one morning to find that the federal government has declared your yard a national park and refused you access across your driveway." The governor had been coaxed by Ray Kreig to fire off a letter in April to Interior secretary Gale Norton, calling attention to complaints in the Wrangells about red tape, access fees, and arbitrary field decisions by park rangers.

But Murkowski was slow to follow up on the specifics of the Pilgrim Family's plight and their federal legal appeal. Key aides inside his administration warned the situation could backfire. The state's main coordinator of federal lands and conservation issues knew the McCarthy scene particularly well: In a former life, she had hosted Labor Day contra dances at the Hardware Store. Sally Gibert was one of a handful of Santa Cruz graduates who migrated to McCarthy in the 1970s. She later put her perspective on Alaska issues to professional use, serving both Republican and Democratic governors as state federal lands adviser. Gibert and others cautioned Murkowski that the legal arguments in the Pilgrim case were shaky, community support was less solid than activists alleged, and the Pilgrim Family's belligerence could undermine the state's long-term interests.

The Pilgrims' court battle was turning out to be no one's idea of a good time. Environmentalists were nervous about a precedent-setting legal challenge over national park access rights involving what was clearly, at one time, a real road. But the state's resource-development-minded Republicans were equally nervous about how the Pilgrim Family facts might suggest to any judge the need for prudent federal oversight of what goes on inside a national park.

IT WAS a funny thing about the Pilgrims: The bigger the stage, the better they looked. From the proper distance—in concert, or in the stories of McCarthy Annie—the family's saga was compelling. Glimpsing them on the front page or the TV news, one couldn't help be intrigued. But up close, the folk-hero luster wore away quickly.

That summer of 2004, the family returned from the Pacific Northwest and the state Republican convention to a showdown in the dusty streets of Old McCarthy Town. Back home, the celebrity musicians' sprawling camp had become an object of universal derision.

Pilgrim seemed taken aback. His family was exposed to so much more scrutiny here in the vast Alaska wilderness than they ever got in New Mexico. In the Sangre de Cristos, the social divisions were deep and historical. People were more guarded, and resentments built slowly. In the Wrangells, everything was new and out in the open. If folks didn't like something, they told you.

Early on, Pilgrim tried to address local tensions with a letter, apologizing for the horses getting loose but blaming the park blockade for everything else. For seven defensive pages he cautioned people not to believe everything they heard. "I read in the Bible how God speaks about it in this wise: 'A man's story sounds good until his neighbor shows up,'" Pilgrim wrote. It was reminiscent of the speech he used to spring the family from trouble in New Mexico in 1995. He described how the conscience of a well-respected McCarthy neighbor was awakened upon hearing Pilgrim's side of things, "released from all his own misunderstandings, his character healed, and we both enjoyed once again the endearment of good neighbor-ship." It was a contrast, clearly, to the "malicious and uncalled-for harassment" from park rangers. The horse manure that people were complaining about was just "grass soup," cleaner than "dog poo." Then he told a story so ghastly that parents hid the letter away: how a Pilgrim horse, tangled in its own rope, was attacked by a town dog: "Sheer terror was in its eyes as the big black dog stood upon its body tearing at its flesh. The blood smeared horse was close to death and shock as it had been eaten alive from anus to its ears."

But Pilgrim's lack of progress toward cleaning up his camp in the public right-of-way had worn out local patience. A heady fragrance of horse manure, burning garbage, and diesel exhaust drifted around town from the Pilgrims' pied-à-terre. Disdain for the modern world was one thing, disregard for friends and neighbors something very different. With no local government, the only recourse was to mining-camp justice. A committee of property owners passed around a petition and presented the Pilgrims a "Notice of Road Improvement" stating that on August 14, 2004, a bulldozer would undertake a road beautification project at the corner of Barrett Way and Donohoe Avenue, presently the site of a wanigan, a horse corral, wall tents, and sundry pallets and storm windows and oil drums.

> Be very clear. It is in your best interest as members of this community to declare your timetable to vacate the community streets. You can only benefit from our respect and by conducting yourselves as you originally declared to the community upon your arrival to McCarthy. . . . After two plus years and clear proof that you do not own the land you occupy, you are in fact homesteading on the community's land and right of ways. We find ourselves motivated to resolve this issue by legal and lawful means.

Walt Wigger was still trying to get the wanigan back from "these would-be pioneers," along with his D5 bulldozer.

"Maybe by now you know this is not a gentle Mennonite family," he told people. "I made them give me the key to my pickup at the airport, but the Park Service found it by the river where the old cars are dumped, with its windows and lights broke out. These are terrorist tactics that they use. They're telling the people of McCarthy if you don't go along with us, this is going to happen to you. They've got this made-up religion. They can justify anything that they do, because the Lord provides for them. I'm still going to move them out of my wanigan, but I'll give you odds two-to-one that after they move out there's going to be spontaneous combustion."

In a town with a proud tradition of bickering, the Pilgrims had suddenly brought everyone together.

It was not just the wanigan camp. It was that the Pilgrims had defied the unwritten rules by which the community always got along.

They had scrapped their little three-wheeled roadster and gone full-scale into the Kennicott shuttle business, undercutting the established local taxi using unpaid family drivers and an uninsured van donated by an out-of-town sympathizer. They built a tourist booth by the footbridge, sold photographs of themselves, and steered tourists toward their own businesses. The down-home neighbors were suddenly apostles of cutthroat frontier competition. They tore up chain speed bumps that a family had anchored across the Kennicott Road to slow shuttle vans passing their cabin. It was a public right-of-way, the Pilgrims argued, without apparent irony. And the Pilgrims, of all people, were invoking state laws and calling the cops.

One afternoon, Papa came upon a group of young women, local summer workers, swimming in a sun-warmed pothole by the glacial river. Once the shouting match had died down Papa called the troopers in Glennallen to report the appalling half-naked sluttiness. The troopers declined to make the four-hour drive in response. A visitor, after hearing this story over a beer in the McCarthy Lodge, spied a knot of Pilgrims in the street and ran out to drop his pants and moon them. This time a trooper did make the trip, telling everyone to stop "picking at each other."

Within weeks, however, the troopers were back, filing criminal charges against two town residents who had crossed the Pilgrims.

The first incident involved an impish bush rat named Mark Wacht, who lost his four-wheeler to the Pilgrims while he was gone on vacation. When he complained, the vehicle was returned with the gas tank empty and his new tires replaced by bald ones. There had been bad blood ever since. Wacht came up with the line, soon famous around McCarthy, that "NPS" stenciled on equipment meant "Not Pilgrim Stuff."

One night that summer, some Pilgrim boys started to goad Wacht by videotaping him and his girlfriend as they walked supplies across the footbridge. He asked them to stop, but they followed him around.

When Wacht tried to drive his girlfriend home to Kennicott, the boys blocked his way with their van, creeping stop-and-go up the road. He tried to pass, hooked a bumper, and went off the road. The Pilgrims called the troopers and Wacht was arrested for assault and reckless driving. It was two months before the prosecutor finally looked at the Pilgrims' videotape and saw the reflection of their stop-and-go brake lights flashing on Wacht's truck windshield, corroborating his version of events. The charges were dropped.

The second incident involved the owner of the riverbank land at the end of the McCarthy Road where visitors parked. Once again the Pilgrims helped themselves to the public right-of-way—this time setting up a tourist-information table in front of Steve Syren's property. Syren noticed food and tools disappearing from his property after he argued with the Pilgrims. His welder was booby-trapped. When he knocked over the table and scattered several children, Papa Pilgrim made another call to 911. The troopers flew out to arrest Syren in a helicopter—knowing, Syren figured, how the phones start ringing every time a trooper SUV drives through Chitina on its way out the road. Once again, the charges were dropped, this time when no Pilgrims showed up in court to testify.

"By all appearances, they're trying to get people to lose their cool," said Jeremy Keller, a dog musher whose family lived eleven miles from town on the Nizina River and somehow managed to get supplies without a bulldozer or an airlift. Keller had delivered the road petition and had to wait twenty minutes outside the wanigan for Pilgrim to emerge. The kids, normally friendly, stood nearby and wouldn't speak to him. "It's as aggressive as passive gets."

PILGRIM CONTINUED to present himself as the victim of persecution. "God says, 'Men will hate Christians without a cause,' and that is what's happening to us in McCarthy," he wrote in a letter to the *Anchorage Daily News,* which he had Country Rose sign. But around town that summer, it became apparent he was bringing on his troubles deliberately. Even the family's closest friends and allies found themselves cut off.

Pilgrim would no longer go by the McCarthy Lodge. He exploded when Neil Darish suggested the family not help themselves to a certain "abandoned" automobile by the river, lest they be accused once again of stealing. Pilgrim called the lodge owner a traitor.

Rick Kenyon got an angry tongue-lashing when he stopped by the wanigan a few days before the road beautification project. The editor/preacher had come on a peace mission. He suggested the family adopt a more Christian approach to business competition in town, mentioning the shuttle van and their footbridge visitor booth. Pilgrim excoriated the preacher for presuming to tell them how to be better Christians.

Kenyon spoke of recent assurances he'd been given by Elishaba. Perhaps he'd misunderstood her?

Joseph turned to the preacher and spat, "Are you calling my sister a liar? I hope you rot in hell."

That evening at the wanigan, Papa bragged to the whole family about Joseph's harsh words to the preacher. But Joseph confessed he had called Kenyon to apologize. Papa was embarrassed and furious. He made Joseph take the phone and call Kenyon to retract his apology. Then he accused his son of betrayal and popped him in the face. With his lip pouring blood, Joseph shielded his head with his arms and wouldn't fight back. His father kept punching. Mama said Papa had gone too far and she made for the phone to call 911, but the children stopped her, terrified that social workers would intervene. Papa grabbed her by the hair and hurled the phone out the door.

Joseph was ordered to leave the family compound. He went off in the woods to sleep under a tree. Mama slept that night in the family bus.

✠

THE SATURDAY morning of the showdown was sunny and hot. Jeremy Keller wore a Hawaiian surf shirt as he led marchers down the dirt street toward the smell of horse urine. Seventy people strode along behind him, a huge crowd for McCarthy. The number included several visitors from the Hardware Store, in town for a writers' conference and surely not lacking for colorful local material. An Alaska State Trooper hung back out of sight at the Wrangell Mountain Air office in case of trouble.

Keller had stepped forward as an organizer to help his friend Stephens Harper, who was feeling heat for his dual role as neighbor and park ranger. Harper had heard there was pressure coming from some congressional staffer to fire him, on the grounds that he was waging a personal vendetta against this family of inholders. The regional director had seen the Pilgrims' camp, however, and was backing her ranger.

The crowd reached the wanigan. Speeches were made, posters and banners waved. Randy Elliott, the local gold miner, rumbled into view atop his Cat—mostly for show in this season of bulldozers and blockades. The old homesteader Jim Edwards was present, though he couldn't hear the speakers' words. Rick Kenyon was there, too, covering the event. After his own clash with Pilgrim, and particularly after Joseph's bizarre apology and retraction, Kenyon began to reflect more openly about things that troubled him. There were theological concerns, and an underlying anger he'd heard about but never witnessed until now. He conceded privately that the fire in the church put out so nobly by the Pilgrim boys—it had been the subject of several sermonizing editorials—might have accidentally been started by them as well. The *Wrangell St. Elias News* would continue to agitate against what Kenyon deemed Park Service abuses in the McCarthy Creek road case, but adoring stories about the family ceased. McCarthy Annie's byline never appeared again. Even Laurie and Keith Rowland's names were on the petition, urging the Pilgrims to abide by local practice and move out of the public street.

One loyal Pilgrim ally who kept his distance from the road beautification project that day was Ray Kreig. To the head of the Alaska Land Rights Coalition, this "greenie lynch mob" was the fulfillment of the government's plan to sow division and turn everyone against the owners of the Mother Lode.

Some blamed Kreig himself for the escalation. Mike Loso, a former head of the Wrangell Mountains Center at the Hardware Store, called Kreig and told him to "take his national fight somewhere else." A wiry, tousle-haired mountain climber with a doctorate from Santa Cruz, Loso had gotten to know the oldest Pilgrim boys that summer when he completed a field study for the park on the family's request to cut house logs from McCarthy Creek. The park had let him hire the Pilgrims and their horses to help with the survey, and they got along well.

Like other well-meaning people, Loso imagined he might be the friend the Pilgrim boys seemed to need so desperately. But then one bright summer evening by the footbridge, as he was introducing his wife to Joseph, Papa Pilgrim himself walked over and tore into Loso about things he'd supposedly told Kreig. Loso had called the Pilgrims evil! Loso protested it was not true. He considered the boys his friends. Papa accused him of being filled with deceit, of trying to tear his children away. He turned to Loso's wife, whom he'd never met, and shrieked, "You're the enemy of my family!" Tears came to her eyes, and Loso pulled her away, saying, "You're out of line and this conversation is over." What shocked Loso the most was that Joseph did not speak up.

On the day of the showdown, the older Pilgrim boys were not at the wanigan. Hunting season had started, and they had already flown off to mountain camps, where they had found work as skilled horse packers. But the rest of the family was in town. The girls lined up on the porch of the little cabin with their musical instruments.

Elishaba's cheeks burned with shame as she watched the angry mob surround them. She saw what had become of her dream of a clean new life with friends in Alaska.

Below the steps, Papa Pilgrim, wearing a battered black cowboy hat, his gray beard trailing down his front, read a statement he'd prepared: "We are absolutely delighted and thankful that *finally* in the last few days we see that we can very soon move to our land west of the river. We want the community to know that we have never been comfortable being stranded in this situation and regret the distress it has caused."

The family had purchased a lot across the footbridge, right at the end of the McCarthy Road, and planned to move the wanigan and camp across the river. Ray Kreig had quietly advanced them funds for the deal. Pilgrim thanked the assembled community for offering to help move them. But they could manage themselves.

People started shouting questions. Papa answered a few, then nodded at his girls on the porch to start playing.

There were more shouted questions, but the only reply was from Elishaba's fiddle. Pilgrim tapped his foot and sang a favorite song, one that had brought smiles in the audience when he sang it two and a half years earlier, during that first concert at the McCarthy Lodge.

I was dreaming of a little cabin, when I heard somebody call my
  name . . .
She gently put her arms around me, oh, an' kissed her little boy
  once more . . .

Elishaba, Jerusalem, and Hosanna did not meet anyone's eyes. Stone-faced, they stared into a middle distance, as though watching a shoreline recede.

The Pilgrim Family Minstrels were never to play in public again.

Later that evening, neighbors held a party to support Stephens and Tamara Harper. Acoustic musicians set up a public address system on the Harpers' porch, just across the storage yard from the wanigan, where the Pilgrims had once blasted music at their neighbors. They had a guitar, fiddle, and washtub bass. Mike Loso played the banjo. A friend handed the Harpers a thousand-dollar check to help with legal expenses in case they had to go to court. He took the microphone and pumped his fist in the air and hollered, "So you can run the bastards out of town!"

"I'm actually getting a little tired of bluegrass," Stephens Harper sighed.

Part Three

Out of the Wilderness

Listening, I could hear
within myself the snow
that was coming, the sound
of a loud, cold trumpet.

—John Haines, "Poem for a Cold Journey," 1966

14

A Quiet Year

T HE PHONE call came at the end of a quiet year.

It was like the Pilgrims disappeared after the wanigan was moved across the Kennicott River. That fall, the controversies and publicity went away. The family came and went quietly through the winter, gone to Anchorage, snowmachining to their place up McCarthy Creek, camping across the river. No longer in the public eye. A big Christian family in the town of Palmer, north of Anchorage, was rumored to be helping them out. By the summer of 2005, when the boys reappeared in McCarthy with their string of horses for rent, they

▲

Along the McCarthy Road

stopped their neighbors to apologize, vaguely, for things that had been going on. Clearly something had changed.

The family had disappeared from my attention as well. I hadn't even gone back to report on the gathering showdown in McCarthy's streets. Those had been Sally's final days. I took time off that summer for my own family. We flew into the coastal range near our home and let Sally's ashes go from a breezy summit. I knew that one of my duties as a father would be to teach Emily and Ethan about things that were important to their mother. Sooner or later, it was going to require a trip back to McCarthy.

One year later, in September 2005, I was back at the desk in my rural one-man bureau for the *Anchorage Daily News*. I had just returned from a conference marking the twenty-fifth anniversary of the Alaska National Interest Lands Conservation Act. There had been a big turnout, as the national parks, no longer poison in Alaska politics, had become important to Alaska's tourism economy. Emily had gone to the conference, too, with members of her high school environmental club. She was surprised to find herself treated like some kind of eco-princess as featured speakers, her mom's old friends and colleagues, greeted her with hugs and whisked her away to shake hands with former president Jimmy Carter.

As I listened to the speakers, I thought about Sally's conservation career and was grateful that our children could still explore vast wild places in Alaska for themselves. A lot of historic choices had been packed into the span of a single generation in Alaska—Native land claims, oil development, the parks and wilderness bill. In the paper the next day I wrote about a Republican congressman from Indiana who got a laugh at the conference introducing himself as a token evangelical right-winger. A history buff, he said that serving on an Alaska conservation oversight committee made him reflect on his own state's past—how the Northwest Ordinance of 1787 opened the West for private development back when the Great Lakes were considered America's remote frontier. "You are going through this two hundred years later. It was fascinating to watch," he said. "The differences were that you treated the Native Americans as partners, and you set aside public lands for the future."

Now I was back in my office, back to the daily journalistic fare of modern Alaska—the volcanoes and salmon wars and bridges to nowhere—when the phone on my desk rang. It was my editor in Anchorage.

"The troopers are looking for a friend of yours," he said. "Robert Allen Hale, age sixty-four, of McCarthy."

A media alert had just been issued. Hale had been indicted by a secret grand jury in Palmer and was being sought on thirty felony counts of kidnapping, assault, coercion, incest, and sexual assault in the first degree.

Alaska State Troopers had flown to McCarthy to apprehend him. The police helicopter landed by the Kennicott River. In the woods nearby was a wall tent with a woodstove, and a dark wanigan on wheels. Troopers checked the wall tent and found the stovepipe still warm.

But Papa Pilgrim had vanished.

15

The Wanigan

T HE WIPERS struggled fitfully as the flatbed truck climbed through dusk and an early season snowstorm. The heater cut on and off. Joshua drove because he had the big-truck commercial license, thanks to Mama reading the exam questions out loud. Joseph sat at his brother's side. The two had been talking with excitement and frustration for hours, most of the way from McCarthy, trying to sort out what was going on with their father.

It was the Tenth Month of 2004—not many weeks after the showdown in the streets of McCarthy. Things remained troublingly

Papa Pilgrim in McCarthy

unsettled for the Pilgrim Family. Papa's behavior was increasingly erratic. They no longer had any friends. They had moved the wanigan,
but there was no more money for plane flights and too little feed for
the horses. Freeze-up was late, and McCarthy Creek was still open
and flowing—no longer summer-gray with silt from melting glaciers
but clear, low, drinkable, and impassable on a snowmachine. When
Joseph and Joshua came out from the homestead, they had to ride
horses, packing two hindquarters of a moose shot by Elishaba and
Israel. Papa's instructions were to stop on their way to Kenai and deliver the meat to a large Christian family in a log cabin on the mountain outside Palmer, the last town on the highway before Anchorage.
Apparently this new family, the Buckinghams, were not experienced
hunters and had failed to get a moose that fall. The brothers recognized the gift of meat as the kind of extravagant gesture Papa favored when making a first impression. To the Pilgrim sons, the effort
seemed so predictable and futile.

The brothers were very different. Joseph, now twenty-seven, was
reflective and stubborn; Joshua, two years younger, was more hot-
headed, more like their father. Joseph had always been the family outcast, though in the last few years, since the time he'd gently pressed
Papa's chest to steer him away from hitting the younger children, his
father had stopped thrashing him. Another time he had pulled a two-
by-four from Papa's hands before he could strike Israel. The eldest son
would come back from hunting camp and Elishaba would have a new
swelling on her face and everyone, even Papa, would tiptoe around.
They were all surprised when Papa gave Joseph that bloody lip in late
summer for apologizing to the McCarthy preacher.

Immediately after that incident Joseph had left to join Joshua at
hunting camp. With no younger siblings to listen in and report them,
the brothers started talking as if for the first time. The conversation
really hadn't stopped since. For the first time they felt like close friends.

Joshua predicted that this new friendship with the Buckinghams would blow up even more quickly than earlier alliances had. The dispute over the wanigan in town had run off the last of their McCarthy neighbors, and Papa, with his angry spirit, no longer even cared. He was fixing once again to be like Noah in the Bible, a man who had no use for neighbors.

Joseph and Joshua had been the first to meet the Buckinghams. Earlier in the fall, they had stopped by a small worship service in Willow with their mother and heard Mr. Buckingham give a fine talk. Papa had not wanted to hear about it. He told Joseph the Bible said not to consort with someone in the military.

Joseph explained now to his brother that the centurion praised by Jesus was a Roman soldier. Papa had read them the story in Luke, but never said what a centurion was. A Christian friend in McCarthy had to explain. So didn't that make it unfair of Papa to hang up on Joseph when he called to say that Mr. Buckingham was in the army?

Once Papa met the Buckinghams everything changed. Suddenly here was the true Christian family they'd always dreamed of meeting. It was all so inconsistent and confusing, and the boys, unable to demand an explanation from their father, could talk in circles for hours about a puzzle like this.

For all their new intimacy, though, there was one subject the brothers dared not bring up. That was the Buckinghams' pretty eldest daughters, Tischaria and Tilaundia. The boys had tried not to stare during that worship service in Willow. Neither of them had ever had a girlfriend. They would be punished severely if they so much as talked to a girl. Regarding marriage, they understood it would be wrong in the sight of God to make a covenant outside the family. But the young men's imaginations usually skipped past such theological obstacles to more practical ones: Living in such isolation, how were they ever going to meet someone, anyway?

Sometimes Joseph daydreamed improbable stories in which he

found a way to marry. The elaborate scenario might involve some girl spoken to only once in passing, years earlier, a girl remembered more as a tremor than a face. Joshua, on the other hand, was given to mad fantasies of running away and meeting someone out in the world, just to make Papa feel bad and shock him into realizing how wrong he treated his family. Joshua burned but did what Papa expected. Papa said if anything ever happened, the family was to follow him or Elishaba. Not Joseph, the family two-year-old, and not Mama, whose jealous heart Papa worked so hard to correct.

Joshua aimed the flatbed down a snowy drive through the woods. The Buckinghams lived in a gambrel-roof cabin built from logs milled on site. It was not a big home for a family with nine children, but to Joseph and Joshua it seemed luxurious. The Pilgrim boys were greeted warmly and invited to stay for dinner. The big kitchen sparkled.

Jim Buckingham was a forty-six-year-old lieutenant colonel in the U.S. Army. Currently he was inspector general for the Alaskan Command. A former instructor at West Point, he had a mechanical engineering degree from MIT, a master's degree from Stanford, and a PhD from the University of Alaska. Yet he and his wife, Martha, studied Scripture every night with their family and believed, like the Pilgrims, in the literal truth of the Bible. It was during an earlier deployment to Alaska, living in a cabin outside Fairbanks, that Buckingham began feeling prompts to turn his family toward a simpler, more pious life, apart from a culture that seemed to have forgotten God. In 2003, nearing retirement, he had returned north for the posting at Fort Richardson and moved his family to Lazy Mountain, above the spreading Anchorage exurbs of Palmer and Wasilla. As they were closing in the cabin that first fall, the family saw a photograph of the Pilgrims in the *Anchorage Daily News* and were struck by certain similarities with their own family, including the modest long skirts and homespun air. But the Pilgrims' unkempt wildness elicited amused commentary

from the two eldest Buckingham daughters, who had recently chosen
to forgo college and remain by the family hearth, preparing to manage
Christian homes of their own.

"Don't laugh," their father had joked. "You might marry one of
them someday."

"Over my dead body," said their mother.

Months later at the Willow chapel, a chance appearance by the
Pilgrim sons, with their leather pouches and buck knives, inspired
fascinated whispers from the young Buckingham boys and suppressed giggles from the older girls. Because Alaska is so isolated and
the number of suitable conservative Christian possibilities is small,
the business of finding a mate is never far from a young person's mind
when a new family shows up. But these big hairy fellows were clearly
out of the running.

Now, however, everyone seemed genuinely pleased to welcome the
same two Pilgrim boys, bearing the gift of winter meat, and to hear
their romantic tales of life in the Alaska wilderness. It was snowing
hard by the time dinner was done, but Papa had been explicit about
not spending the night. Joseph and Joshua were to continue to Kenai
for supplies. The brothers drove off sadly into the storm.

They had gone less than a mile down the mountain when the
headlights of the hay truck flickered and died. They pulled over and
struggled with the wiring, the snow, and with their softly accumulating guilt over wanting to turn back. Then they noticed one of the bald
tires was nearly flat. Guilt turned to joy at being able to acknowledge
some design at work more irresistible than their papa's will. They
followed their own snowy tracks back up the mountain through the
dark. When they opened the door, the cabin was bright and the children came running from their bedrooms. Everyone was smiling. But
the only smile Joshua saw was beaming from the face of the eldest
daughter, Sharia, and Joseph was already constructing elaborate daydream scenarios around her taller sister, Lolly.

Within a few weeks of the moosemeat delivery, the entire Pilgrim Family had been moved by Papa into the cabin on Lazy Mountain. Jim and Martha Buckingham sensed the desperation of the situation in the Wrangells. They offered to take the family in for Christmas and corral the Pilgrims' horses for the winter in Palmer, where hay could be purchased locally. The grown sons of both families nailed together fencing and bunk beds and figured out ways to make a cabin that was small for eleven work for twenty-eight. The children got along well. The young hosts were fascinated by the horseback adventure stories and amused by their visitors' simple unworldliness. Some of the Pilgrim children didn't even know about ironing clothes—they had spent their lives pulling garments out of a pile. For the Pilgrims, the intimacy of the following few weeks came as a shock. They learned so many new things—for instance, how to pronounce the bulldozer name, "Caterpillar." The children thought the word was "Callapitter," because that was how their papa said it. Elishaba, accustomed to eating on her feet as she fed the family, fidgeted while sitting with a plate before her, certain everyone was watching to see how she chewed her food.

They were also surprised and scared, even a little jealous, seeing the openness in their hosts—in personal choice, in worship, in family relations. The Buckingham children did not seem to be performing under stress. They actually talked together as a family about parenting choices, about whether the older Buckingham children had been raised too strictly or the younger ones spoiled. The Pilgrims sat wide-eyed and offered no opinions. At dinner, Papa interpreted God's word with such authority. Mr. Buckingham threw everyone off balance by asking questions directly of the children. One night, Sharia challenged Papa over whether a child can go to heaven if the name of Jesus Christ is not uttered during baptism. The Pilgrim children held their breath.

This was not going to end well.

"Don't be surprised if we just disappear in the middle of the night," Moses later whispered to Jim Buckingham.

It had always been that way. The darling Pilgrims, the generous hosts, the rosy intimacy in the Lord Jesus. Papa speaking in his calm, soft, wooing voice. His children peering into any unnatural silences to check on the simmer of his anger. The Pilgrim children could only hope Papa would be slow to react this time, reflecting perhaps that the alternative was cold poverty in the mountains. They understood the burden of the righteous life they were privileged to lead. But was a solid Christian family such as the Buckinghams truly doomed along with the rest of the world?

Elishaba bunked at first with the other girls. She felt a lighthearted joy those first nights, sleeping away from her father. But one evening Papa summoned her into the basement. She lied to her friends, saying she needed to massage his feet. When he was done with her he sent her back. But she felt so angry and ashamed and exhausted that she put on her winter coat and went out in the dark to hide. Curled inside a vehicle, Elishaba awoke to the sound of voices calling her name. Your father is looking for you, the Buckingham girls said. They hugged her and asked what was wrong, but she tore away and went inside. She slept every night in the basement after that.

Papa began to take over the Buckingham home. He ignored the army-strict timetable for going to bed and rising and eating meals. He sat up until two talking about God's purpose, and his children stayed up with him. The short haircuts of the Buckingham sons showed they were not walking right with the Lord, he said. He hung a towel over the bathroom mirror to guard against vanity. In the presence of such virtue and humility, the Buckingham daughters began to doubt themselves—had their own parents indeed let them grow away from God, in pride and egotism? The Buckinghams were reckless with graven images. One afternoon Papa plunked a table grape in his mouth and, finding it made of rubber, scooped up the entire decorative arrangement and threw it in the trash. A heaviness descended. Papa remained in the basement when dinner was served. Country Rose and the children waited before empty places. Finally one night, Pilgrim laid out a string of theological challenges to Jim Buckingham. The host said he did not want to be in confrontation, as he put it.

Early the next morning, though, Buckingham took his wife and nine children with him to work at Fort Richardson in Anchorage.

The Pilgrims, waking to an empty log cabin, departed for Kenai.

FAMILIES WHOSE hearts are not right will try to lead them astray. The Buckinghams were like those travelers in *The Pilgrim's Progress* who wander off the trail while the hero, Christian, follows on to the Celestial City. John Bunyan's allegory had remained the children's guidebook in the wilderness of the Wrangells. The seductive short-cut seekers, Formalist and Hypocrisy, coming to the Hill of Difficulty, take easy-looking detours that lead to Danger and Destruction. These were metaphors to live by, and also practical lessons for the commute through God's bear-infested creation.

Meanwhile, the line drawings in the book on Papa's lap—the Delectable Mountains, the Valley of the Shadow, the Slough of Despond—had given dramatic portent to Alaska itself. They had learned their own valley intimately. They knew where birds nested along McCarthy Creek in summer. But when the valley fell silent at freeze-up, they could not say where the birds had gone. Their minds remained like the early topographical maps of the Wrangells, sharply delineated around settlement zones but elsewhere showing vague contour lines every thousand feet, or vast blank icy spaces.

The children had hoped this new land would change their father's heart. The mountains were so white and pristine it was easy to picture Christ's descent. Instead they feared Papa all the time now—the way he would kick or swat at them as he passed by. One time at their Copper River fish-wheel camp, Israel grabbed a phone from Elishaba and gave her a bloody lip. Papa struck him and then, after pausing to consider, kneed him and kicked him and shoved him in the river, then pulled him out and beat on him in a corner of the shed for twenty minutes. They had seen Papa drag Mama out the cabin door headfirst, then return and nail a handful of her graying hair to the cabin wall as a warning. Sometimes the younger ones heard Papa hitting at Elishaba in the bed she shared with him and Mama in the middle of the cabin, the mattress surrounded by a curtain. When he was ten, Noah woke up on the couch one night as Elishaba rolled out from behind the curtain. He watched Papa stand and beat her on the floor with his braided leather thong. Papa was wearing just a robe, and the robe fell open and Papa was naked within. The family was never supposed to see that—it was the first Noah, in fact, who laid a curse on Ham and Canaan for seeing their father naked in his drunkenness. Papa turned the thong that night on Noah as well.

Papa was no longer drinking, at least. For a while in Alaska, he had been drinking whole boxes of wine in a day. Once he rolled a truck off the McCarthy Road by the historic Kuskulana River bridge, and it was only by God's grace that the trees caught them before they tumbled into the 300-foot canyon. If you dared use the word "drunk" around him, you were disciplined severely. He drove their old Suburban to Fairbanks, and when Elishaba tried to make him surrender the wheel he ordered her to climb on the roof with Joshua and listen for a troubling noise he'd suddenly detected. Brother and sister squeezed a thin aluminum strip to hold on as he raced around corners on a quiet dirt road. When Joshua looked over and saw Elishaba was going to let go, he commanded her to hold on. The happy surprise that her brother loved her saved her life, she said later.

The very next day at a for-pay shower, Papa started throwing up blood. The doctors told him his damaged pancreas was going to kill him. He had drunk no alcohol now for several years. He said with pride this proved the source of his anger was not alcohol but rather a righteousness like that of the Lord Jesus when he turned the moneychangers out of the temple.

From this righteousness none were exempt, not even baby Jonathan, the gift of Jehovah whose birth at the Mother Lode he had heralded two years earlier. *Thoughts pierced my heart as I saw this child,* Papa had written in his community letter, *my fingers caressing its head, so small, so new, so holy, such promise, such love.* In fact, he'd been staggeringly drunk when he got home for the birth. The boys had to roll him out of the tracked vehicle. The florid letter had been his way of rearranging the past into a new official story. Now if baby Jonathan started crying and wouldn't stop, Papa asked to hold him and pinched his mouth and nose until Jonathan fell silent and his feet kicked and his cheeks turned blue. Papa would sit in the rocker in the cabin's kitchen holding Jonathan until he started to pass out. It scared the young boys to see their baby brother smothercated that way. It scared baby Jonathan, too, and he cried and tried to run whenever his father picked him up. This was handy because if Mama or anyone else was being contentious Papa would take Jonathan onto his lap and hold him until everyone in the family had fallen silent.

THE BUCKINGHAMS fasted and prayed and then drove down to Kenai and invited the Pilgrims to return. Papa agreed, and they came back on Christmas Day. The reunion was joyous. Joseph and Joshua resumed daydreaming about the Buckingham daughters.

But a great shock awaited. Jim Buckingham said he had business with Papa. He drew Papa aside in the basement, with the two eldest Pilgrim sons as witnesses. Mr. Buckingham said it appeared to him that Pilgrim had an unhealthy relationship with his oldest daughter, possibly even one with physical and sexual overtones.

Papa was appalled. He challenged Buckingham to ask his sons if anything was going on. Joseph and Joshua insisted there was no sinful relation between their father and their sister. They knew well, from the whippings in New Mexico, how strongly their father felt about the sin of lust. In truth, the possibility of such a relation did not even have a name by which they could conceive it. But hearing Mr. Buckingham's words, a notion did begin to take shape.

As this conversation unfolded, the girls were all out walking together along the wooded road, talking like sisters about the future and marriage. When they got back, Martha Buckingham said there was business under way in the basement. Elishaba followed the Buckingham girls up to their room, suddenly petrified. Her father would take it out on her for being gone so long. She got an idea that if she put her time to use in a way her father approved, he would feel merciful. She sat down with the other girls and started preaching to them the lesson her father had taught, from 1 Corinthians, about how only a virgin can attend to holy things. Therefore, despite what they'd been discussing, none of them should ever get married.

The Buckingham girls seemed surprised. Well versed themselves, they explained the Scripture differently, saying it was one of those rare places in the Bible where the writer, Paul, declares he is giving his own opinion, not the word of God. He wasn't saying they should never marry, only that the Christians of Corinth might want to hold off during the "present distress" of Roman persecution. Sharia added that later, in Timothy, the Bible even warns against false prophets who would forbid marriage.

A lesson that had always seemed harsh to Elishaba and difficult to reconcile suddenly uncoiled. She saw that she was in big trouble.

That night, as the Buckinghams said grace before dinner, Elishaba burst into tears and ran to the basement. She buried her face in the bed, and looked up when she heard sniffling. The three oldest Buckingham daughters stood outside the door, concerned over their friend's inexplicable strife. For a moment they were a tangle of arms and hugs, and then Elishaba pulled free and ran up the stairs, hoping

Papa would be pleased to see that she had come back to the meal on her own. He was not. He took her by the arm and led her back down.

"I told you not to show them you were upset," he said as he closed the bedroom door.

Afterward Papa took her for a walk outside. Joseph and Joshua worried as they watched them go: No matter what Elishaba had said to aggravate him this time, usually Papa was more in control, more careful around others. His recklessness, and hers, threatened them all. When they got back, Martha Buckingham saw the bruised swelling on Elishaba's jaw and was told she had slipped on the ice. Papa announced they were leaving immediately for McCarthy. He put Elishaba in the pickup truck and drove away.

The nights are long at that time of year, and few headlights broke the darkness on the highway to Glennallen. Through the pass, Elishaba stared out at the dark mountains and thought about how hard she still wanted to please her father, even after all she had seen at the Buckinghams'.

She still tried to soothe his anger, though she knew her motives were not always pure. Like the time with her beautiful fiddle. He spent seven hundred dollars on the violin, a figure that astonished her brothers and sisters. You could buy a truck for that kind of money. None of them had ever possessed anything so precious. Then one night Papa was raging that she did not love him and did not want to please him. She said it was not so. He accused her of loving her fiddle more than she loved him, and she swore she did not. He told her it was true because she would not hurt that instrument even if he commanded her to, and she took her beautiful fiddle by the neck and swung it down over the back of a wooden chair. In her heart, Elishaba knew she had done it less from love than from anger, to show how wrong he was and to push him to repentance. And it almost worked—in the moment, he was shocked. He brought in the violin for repairs and said it had been dropped accidentally, but the instrument maker looked at the two pieces and said this was no accident.

Later Papa took glory in the broken fiddle, as he did in all her bruises.

Now as they drove east toward the Wrangell Mountains he kept asking questions about the Buckinghams she couldn't answer. This confusion came over her often these days, made her feel clumsy and stupid. She could hardly listen to what he was saying. She woke when Papa pulled over beside the highway. Before long, one whole side of her face was swollen. She combed her long dark hair down over that side as he told her to.

The rest of the family followed in other vehicles. They reassembled the next night at a cabin by the Copper River. Papa kept them up nearly until dawn, explaining how the devil was at work on Lazy Mountain. Everyone was upset at being torn from the Buckinghams. They blamed Elishaba.

After the sun came up, Elishaba put on a light coat and shoes and walked down to the river. The canyon was wide here where the channels unraveled through the gravel bars. The temperature was below zero. Floes of ice pushed by on the water, and clouds of blowing snow drifted along the flats in the weak winter sunlight. Elishaba stepped onto the gravel and started crunching across the ice. There was no way she could ride the rest of the way home with Papa. Instead she thought she would follow the frozen river bars to McCarthy—130 miles away.

WAS IT blasphemy to wonder if what her father said about the one special daughter was true? Unlike her siblings, Elishaba had learned to read as a child, however haltingly. She had sneaked to the Bible shelf to see what Scripture said. But he caught her searching through the Bible and he beat her for that, too.

Sometimes when they were alone she would dare to resist. This made him impatient—did she not love him? He would push her hand aside and accuse her of not trusting him. He would pound her with a vigorous fist and then tell her, "I forgive you," and make her show what she would do for his mercy. He found new ways to punish her when she did not perform to his expectations. He would make her apply the thong to her young brothers and sisters. She could be angry and cruel and this pleased him. He learned to single out Abraham, with whom Elishaba was especially close, having raised him up as a baby after he was taken from Mama as punishment. She would beat on her little brother as told, and when she was done she would take him aside and they would cry together.

Papa brought her regularly to Anchorage. They would stroll through the Fred Meyer department store and he would take her hand like they were married, which made her flushed and dizzy. He would drive around all night in an agitated state, expecting her to keep him company, and if she fell asleep he would drag her by her hair to kneel in the headlights and push her face in the crusty snow. He counted her bruises boastfully and told her she was blessed to have someone like him. He hit her until she said she wanted to do whatever it was he wanted. This seemed important to him, to hear her say this.

Her brothers and sisters did not know. They assumed she had been rebellious and that's why she was being corrected. Elishaba could say nothing. They did not even seem to have formed a suspicion about what was happening, despite someone occasionally stumbling on father and daughter together. Any inkling could be brought only to Papa, who could explain it away. Papa would keep talking about an event they had seen, describing it in his own way, until they had a hard time remembering anything other than Papa's description.

But Mama knew.

Mama even talked about it once at the Buckinghams'. Elishaba had grown brave enough to go to her in secret to ask if what her father did was right. Mama said it was against the Bible but couldn't be helped. Mama said she had fought and fought, but she had given up fighting so she could go on being a mother to the other children. She put her arms around Elishaba and said she felt bad about it but was forbidden from saying more.

Sometimes the three of them would lie together inside the curtain in the Marvelous Millsite cabin. Mama would rest quietly until Papa was ready. Papa told Elishaba not to be upset, that Mama understood the spiritual nature of their relationship. He explained he no longer felt desire for Mama Rose, for she was old and ugly at forty-six and when he was with her his body did not do what it was supposed to. And yet God wanted him to have twenty-one children. Elishaba's duty was to help keep his flesh working, and when it was time, to bring forth his seed for Mama. If Elishaba didn't do this, if she didn't help him get Mama pregnant, she would be a murderer, killing the brothers and sisters that God wanted her to have.

Elishaba did not want to kill babies. What she did want—though she could not put the desire into words as she set out that morning in a daze, on foot and lightly dressed, to follow the Copper River home during the coldest days of winter—was to kill herself.

SHE DID not get far. Her brothers found her on the river ice and brought her back. They continued on through lonely McCarthy, and started up the narrow valley on snowmachines. Elishaba felt herself being hauled into a wintry tomb.

After a few days, Papa decided to return to McCarthy to gather supplies from the trucks. Elishaba refused to go, in the new spirit she had felt since Christmas at the Buckinghams', but he insisted she come with her older brothers. When they got to town, they went directly to the wanigan, on their new property across the river. The shack was no bigger than when they had taken it over from Walt Wigger—twenty feet long, dark brown boards on the outside, and dark inside with small windows, kitchen shelves, and a small woodstove and a bed. It sat back from the road in the woods.

A cold subzero spell was settling over the valley. Inside, the woodstove roared. Elishaba baked fresh cinnamon rolls to make things homey. But no one could get along. They argued about the Buckinghams and any other subject that came up. Papa boasted about how he'd told Israel to move the corner stake to expand this new lot. Joseph quoted Jim Buckingham about obeying the law. Deuteronomy said the man is cursed who removeth his neighbor's landmark. Papa replied he did not need to obey that law because it was in the Old Testament. Elishaba told him his unneighborly attitude toward the people of McCarthy was against what he had taught them and was hurting their whole family.

Papa sent his sons off to start unloading the trucks.

As usual, the argument about one Bible verse led to another. Elishaba went farther this time. She brought up the passage from 1 Corinthians about virgins and marriage. Papa had not been teaching what the Bible really said.

Soon David came running to get his brothers. He said Papa had taken out his belt and was correcting Elishaba in the wanigan.

When Joseph and Moses got back to the clearing, they heard their sister's screams. The building shook. Their father came to the door and threw the cinnamon rolls into the snow. He was sweating and his hair was flying in all directions. He did not seem to notice the boys standing there. The yelling began again, and the boys did not know what to do. They could not imagine what Elishaba had done this time.

Elishaba had grabbed Papa's belt when he wasn't looking, opened the woodstove, and thrown it into the flames. She dashed for the door, but he grabbed her by the hair and pulled her back and said leaving her father was the worst sin of all. As he nailed the door shut, she reached for the phone to dial home. She could leave the phone off the hook so they would hear what was happening. But he tore the receiver from her hands, pulled out the plug, and accused her of trying to call 911. He began to beat her with his fists and said she would never want to fight back again. If she was quiet, he punched her. If she said something, he punched her. She saw at last that God had abandoned her. She saw lights flash and reached up to feel the side of her face because she could barely see out of one eye. Don't worry, he said, he would take care of the other side.

Moses went up onto the porch and listened. He heard their father say, "I'm going to strip you down pink like a chicken." They heard dishes flying, and somebody banged against the door. Papa yelled about Elishaba being rebellious and ordered her to hush her mouth. He called out for the boys to leave.

They waited. Things seemed to quiet down. After a while, the boys got on their snowmachines and headed up the valley toward home.

Elishaba had fallen on the bed and passed in and out of consciousness. When she awoke, she could tell that Papa was aroused by the fighting. He raped her every way he could. Then he kept her in the wanigan for three days, waiting for her swelling to go down. It was almost forty below and Papa called the family to say that even using coals from the stove they couldn't get the snowmachine warm enough to start.

When they finally got home, Elishaba wore a ski mask. Her father told her to keep it on and not try to make everyone feel sorry for her.

MANY YEARS ago, when she was very young, Jerusalem had gone to Papa with something that troubled her heart. Papa said he was very sorry that she had so misunderstood seeing Elishaba naked in bed with him, that Elishaba was helping Mama and Papa with something, and that indeed it was very wrong for Jerusalem to have had such thoughts. He wouldn't stop talking to her about what she had really seen, and then he punished her for the presumption she had allowed into her heart. She felt racked for years by guilt, fearful that God would judge her harshly.

Now Jerusalem was sixteen and the memory returned. She made her sister peel off the ski mask. Elishaba's face was so swollen and discolored, Jerusalem hardly recognized her. She shared her suspicions and Elishaba would not deny them. Her brothers were shocked to see how badly she was bruised. They told her Papa was wrong to go so far.

Somehow this gave her strength. The next morning, alone in the curtained bed, her father asked, as he often did, why didn't she love and accept him as much as he needed her to love him? She told him she had to make a confession. All the times she said she did love him had been lies. She only ever said that because she was afraid of him. She did not want what he wanted.

He looked at her coldly for a long minute. "Go get the whip," he said.

She pulled back the curtain and what she saw lifted her spirits. Her whole family was sitting there in the room, listening. "We're praying for you," one of them whispered.

Her correction that morning did not hurt so bad.

When Papa went off on a snowmachine to get a load of firewood, she pulled Joseph and Joshua aside, though she had been put on silence. She believed that if she didn't use the actual words, no one would have to lie under interrogation, so she only hinted: Papa had been treating her like a wife, only a hundred times worse. It was as bad as they could imagine, she said. They needed to say something to make him stop. Mr. Buckingham's words came back to them and the truth found its shape.

That night when Papa came in, his children confronted him in the kitchen of the cabin.

Do you not love your own father? Papa asked them.

They didn't answer.

I'm asking you not for the seventh time but for the seventy-seventh time. Do you love your father?

No I do not, said Joseph.

Why would you say such a thing?

Because you're having sexual relations with your daughter.

Papa turned white and Joseph knew it was true.

Do you want to know what happened at the wanigan? Tell them, Papa said to his daughter.

Elishaba stammered. She didn't know where to begin.

I don't even want to hear another lie, Joseph said.

Papa's fist tensed. Just go, Moses said to his brother.

Papa asked again if they wanted to know what happened in the wanigan.

Joseph turned and left the cabin. It was what their father had taught them to do when someone tells a lie—walk away.

I was only trying to correct her disobedient attitude, Papa said. Tell them.

Elishaba said Papa had beaten her to get his way.

Joshua, the favored son, stepped forward and told their father he was deceitful. It was the most blasphemous thing anyone had ever said straight into Papa's face.

Country Rose tried to get between them but Papa pushed her aside and dropped Joshua to the floor with his fist. Joshua rose twice and each time was knocked back down. His nose was broken. It was a sucker punch, the other children said later, like when King Saul tried to kill David with the javelin. Joshua felt good, lying on the floor with blood pouring from his nose. He sensed a shift in sympathy and allegiance as his young siblings jumped up and grabbed at Papa to make him stop.

Pilgrim kept the family up until six the next morning. He preached that it was a right perfect and beautiful relationship he had with his daughter. He explained how Elishaba's help would give them more brothers and sisters. He argued that the father-daughter relationship is the only exception allowed in the Bible—that Leviticus, which goes to great lengths listing whose nakedness within relations shall not be uncovered, expressly skips the one category of daughter. He reminded them how Lot's daughters slept with their father after their mother had been turned to a pillar of salt. He described how the law of Moses gives a father special authority over his daughter while she is young and still in her father's house. He challenged his children to show him in the Scriptures where what he said was wrong.

His preaching continued thus for days.

Joseph and Joshua ignored him. They knew the punishment for adulterers and refused to eat in the same room.

They felt a new sympathy and tenderness toward Elishaba. All this time she had been trying to protect her brothers and sisters. *Please don't give up,* Elishaba begged them. Joseph warned this would lead to the breakup of their family. Elishaba disagreed. She believed Papa could yet be shown how wrong he was. She blamed herself for failing to do enough to make him the person her heart still wanted him to be.

The only thing left for the boys to do was leave. It was how they had been taught to respond. They urged their sister to flee as well. "You have to run like the devil's chasing you," Joshua told her. The older boys slipped out one night. Elishaba was on silence but she snuck a loaf of bread out the kitchen window to say good-bye. Joseph, Joshua, David, and Moses pushed two snowmachines down the trail so Papa could not hear them starting up.

A new chapter was beginning, and Elishaba felt her heart turn cold.

Now it was Israel and Jerusalem's turn to object. They discussed their father's actions one afternoon as they shivered outside in a snowfall, where everyone had been sent so Papa could be alone with

Elishaba. When their conversation was reported, Papa made them fast for seven days. At night, the teenagers were roped together on the wood floor in the living room without blankets, tied to the barrel stove. As the stove went cold and wind blew under the crack of the door, Papa called to Jerusalem: "What's the matter with you, little wimp? You act like you're going to make me feel sorry for you. I can't sleep with you acting like that."

He declared his sons lost to the devil. They would not be allowed back to poison the younger children. Papa seemed relieved, in a way, that he could be more open now about his relationship with Elishaba. She had new bruises every day. He reminded her she would come with him to the Kingdom. He warned her never to try escaping out that door like her brothers. He said he would tear her to pieces.

She wrote down a line from Psalm 27 and posted it in the living room: WHEN MY FATHER AND MY MOTHER FORSAKE ME, THEN THE LORD WILL TAKE ME UP. It was the kind of thing Papa would do, posting a lesson from Scripture. He left it up as evidence of her rebellion.

"Just tear me up," Abraham heard her cry behind the curtain. "Just tear me up."

She looked out at the snowy peaks around their home and prayed that God would take her up. She thought about climbing to Him, but the snow was waist deep and she would be easily tracked, unless she was lucky enough to be dead before she was found.

Mama, too, told Elishaba to run away. But Elishaba could not move. She was afraid of what Papa would do if he caught her. And she couldn't shake the lesson etched in her soul that going down from the mountain was unforgivable. She would never evade God if she went out alone in the world. Her twenty-nine years of working for salvation would be squandered. The laws of the world would surely condemn her, too—for how many times had they all seen truth disappear in humble apologies, exasperated sighs, heartfelt sharing of the Gospels, or red-faced anger—whatever it took to turn black into white? Papa would lie to the faces of their neighbors and the police. He had done it hundreds of times, and boasted about it afterward. They would return Elishaba to his mercy.

At last she remembered the old hippie commune cabin at the mouth of Chitistone Canyon. The cabin was farther inside the national park, below the Mile High Cliffs. Before long it would be springtime breakup. The frozen glacial rivers would reopen and become impassable. Her father would not be able to track her then. Her body and soul would both be safe.

Elishaba developed an escape plan. She would run deeper into the wild.

16

Exodus

E LISHABA'S CHANCE came in the Third Month. The family had run low on gasoline for the generator and Papa had to go to McCarthy. He did not want to let Elishaba out of his sight, but he could not bring her because her brothers might be in town. He commanded his wife to place a hand over her mouth and not move it until he returned. His daughters were to speak only of their work on the woodpile. He rigged a sled with an oil drum and placed Job and Noah

Moses Hale crosses the waters of McCarthy Creek beneath the white-mountain throne of the Wrangells.

on the family's biggest snowmachine and disappeared down the valley toward town.

Elishaba announced she was going away. She wouldn't say where because she knew Papa would find out if she did. Jerusalem listened with concern. Old feelings of rivalry had vanished. She had never really known her sister's heart. She worried Elishaba might not try hard enough to keep herself alive. Jerusalem insisted on going along.

Mama rushed to an outbuilding and got the antenna working on the remote phone. Papa had disconnected it weeks ago, but Mama had been using it to keep in secret touch with her sons in Glennallen. She had made sure one of the younger boys removed the bullets from the pistol strapped on Pilgrim's snowmachine. Now Mama called Joseph from the cabin. Even in the midst of her mutiny, Elishaba felt deceitful speaking into the phone. Her brother urged her to give up her plan, to meet him instead in McCarthy. She agreed to try. But she would have to avoid meeting Papa on the trail.

They pulled and pulled on one of the Tundras but couldn't get the snowmachine to start. Hosanna figured out that the spark plug had been removed. They found a replacement and said good-bye. The fan belt broke right away, and Jerusalem postholed back to get the second Tundra. When that one ran out of gas because of a fuel line leak, they switched to a third snowmachine. They turned away from the main trail and hid in the trees under white sheets. They could hear Papa's snowmachine coming.

Elishaba could think of no explanation that would stopper his rage if he found them. She concentrated on words from a Psalm: Be still and know that I am God.

Papa drove on by.

As the angry whine faded, Elishaba told her sister it was time to put their hand to the plow. She recalled Joshua telling her, "You have to run like the devil's chasing you." She had half an hour at best.

The girls raced down the trail and into McCarthy—there was no one around to see and report them—and across the Kennicott River. They knew it wasn't safe at the wanigan. Employing another of her father's tricks, Elishaba drove into an area where people had been busy cutting firewood and circled until her track was mixed illegibly with others. She hid the snowmachine in thick brush and covered it with a sheet. Jerusalem had worked out details for a rendezvous over the phone that morning. But their brothers were missing. Maybe there had been a misunderstanding, she said. The sisters started out the McCarthy Road and climbed into the woods where they could watch for traffic. They hid where there was no snow under the boughs of a spruce tree.

Their brothers did not show up.

Before long, they heard Papa's snowmachine searching the streets of the ghost town, past the lodge and the Hardware Store, across the river and around the wanigan and the few houses on the west side, circling.

Elishaba and Jerusalem waited under the tree for five days, eating cold cheese and raisins, with temperatures dropping to twenty below at night. They had sleeping bags but no tent, and they did not dare build a fire.

As she waited, Elishaba worried about the brothers and sisters she'd left behind. She couldn't keep from worrying about her father's health as well. He always said he depended on her to keep his medicines straight. Would he die because she had left? She knew that if she saw him, she would crumple at once and go back. More than ever before, she felt like a wild thing scared of humans. Jerusalem, meanwhile, couldn't stop talking about going to see the Buckinghams. Elishaba finally snapped at her sister and said she would never go live with them, because that would prove to their father that she had left in rebellion.

They decided to sneak down to the wanigan in the dark to use the phone. The icy trail was crunchy so they took off their boots and crept to the gypsy trailer in their sock feet. There was no sign of their father's snowmachine out front, but they knew he was tricky so they kept quiet and looked around back in the trees. Sure enough, he had hidden his vehicle there. He was inside. Wide-eyed, they tiptoed back down the trail to the road, put on their boots, and ran back to their hiding place. They said they felt like David sneaking out of the cave past a sleeping King Saul.

The next day they entered another cabin and phoned Glennallen. It turned out there had been confusion over the rendezvous point: There were two national park information kiosks. Their brothers drove straight to McCarthy and gathered them in.

When Mama told them on the phone that Papa was taking a bath with fifteen-year-old Hosanna, Joseph drove back to McCarthy and snowmachined up to the homestead and took her away, too.

THE PHONE calls from Glennallen were gravely troubling to Jim and Martha Buckingham. It was a delicate thing to challenge the authority of a father. The Bible said children were supposed to submit, and outsiders to defer. But there was an exception in Matthew if a parent is leading a child away from God: *He that loveth father or mother more than me is not worthy of me.*

They told the Hale children they could come to Palmer for a visit. During the drive, the siblings agreed to say nothing about the worst things that had happened. They still feared the intervention of state child welfare and the ruin of their family. It seemed possible Papa would come around now, faced with the ultimate defections. As they approached the Lazy Mountain cabin, Elishaba panicked. She felt a lowly fraud around the Buckingham girls. But everyone was lined up on the porch as the van approached, and when the girls rushed forward to gather Elishaba with hugs she had a shocking revelation: She did not have to look over her shoulder and worry about her father's reaction.

Elishaba's face was still badly bruised. The Buckinghams told her she could stay when the others returned to Glennallen. After two days, she asked them to adopt her. She said she felt like an orphan. They smiled and said she could stay as long as she needed but reminded her she was twenty-nine years old. Still she would not tell them what her father had done. The Buckinghams' worry about overstepping was now matched by an opposite worry: Were the seven younger children still up McCarthy Creek in danger? Would the Buckinghams be responsible before God and man for not doing even more?

After a month, Jerusalem and Hosanna arrived in Palmer to join their sister. The three sisters lived at Lazy Mountain through the summer. They cooked and worked in the garden and shared the clothes of their hosts' five daughters, while Jim and Martha Buckingham worked to win their trust. It was slow going. When Martha Buckingham sat down with Elishaba to describe the ways of a true marriage, Pilgrim's daughter wept quietly.

The older Pilgrim boys were in McCarthy for the summer, running the horse ride business and the Kennicott shuttle. Pilgrim traveled between the homestead and his doctors in Anchorage and took care to avoid his sons.

The Buckinghams did not want to see the boys, either. Jim Buckingham told them to stay away. He was concerned about having his daughters in the presence of these untethered sons of an abusive father, rough, longhaired, bearded, smelling of woodsmoke. But gradually the Buckinghams softened. The boys were sheep without a shepherd. Yielding to what he called "the gentle press of God," Jim Buckingham rented a plane in July 2005, flew to McCarthy, and handed the boys a letter outlining the strict rules by which he would be willing to take them in. They could not read the letter. Buckingham read it aloud. The boys agreed to keep their distance from his daughters and made plans to move to Palmer when the fall hunting season was done.

At the Mother Lode, Pilgrim was struggling to reorder his world. He tried to be nice. He let Hosanna go off to visit her sisters, and was shocked when Joseph called to say she wasn't coming back. You can't steal my daughter, Papa said. But it was a different Joseph talking back to him. If you want her, Joseph replied, call the state troopers. He was hoping to scare his father. You could go to jail for what you did with Elishaba, he said. Papa said it wasn't so, because she was eighteen before anything happened. That was the legal age. Papa did not repent, but neither did he call the troopers to claim Hosanna.

He launched a campaign that summer to win over Job, Noah, and Abraham, his three adolescent sons, showing new generosity, taking them fishing, and buying used four-wheelers for them to ride around. There would be no more beatings, he said, thanks to the grace of God. Rose interpreted this to mean that if the beatings resumed, it would be God's fault. She prayed her husband had finally changed.

In quiet moments, Pilgrim was restless and depressed and talked of moving on. Where else could he go, after the end of the road in Alaska? Maybe back to New Mexico. He started making plans.

Then one late-summer afternoon the children were tossing rocks into a bucket, and little Jonathan, now two, threw a rock that hit Lamb. He ran over to hug her and apologize but Papa grabbed the thong and started flailing at him. The child writhed in the dirt, and it became one of those times when Papa wouldn't stop. He pushed away Psalms and Bethlehem as they grabbed at him. Mama came running from the laundry and pulled her husband away by his shirt.

Country Rose told her husband he had to go. Pilgrim said he was leaving anyway, that it was time to fly out for a hernia operation. When the plane came to get him, Rose pulled aside the pilot, Gary Green, and said, whatever you do, don't bring him back up here.

A FEW weeks later, on Labor Day weekend, Neil Darish was sitting in his van by the footbridge, windows down, waiting as guests unloaded their car across the river. He was lost in thought, listening to music, thinking about his breakup with Doug Miller that summer and his promise to buy out his partner's share in the lodge within six months. Suddenly there was a thump on the passenger door and one of the longhaired little Pilgrim boys was panting and looking in the van window frantically.

"My papa's after me," he cried. "Have you seen Israel?"

At the sound of an approaching four-wheeler, the boy ran on toward town.

A moment later, Papa Pilgrim was at the window on Darish's side. He, too, asked about Israel.

"He's disobeyed me, and he's telling lies," Pilgrim said. He hesitated, and it seemed to Darish, especially thinking back later, that Pilgrim waited to see if the lodge owner had a question for him—that he was calculating how much Darish might already know.

"He's going to say evil things about me to the troopers," Pilgrim added.

Seeing no sign of his son, he got back on his four-wheeler and headed on toward McCarthy.

Darish sat there, thinking: *As an Objectivist follower of Ayn Rand, I am supposed to be cool and rational. I hope I haven't been romanticizing this family.*

PAPA HAD come back from Anchorage earlier that day. He had Noah and Job with him.

Israel had come down to McCarthy from hunting camp at the same time to meet a client. He called the homestead, and Mama told him how Papa had beaten Jonathan half to death. She said she had told Papa not to come back, but he had taken Noah and Job. She told Israel to get the boys away from their father and send them home to safety.

Israel found Noah first and hid him in the woods. He was shoeing a horse near the wanigan when he saw Papa coming with Job. Israel was now eighteen and tall and was considered the strongest and toughest of the sons. He was the one Papa always beat the worst, but Israel had never fought back.

Now he stood up with the hammer. Papa demanded Noah, and they started shoving each other. Israel said, If you hit me I'll call the police. Papa kicked the horse, and Israel pushed his father to the ground. It was the first time one of his sons had laid a hand on him! Papa got up and grabbed Israel and punched him twice. Israel ran away to the footbridge and dialed a number on the pay phone before Papa caught up on his four-wheeler, grabbed the phone away, and pushed Israel down. Call the troopers, Papa said. They'll tell you I'm right. You can't keep my son from me.

Israel ran across the footbridge and past Neil Darish in his truck. Job chased after him, pursued by Papa on the four-wheeler. Israel ran into Rick Kenyon's church and locked the door. His lip was bleeding. In the basement of the church was a phone. Whenever Papa got mad at someone these days, he called the troopers. In spite of everything, Israel couldn't bring himself to call the police against his own father. Instead, standing in the church and shaking, he dialed the one person who might be able to help.

Jim Buckingham was putting shingles on his porch roof when he got the call. Israel recounted the fight in a trembling voice. He had not turned his cheek. What should he do now? The phone was silent for a long minute, as Buckingham stood on the roof of his porch and prayed for wisdom. Then he told Israel to call the troopers. Tell them about the fight, and tell them everything else, Buckingham instructed. You need to do that to protect your family.

Two troopers in a patrol car were soon headed out the McCarthy Road. They met Robert Hale near the Gilahina River trestle. He was already on his way back to Anchorage with Job and Noah. The troopers took statements from everyone. It was just another small domestic matter. Israel had told them over the phone about the fight near the footbridge, but that was all. He still couldn't talk about the rest.

The troopers reported that Robert Hale was calm and didn't appear excited. He told them Israel had been trying to hide his brother and had pushed his father to the ground. He had always been an aggressive boy, Robert Hale said. He felt a certain responsibility as a father and was forced to strike Israel in the face, to show him what could happen if he didn't quit being so violent. He had asked Israel's forgiveness and told his son he needed to have a forgiving heart, just as Hale himself had forgiven Israel many times for his aggressions.

Papa Pilgrim was allowed to go on his way.

But Elishaba had heard enough. She had listened as Mr. Buckingham talked on the phone to her brother hiding in the McCarthy-Kennicott Community Church. He had told Israel to protect his family. Something unlocked inside her. She saw what she had to do.

17

Pilgrim's Last Stand

I T WAS like flying into the heavenly kingdom. The young assistant district attorney from Palmer had never seen anything like it. The helicopter, dwarfed by the glaciers and peaks, flew swiftly toward the ice spilling off the face of Mount Blackburn. The closer they got and the higher they flew, the bigger the mountain looked, and they never seemed to arrive—the whiteness just kept expanding, like the face of God. Richard Payne felt himself lifted momentarily from his grim mission.

The Alaska State Trooper pilot had steered up the glacier to avoid

The ruins of Kennecott Copper's mill town and the moraine-strewn ice of the Kennicott Glacier

flying over the buildings of McCarthy. They didn't know if Robert Hale might be in town. At this point, only days after the Buckinghams alerted the authorities over what they'd been told by Elishaba, they were still trying to keep their investigation quiet. Veering from the white mountain at last, they left the glacier and flew above the red tinder ruins of the Kennecott mines. The pilot circled, purely a grace note. Payne gazed into his own family's past.

The prosecutor's father had been a Kennecott man in Utah. His grandfather and great-grandfather, too—three generations of copper miners descended from original Mormon pioneer families. Payne had seen old photographs of the Bingham Canyon mill outside Salt Lake City where his ancestors worked. They were timber buildings like the ones below, erected with profits from this very mountain. The Utah buildings were gone now, of course, the canyon buried in waste rock from the deepest open pit mine in the world—a hole visible from outer space, as the local chamber of commerce liked to point out. Payne grew up expecting to work for Kennecott Copper like everyone else. When he was a teenager, though, world prices plunged, the pit shut down for a while, and in the turmoil of unemployment and divorce that followed Payne found a job in the law office of a second cousin. He wound up pursuing a university scholarship.

He was now thirty-five years old. He had lived in Alaska for nine years. He had married here and started a family, but had never before made his way out to Kennecott's birthplace. Now that he was here, he was thinking he should get out to the real Alaska more often. The sharp crags above the mines reminded him of the Wasatch Mountains in Utah, but beyond these were altogether different summits of celestial winter, taller than anything in the lower forty-eight. The helicopter swept up the slope above the mining camp, climbing past reds and yellows of autumn tundra to a serrated ridge. As the far side of the mountain fell away, Payne could imagine his pioneer ancestors looking down on Zion for the first time.

They started their descent. The horizon disappeared, pinching off the grandeur. As the cabins beside McCarthy Creek came into view, they looked tiny and alone, hidden away. His mood changed. Payne remembered how he'd felt when he first read through the trooper interviews. As a churchgoing father of three young children, he'd found the stories sickening—the worst sort of domestic violence he could imagine. He was eager to get before a grand jury. But he still needed to know the scope of the case.

Payne had called ahead, reaching the cabin over some sort of remote phone, and the mother would be down there waiting. He had flown all this way to interview her and find out how such things could have gone on. How to measure her guilt in all this? He was also unsure about the oldest sons, whose whereabouts were unknown. They were reportedly away at a hunting camp, but he'd been glad to have two armed trooper investigators in the helicopter when they stopped to fuel up in Glennallen.

The helicopter landed in a clearing by the Marvelous Millsite camp. Cute little children scrambled over when the rotor stopped. The pilot invited them to look inside while Payne and the two investigators followed the mother to a cabin. She said she was glad it was finally over. They sat and talked for several hours. As Country Rose described how her husband ordered their daughter to do a dance and get him ready to bring forth his seed, Payne felt the hair prickle on the back of his neck.

ONCE THE hunt for Papa Pilgrim commenced, sightings were called in from all over the state. None were helpful. Longhaired, graybearded men were more plentiful in Alaska than anyone expected. One old-timer from the ghost town of Hope, driving a van around Anchorage to gather supplies, was stopped by police three times in a single afternoon.

The sound of a helicopter landing by the footbridge had evidently given the suspect time to slip away on a four-wheeler held at the ready. Despite his feeble health, he had somehow managed to sneak back after the troopers left and drive his dark blue Dodge Ram camper van out the McCarthy Road without being spotted. "We were expecting this to go nice and easy, and apparently Mr. Hale had other plans," a trooper spokesman said. "Maybe we underestimated him."

Alaska, however, is not an easy place to make a getaway. The airports and ferries are easily watched. There's one main highway out to Canada. A fugitive on wheels can only pinball among Anchorage, Fairbanks, and the border post at Tok, basically a highway triangle with a handful of road stubs leading to dead ends in the wilderness. And winter was closing in.

After a week the troopers announced they were easing off the intensive manhunt. They were confident their quarry was still in Alaska and would turn up soon. "We don't have the resources to be driving up and down the highway looking behind every tree," the spokesman said.

On October 5, 2005, twelve days after troopers had found the stove still warm in Pilgrim's tent by the Kennicott River, an Alaska Railroad security agent came across the dusty blue van on a dead-end service road north of Anchorage. The agent was making a routine patrol near the tracks, through one of those weedy urban pockets where people sometimes go to disappear in more settled parts of America. The van's driver tried to turn around but the agent used his pickup to block the way. Robert Hale's long gray beard was tucked in a purple scarf around his neck. The fume-filled van carried a canister of extra gasoline, boxes of food, and eleven Bibles.

The fugitive was cooperative as he was handcuffed. He waited on the pickup's tailgate for troopers to arrive. In an Anchorage police video of the arrest, he seemed tired, his head sunk. He mumbled about a recent operation, his knee problems, and diabetes. He asked to see the wanted poster with his photo on it. One of the search warrants left at his tent in McCarthy was found in the van with "self defense" written across it, but Hale told authorities he had only just discovered he was wanted and had been on his way that very morning to turn himself in.

The superior court in Palmer has jurisdiction over state criminal cases originating in the Wrangell Mountains. The suspect appeared there the next day to be arraigned and assigned a public defender. He peered out uncertainly through round wire-rim glasses, his long white hair thinning, his yellow jail suit looking a few sizes too large. In legal papers, and among the newspaper and television reporters who turned out in force, he was no longer known as Papa Pilgrim.

The judge asked Robert Hale for his occupation.

"I'm a father," he said.

THE CRIMINAL case against Robert Hale raised several unusual challenges for the Palmer prosecutor. The defendant insisted he had done nothing wrong. Everything had been consensual. Richard Payne knew a jury was going to have some questions. If things were so bad, why didn't Elishaba simply leave? Why didn't the mother help? Indeed, how could such a big secret have been sustained in such a small cabin?

Medical examiners found no lingering physical evidence of abuse. They confirmed that Elishaba had never been pregnant. There had apparently been a memory stick of digital photos, which Hale hid on his Bible shelf, but the boys had destroyed them as vile. Troopers had hoped at one point to trap Hale on the phone. But Jim Buckingham refused to allow a phone tap. Hale had often secretly taped conversations in the cabin, then turned his children's own words against them. The Buckinghams were trying to teach the children to give up such deception.

Without physical evidence, then, Elishaba's testimony would be crucial. But it was going to be necessary to paint a fuller picture of life in the cult that Robert Hale had raised around himself. The oldest son, Joseph, had turned out to be particularly helpful in describing for investigators how his father used starvation and other techniques—Joseph called it "brainwashing"—to control the family. Payne filed a motion spelling out how his case would involve testimony from Kurina Rose, the older children, and the Buckinghams to explain the ways this unhappy family was like no other—how Robert Hale had made himself into a feared "quasi-deity" for the purpose of controlling his family, and then ensured his conduct would not be discovered by isolating them and adopting the guise of a man pursuing a dream in the Alaska wilderness.

Some people seemed ready to explain Hale's God as the grandiose fantasy of a pathological narcissist. But Payne was starting to believe the whole religious guise was phony. It was so riddled with contradictions. He also had doubts about Hale's purported pacifism. With all those guns around, there was no telling how the story might have ended if the sons and daughters had not found the courage to escape when they did. Payne followed the trail back through Hale's life. He found the death of Kathleen Connally particularly suspicious, given the absence of fingerprints and the gunshot wound to the back of the head. Hale's family told Payne they believed the shooting was truly an accident. In his early Christian life, they said, their father would have confessed such a serious sin in hope of clearing his soul. Payne wasn't so sure. That kind of soul-clearing confession can put a person away for life.

So far, the general public knew little about what had gone on inside the Pilgrim Family. The state's charges—separate counts for each year the family had lived in Alaska, plus multiple counts of rape, assault, and kidnapping for the January 10, 2005, incident at the wanigan—were laid out in brief, neutral, boilerplate language. Because the accusations involved sexual assault and the exposure of minor children, no detailed charging document had been filed. The grand jury testimony was locked away. The family members, all of whom had now moved into the Buckinghams' home in Palmer, were being shielded from reporters. It was not even very clear that the charges involved a single adult victim, someone referred to misleadingly by her legal initials, B.S.

My newspaper went along with the general blackout, following policies against naming rape victims. There was no worry this criminal case might slip through the cracks, as there would have been if the complaint were in the hands of the state's office of child protective services (which continues to this day to cite the confidentiality in its statutes in refusing to discuss how at least six formal investigations of the Pilgrims had been opened through the years in Alaska with no action ever taken).

The date of the trial, when secrets would finally be revealed, was pushed later and later into 2006, as Hale's public defenders won repeated delays. Gradually, in court filings, the defense's legal strategy emerged: His lawyer would argue that sexual activity with the adult victim had not been forced; that Jim Buckingham, the real Svengali in the story, had stolen away the defendant's family and planted stories in their minds; and that the state was unfairly and selectively singling out Robert Hale for prosecution, ignoring other allegations of thievery, incest, and child abuse perpetrated by the children themselves and offered up freely to investigators in the detailed stories they told of their lives.

The first two arguments were to be expected. The last one infuriated Payne. He saw it as pure mudslinging—an effort to intimidate the children by threatening to drag the family's ignorance and confusion into the courtroom. Payne needed the children to testify without fear. He was prepared to bring in clinical experts who would talk about sexual grooming and the way victims came to identify with their captors, and how these factors were heightened in this case by religious domination and social and geographic isolation. But such expert testimony would be useless without the children's own stories.

He had decided not to file charges against Kurina Rose. His helicopter visit to the Mother Lode convinced him she was a textbook abuse victim herself, making crazy desperate trade-offs as she struggled to protect herself and her younger children. Charging her would give the case too many confusing vectors. Going after both parents would also fulfill Robert Hale's pseudo-prophetic warnings about state social workers, conceivably upsetting the family to the point of destroying the criminal case against the real perpetrator. But Payne knew a jury trial was going to put Mama Pilgrim in a difficult position.

He worked to nurture his relations with the family. He brought his wife to dinner at the Buckingham home. His open Mormon religiosity was a helpful bridge: The Buckinghams and Hales said it felt like the Lord himself had brought Payne to their assistance. Payne also brought in assistant district attorney Rachel Gernat, a young soccer-playing mom whose sunny demeanor belied the darkness of her experience as a sex-crimes prosecutor in the rural meth belt of the Palmer-Wasilla valley. Gernat was not at all religious, but she came back early from maternity leave to work with the children of Papa Pilgrim, especially the females. She prepared them for the kinds of questions they might hear on cross-examination. She explained the difference between a witness statement and soulful testimonial. She listened to their stories. The children had visited no psychologists and received no conventional trauma counseling, and the lay reassurance of a state lawyer who had seen these things before was undoubtedly valuable beyond the practical purpose of putting their complicated experiences into words the court would understand.

"Victims have to feel safe before they will tell you what happened," Gernat told me privately. "What if no one believes you, and then you have to go back to the abuser? Because now you've told, and it's going to be even worse for you. At the same time, they've been taught to fear the state. That's very common among abused families: 'Children's Services and the cops are going to take you away.' What was unique in this case is that he expanded it to all government, including the National Park Service."

The case was distinguished, too, by the victims' efforts to reconcile their rescue with the religious faith in which they'd been raised. For many abuse victims, an important part of recovery is constructing a narrative to explain their trauma. In the case of the Hale children, this meant persuading themselves it had been God's plan all along to guide them through their wilderness trials to safety, learning hard lessons along the way about grace and redemption. Gernat found the Bible lessons and sympathetic ear of Jim and Martha Buckingham had been remarkably helpful at leading the children out of the valley of the shadow of their father's megalomania.

"I don't think he ever thought his own children would go against him," Gernat said. "He was too narcissistic; he couldn't see his own potential downfall. I know he still has a hold on them. Maybe in the courtroom he thinks he can exert his power. I don't think it will work. At this point, they just want to hear him ask forgiveness. Most victims want to hear the words 'I'm sorry.' "

Gernat understood that the children would see the defense table bathed in a holy light. "They will look at him and wonder, how could he not repent?"

THE IMPRISONMENT of their poster child had not been helpful to the property-rights campaigners fighting the Park Service.

Activists struggled to distance themselves from the man who had conjured such happy images of living off the land. The American

Land Rights Association issued a press release calling the criminal charges against Robert Hale "appalling and tragic." Chuck Cushman, the association head who had helped set up the family's Pacific Northwest concerts, noted that ownership of most of the McCarthy Creek inholding had always been in the names of the victimized children anyway (a ruse, he may not have known, to ensure that assets in a parent's name did not interfere with the family's eligibility for welfare).

"In working with the family over the last two years ALRA never observed anything out of order and we had no reason to believe that any misconduct by Papa Pilgrim was taking place. . . . The American Land Rights Association will stand by these children and all other Alaskans that are facing unjust access restrictions to their lands affecting their daily lives."

Kurt Stenehjem, the airlift "angel" who once fell into Hillbilly Heaven, showed up at Hale's arraignment in Palmer, appearing stunned at the ground loop his memoir's story line had taken. Stenehjem was interviewed on the evening news as a former admirer.

"I enjoy families, large families," he told the cameras. "You hope for the best. You're curious and try not to be cynical, but the accusations would perhaps answer a lot of questions."

In McCarthy, the greatest surprise was expressed by those who had claimed to know the family best. Investigative records later revealed that some of these friends told troopers they'd often wondered how such competent and strong children could be so bruised up all the time.

The *Wrangell St. Elias News,* which two years earlier had run a cover story called THE DARK SIDE OF NPS, now ran a cover story called THE DARK SIDE OF ROBERT HALE. "His accusers are not the National Park Service, but rather his own family," Rick Kenyon wrote. "*WSEN* strongly supported, and still strongly asserts, the validity of the family's right to access their home—to Hillbilly Heaven, a term the family gave their mountain property. But, unknown to us, their heaven was becoming anything but."

The Hales sent a letter to their neighbors in the Wrangells, signed by Joseph, to be read aloud at the next meeting of the McCarthy Area Council:

> We well remember the day we drove into McCarthy. Our hearts were overwhelmed by your kindness, and we fell in love with your town. You were gracious to us and we wanted to reciprocate, but we truly did not understand what it meant to be a good neighbor. Our hearts weep for the pain and misunderstandings that we have caused in the town, and we want to ask your forgiveness individually and collectively. We need your help to be the people that we want to be, and though we don't deserve it, we beg for your patience and understanding. It took years for us to become the people that we are, so we know that it will take some time for us to adopt a manner of living that is truly acceptable before God and man.

Joseph wrote that the family hoped to return to McCarthy the following summer to run their horse-ride business but planned to remain for the time being in Palmer, "to round out a bit of our educational needs." Reaction around the valley was generally sympathetic, though some wariness lingered among those who thought they detected in the prose style a trace of Papa Pilgrim's florid promises.

The Hale family had already taken a step away from McCarthy. While holding on to Hillbilly Heaven, they had sold the copper catacombs on the mountain above to Ray Kreig.

From their home in Anchorage, Ray and Lee Ann Kreig were aware, months before the arrest, that something big was going on. They knew the older children had moved out. Plans for a tourist lodge were forgotten. Elishaba, Joseph, and Joshua came by in May 2005 to sign the Mother Lode sales agreement and got Papa on the speaker-phone from McCarthy. "That's the first time I've heard his voice since I left," Elishaba said. She gave Lee Ann a hug as they departed and whispered, "We left because of me."

The Kreigs nevertheless stayed on friendly terms with Papa, visiting him in the Anchorage hospital a month before the indictment. Shaken when news of the manhunt came out, Ray Kreig asked Joseph what to do if his father tried to get in touch. "Do what I would do. Call 911," Joseph told him.

Sure enough, one morning the fugitive called from a phone booth. He asked Kreig to save newspaper clippings about his run from the law. He didn't say where he was, and the call time expired. Kreig called the police and told them what he could.

Robert Hale's arrest did not diminish Kreig's outrage over the government effort to close the Green Butte Road. When the federal appeals court finally endorsed "reasonable" regulation of inholders and environmental review of certain access plans, Kreig protested on his War in the Wrangells website. The appeals court judges had decided on their own, he complained, that winter access up McCarthy Creek was the best solution—details the trial lawyers had never gotten around to arguing. The Pacific Legal Foundation appealed to the U.S. Supreme Court, but eventually their petition was turned down. Thus ended the legal test of the limits of Alaska exceptionalism in the first generation to come along after the epic 1980 conservation act.

There appeared to be little public energy left for defending the pioneer lifestyle of Papa Pilgrim.

FOR THE first time in her adult life, Kurina Rose Hale was out in the world. She had a little cabin of her own, not far from the Buck-inghams'. She attended Bible study classes and a class on victims of violence, where she heard stories of abused women and their embarrassments, fears, and foolish hopes. She also learned about something called bipolar personality disorder: *Grandiose. Intolerant. Euphoric. Volatile. Jekyll and Hyde.*

As far as she could tell, such erratic behavior had been part of her husband's makeup since he was young. It was crazy rage that got the best of him with Kathleen Connally, he had always insisted, and the poor confused girl couldn't take it—pregnant, a disappointment to her father, trapped in a dumpy apartment far from home with a husband furious about a bathtub ring. Bobby felt guilty and searched twenty years for answers before he found Jesus. But it was like the parable in the Gospels about the house that has been swept clean, Rose thought. Her husband's evil spirits were banished and went away into the wilderness, until he allowed himself to become proud in the mountains of New Mexico. The devil found a way back in. And he came back, as the Bible says, bringing seven spirits even more wicked. That number again.

Rose wished she had known something about manic depression. But she was only sixteen when Bobby Hale took her in, and young even for that, too eager to build a rebel lifestyle all her own, too proud to admit a mistake, too foolish to see the warning signs in an older man who never got over another innocent sixteen-year-old.

This was how things began to look to Rose when she gazed back on her life. But people didn't want to hear her say anything that sounded like she was explaining or defending her husband. She tried to keep her mouth shut.

A YEAR after Robert Hale was arrested, I received a jailhouse letter addressed to Neighbor Tom. The defendant wanted me to know he always felt I had done an "Honest and Admirable job of Reporting." He added: "I held you in heartfelt prayer as I recall the hardships and sorrow you personally went through in your life—I'm not writing but to say that you now could pray for me, that the Truth of my situation will be brought forth."

Actually, he wanted something else from me: a photo of his family. He dangled the possibility of an interview and signed the letter "Papa."

I went to the jail but was turned away by orders of his lawyer.

Several months later, though, I was invited to visit the Buckingham home. It was right before Christmas 2006. The trial, after many postponements, was scheduled to begin in two weeks. The Buckinghams decided it was time to let people see how the children were doing.

I arrived at Lazy Mountain early, in time for morning chores and Bible study. I squirmed through lessons from Thessalonians and Luke, watching for the first light of winter solstice and trying to recall my own distant Sunday school days.

The Buckinghams had doubled the size of their log cabin to accommodate the Hales. A nave-like log addition perpendicular to the original provided a living room ringed by comfortable old couches. Counting Martha Buckingham's parents—former missionaries in New Guinea—the cabin had become home to twenty-eight people. Eight girls shared a bedroom upstairs and hung their thrift-store clothes outdoors on a balcony. The boys bunked in cramped basement rooms down a stairway choked with overcoats and coveralls.

Breakfast, including four loaves of freshly baked bread, was ready at eight a.m. sharp. The house was managed with military punctuality: Every room had a wall clock, synchronized with such precision that even the second hands seemed to march in step. Homeschooling started at nine. Martha's missionary mother taught reading and phonics ("Parts of speech are a wonderful gift from the Lord"). Older boys sat around the big dining table with their little siblings. Apart from Elishaba, none of the Hales was able to read much past a second-grade level when they arrived.

The Hale boys were shorn and scrubbed and smiling. The girls from two families sang hymns in the afternoon as they frosted cookies in the kitchen. There was no Christmas tree—a tradition of Teutonic nature worshippers—but they strung garlands and lights on the log beams. If the tableau felt a bit staged, it was no more than most American households might contrive for a holiday visitor.

They thanked me for the stories I'd written. They made me feel I had played a small supporting role in the rescue narrative they were using to rebuild the children's lives. The newspaper's front-page photographs had first brought the Hales to the attention of the Buckinghams. The stories had dragged hidden things to light, prodded authorities, and provoked conversation inside the family. Joseph told me about his brainwashing joke and how mad his father got.

Everyone called Mr. Buckingham "Papa." They conceded this was a little strange, but no other designation had stuck. They referred to their biological father as "Pilgrim" or "Mr. Hale." When we found space upstairs to talk privately, Jim Buckingham was grave and on message. Martha, who radiated more emotion, participated fully in our conversation and in managing the entangled families' complicated lives.

The Buckinghams said they were not sure how long the housing arrangement was going to last. They were still trying to sort out God's plan. They said the children faced many fears and difficulties. They were still tempted to lie and hide things to stay out of trouble. There were, too, the strains and jealousies of blended families: the grown Hales chafing at new rules, the clash between the Hales' rugged sledgehammer approach for dealing quickly with problems and the Buckinghams' overly deliberate style. They were learning from one another.

Jim Buckingham had little to say about the crimes of Papa Pilgrim. That was for the trial, he told me. Only later did I realize how angry he was, when I saw a letter he wrote to Pilgrim around this time in which he called the man a fake and a charlatan, and described the horror the children lived with "behind closed doors under the pretense of your being a godly old sage that had forsaken the world to protect his family." The children were praying and fasting, he wrote, in hopes that their father would repent. He deplored Pilgrim's response: "that you are willing to go to jail and possibly die there to protect the now shattered image of the enigmatic leader of the Wilderness Pilgrim Family rather than openly embrace the truth of your sins and your crimes and begin the process of reconciliation with all those you have hurt so badly."

Kurina Rose stopped by for dinner. Afterward, everyone found seats on the perimeter of couches for even more Bible study and lessons about character building. Today's lesson involved initiative versus idleness. Then Jim Buckingham read from Proverbs.

" 'Trust in the Lord with all thine heart; and lean not unto thine own understanding.' What does it mean, to trust the Lord?"

Elishaba was the one who answered.

I could not yet appreciate how hard the long wait for a trial had been on the leading witness. Later she told me how she had come down from the mountain in the Wrangells feeling stupid, worthless, soiled forever. She blew up and said hurtful things. She woke up screaming at night from dreams about New Mexico and getting beaten in the head. Yet the thought of testifying and bringing her father to ruin terrified her.

Angry and depressed, she ran away from the Buckingham home several times to live in the woods. The last time out, hiding from the rain under a spruce tree as she read her Bible, a description of lost souls as lambs brought a happier memory from the Sangre de Cristos, of a time they had all gone out to hunt a missing lamb. It was a little black newborn that no one had bottle-fed or cuddled yet, so there was little hope it would respond to their calls. The coyotes would finish it off in a night. But as they hiked the cliffs at dusk, bleating their calls, they heard a reply and found the black lamb huddled in dense brush.

As Elishaba sat alone, remembering the hunt for the lamb, she heard her brothers calling across a canyon, and she cried out. David, Moses, and Jonathan delivered provisions and a message from the Buckinghams, who suggested she let go of her anger at her father and look instead at her own failings. It seemed to help. She returned to live in an outbuilding, and eventually moved back in to the main house.

Elishaba spoke now with her cowgirl twang over the soft click-click of knitting needles: "Trusting the Lord means God doesn't do evil to us. He forgives us as we reach out to Him. He gives us trials, so we can learn to know Him better."

All day I had struggled, I admit, with how the family still looked to heaven to sort out their lives. "God's grace" sounded like more magical thinking to me, a catchall explanation for good things that happened, the way "God's plan" offered a consoling shrug when things went awry. But grace, at least, was something the children could reach for. It was shaping their recovery. Whatever the Buckinghams were doing, it was working. The family had not yet produced any drug addicts or felons, nor even any apostates. They had found a perfect Christian halfway house.

After the lessons there was time for music. The Pilgrim Family acoustic instruments remained packed away, mournful reminders of a time of strife and false appearance.

This time it was the singing of hymns and Christmas carols. At the request of the boys, the seven oldest girls—Elishaba, Sharia, Lolly, Jerusalem, Hosanna, Christina, and Maryanna—harmonized a cappella:

Well the winds of despair were blowing in my face
Til the day I felt the gentle breeze of "Amazing Grace."
Then I charted a brand new course,
Let the Savior be my guiding force
And put my anchor down in Peaceful Harbor.

✠

TWO DAYS after Christmas, Robert Hale agreed to plead no contest. There would be no trial after all.

Richard Payne had initially resisted any kind of plea deal. The more he learned, the more heinous the father's crimes seemed. The family members were resolved to tell their story, and to Payne it seemed an important story for the world to hear. Their escape would inspire others in desperate domestic situations, he thought. Who could feel more trapped than the children in Hillbilly Heaven? Plus, Payne looked forward personally to boxing the old hypocrite's ears, partly as society's avenger, and partly—he felt a twinge of guilt about this—as a lawyer planning to go into private practice after the show-trial prosecution of a widely loathed figure.

It was Payne's wife who softly but persistently urged him to offer a deal. She said it was right for the children. In court, the defense would surely attack Elishaba and raise humiliating allegations about others in the family. So Payne talked to doctors about how long the sixty-five-year-old defendant was likely to live, given his many medical problems—diabetes, blood clots, infection, advanced cirrhosis from so much sacramental wine. Payne did a complicated piece of legal math, doubling the prognosis and calculating good time and other factors. He figured a sentence of fourteen years would keep Hale in jail until he was dead.

Hale might do much worse in a jury trial. He discussed the offer with his public defender. Frail and in a wheelchair, Hale then appeared before the judge and said he didn't have long to live and had decided it would be best for his family if he pleaded no contest. But, he added, "I want to make it clear that I never in any kind of way sexually assaulted anyone."

The lawyers started to prepare for sentencing. But Rose and the children, noting the absence of repentance, weren't so sure.

They feared Pilgrim would find a way to keep himself the center of attention.

"Nobody is breathing a sigh of relief that this is a done deal," Jim Buckingham told me.

They were right to worry. In April 2007, one week before his sentencing date, Hale dismissed his public defender. Acting as his own lawyer, he asked to reverse the plea, saying he had been heavily medicated and confused when he agreed to Payne's offer.

The canny prisoner had picked apart the legal code in the same way he teased lessons from the Bible. Hale had found a legitimate justification for getting out of a plea agreement. A court date was set to consider his new request, and an independent lawyer appointed to represent him. His family could not relax. Even from jail, Papa Pilgrim had extended his control over their anxious lives for two full years.

In September, the Hales and Buckinghams filled the gallery in a small Anchorage courtroom to hear Robert Hale argue for the chance to change his plea back to not guilty.

They were in for a surprise. The public defender's agency, accused by Hale of inadequate counsel, showed up in court with boxes and boxes of documents and phone logs demonstrating extensive efforts on behalf of an exceptionally demanding client. The court recessed so the lawyers and judge could talk privately. When they reconvened, a gaunt and slurring Hale reversed course yet again, dropping his request to change his plea. The court could sentence him as a guilty man.

Superior court judge Donald Hopwood asked several times if the defendant understood what was going on and was sure about his decision. Each time, Hale hesitated, letting his eyelids droop and touching his worn Bible, before saying he understood.

So it was nearly over. The courtroom was reserved in November for a two-day sentencing hearing, at which point family members would finally get the chance to speak in public. Their father would have a last chance to speak as well. At the bang of the gavel, the children rose and filed out, never looking over their shoulders. Hale watched from his wheelchair, his face collapsing in a look of anguish, and cried out, "Family, don't turn your backs on God!"

18

The Man in the Iron Cage

THERE WAS not much at issue when Robert Hale was wheeled into the courtroom for the November sentencing clutching a Bible. He turned to make eye contact with the front row of spectators but did not risk a smile. The youngest children stared back. They had not seen their father in two years.

Hale had agreed in the end to plead no contest to three consolidated counts of twenty-seven charges of rape, coercion, and incest, all involving Elishaba. Judge Hopwood had only to decide whether to add an additional suspended sentence and any conditions on

Elishaba at Hillbilly Heaven

probation—mere technicalities given that no adult in the room expected the ailing inmate would ever leave prison alive.

Under Alaska law, however, crime victims get a chance to speak before a sentence is imposed. They are invited to court primarily to address sentencing conditions. But sometimes they are allowed to speak directly to the guilty party about what is pent up in their hearts.

Hopwood had a reputation for running a tight hearing. It wasn't clear how much rein the family would be given. The judge had already turned down a request by Jim Buckingham to speak.

The Anchorage courtroom was small, with just three rows of spectator benches. Hales and Buckinghams filled the first two rows. I sat against the back wall, next to Kurt Stenehjem.

For four hours, we watched transfixed as the Pilgrim Family talked back to Papa for the first time in their lives.

Kurina Rose Hale was the first to speak. She addressed the judge directly.

"On the outside, we looked quaint and could be quite charming when it suited us. But behind closed doors, a battle was always raging," she said.

Her notes trembled in her hands. Life wasn't easy in a small cabin with a husband who "always made life sound so different from what you thought it was," she said. "He demanded complete attention when he spoke, and he could go on for hours. Sometimes he would not allow me to feed the children their breakfast until way after lunchtime, because he had so many things to say about the Bible. The children learned to sit almost motionless, like in a trance, while listening to him."

The boys, she said, were trained to take the beatings. They turned the other cheek and never dishonored their father by fighting back.

"He began to teach the family that if we sin we do not go to heaven. . . . He tried in every way he could to convince us that he himself was not a sinner, and that if we perceived that he had done something wrong we could be sure he was doing something God told him to do. . . . It took me a long time to grasp this doctrine, but the children were taught it from the time they could talk and so they always lived in fear of what it meant."

As she described how he punished her for showing disrespect, she broke down weeping. She apologized, saying she had never been able to speak of such things in his presence without fearing for her life.

"Words cannot express how women like me need others to reach out and help us in our desperate situation. How different our lives would have been if I had a friend to reach out a helping hand. I have asked God and my family to forgive me for not making more of an effort to get help."

After thanking those who did help bring them out of the wilderness over the past two years, she said she had only one thing to say to her husband. "I'd just sort of like to know where he's at in his 'progress.' "

She asked to read a short excerpt from *The Pilgrim's Progress*. It was the story of "The Man in the Iron Cage."

The book's pilgrim, Christian, is introduced to the caged man. The man was once a flourishing Professor, making fair for the Celestial City, but is now trapped in despair for having "laid the reins on the neck of my lusts" and sinning against the light of the world. It was not his sin, though, that has built his iron cage, but rather that "I have hardened my heart so much that I cannot repent."

Hale's court-appointed attorney stood to object.

"To be read a long passage from a book to inflict whatever she's trying to inflict on Mr. Hale adds nothing to the proceedings," he said.

Richard Payne responded that the book was a key to understanding the family's story.

"This individual names himself Papa Pilgrim. He derives that name from the book from which she reads. I think it's very important for her to express this in words that I think are very well understood by the other victims in the family and by Mr. Hale."

The judge overruled the objection. Rose finished reading:

MAN: I have despised his Righteousness, I have counted his Blood
    an unholy thing, I have done despite to the Spirit of Grace:
    Therefore I have shut myself out of all the Promises, and
    there now remains to me nothing but Threatenings, dreadful
    Threatenings, fearful Threatenings of certain Judgment and
    fiery Indignation, which shall devour me as an Adversary. . . .
CHRISTIAN: But canst thou not now repent and turn?
MAN: God hath denied me Repentance. His Word gives me no
    encouragement to believe; yea, himself hath shut me up in
    this Iron Cage: Nor can all the men in the world let me out.
    O Eternity! Eternity! How shall I grapple with the Misery that
    I must meet with in Eternity!

Then came the children, from young to old, starting with Alaska-born Bethlehem, who managed only a few words before crumpling into tears.

Unlike their mother, they spoke directly to their father. Much of what followed was plain description of life inside the family, which one of them called "an occult"—the anger and the drinking, the braided thong, the scriptural support for stealing, poaching game, and lying to authorities. Some carried written statements that Rachel Gernat read aloud. The way the older boys stumbled as they tried to read their own simple words was perversely eloquent. Each child carefully included a request that their father forgive them—for some past moment of pride or disobedience, or for holding bitterness in their hearts. Each apology was a reminder that this might be their final exchange, their moment to say good-bye.

"I remember I would try to get my sisters to do bad things so you'd like me as a special one," said one of the little girls. When she was bad, he had forced her to do push-ups under the family table until she fell asleep. Another of the little girls said, "I remember how, on my birthday, you held me for a very long time on your lap. I have been trying to get that out of my mind for a very long time."

Their father sat silently in his wheelchair at the defense table, scribbling furiously on a gray legal pad. He looked healthier than at earlier hearings.

The older children spoke of their embarrassment at being unable to read and do math, and at people knowing all about their father's sins. Jerusalem, who had learned swiftly to read, described her childhood and the shock of going out in the world:

I would get on my knees at night and cry in my pillow and ask Jesus to show me the big miracle that was supposed to happen in my life. I thought I was going to be a new person and feel a natural desire to do what was right. . . . There are no words to describe what it means to think you are better than everyone else in the world—and to find out that you know nothing, can do nothing, and aren't appreciated for what you can do because no one lives like we lived anymore. Plus, all the bad character that we learned from our primary examples is character that has had to be changed. . . . It has been very confusing to think back on memories and try to discern what really happened. So often a story would be carefully told as to how you would think it should be told, and we all told it over and over again until we believed that it really happened that way. . . . Please forgive me for not taking a stand because of the fear that gripped my heart. I believe we all would have taken a stand earlier, but we were all under your spell, just like a small mouse is trapped by the glaring eyes and swaying head of a poisonous snake.

Her older brothers told about the years of beatings and the whipping barrel. They expressed terrible remorse over their own ignorance and fear. They were astonished now at the confusion that had held them outside the door of the wanigan listening to their sister's screams. Joshua grimaced and lost control trying to apologize—"I don't know what possessed me. I beat my chest and weep," he cried, his voice rising an octave as his family in the gallery burst into loud sobs.

Finally it was Elishaba's turn.

The cowgirl seemed transformed by two and a half years away from Hillbilly Heaven. She wore a long pink patterned dress with maroon sleeves and a white lace collar, her dark hair pinned neatly back. Even some of her Texas twang had fallen away. Reading from a statement, and looking up periodically to elaborate, she addressed her father directly.

> I have tried so many times to tell you about the deepest concerns in my heart, about the things done in secret. Things that I felt were wrong. Things that you insisted were right before God. . . . My eyes have been opened just like Eve in the garden when she bit into the apple and her eyes were opened to her nakedness. When my eyes were opened to the truth of my relationship with you, I found myself naked and unclean before God and before man. As you knew it would, this truth devastated me. . . . You took for yourself the very things that I held so dear. You knew that I wanted so badly to be pure and godly and to make it to heaven. In fact, you even encouraged that spirit in me and then turned around and used my desire to be right before God to get your own way with me. . . . I was just a little girl who wanted to please her papa.

Elishaba spoke of growing up in the mountains, of the punishments and the false picture their family presented to the world.

All your life I've watched you twist the truth of things to always make yourself be the one in the right. If you could manage to shift the blame on someone else you would feel you had won a great victory. Woe it be to the one who ever accused you of anything— they would be sure that you would turn the table around and they would be the one who would look guilty in the end.

You carefully made up signs and visions which you used on me whenever I would show the least bit of resistance to your physical advances. You would remind me that God was the one that approved of our relationship, and yet to me, it often seemed like you would just make up the vision with the forethought of needing to use it later to get your own way. Of course I would never have dared to speak of my doubt openly because you said to question you would be the same as blaspheming the Holy Spirit of God, and that would be a sin that could never be forgiven. . . . There was no end to the ways you could think of to punish me for not meeting up to your physical demands. It seemed like you would do anything to find an excuse to beat me up. In my weakest state I would always end up giving in to the pressure to once again meet your sexual desires. You got a sick delight in looking at all the bruises you had put on me when I resisted you. You would boast of what you had done, as if there were some secret delight in being able to overcome my resistance. All this you did in the name of God and love.

Elishaba paused more frequently now to draw fresh tissues. She talked about what happened in the wanigan, describing the beating though not the rape. Then she told of the violent nights alone with her father that followed the family's showdown, her voice rising higher and tighter as she tried to recount his threat to tear her to pieces. She gasped with overflowing emotion and took a deep breath.

You taught me that going to the world, which meant if I left you, would be my damnation and that I would be lost forever. Even though I didn't have all the right words and made a fool out of myself trying to tell you why it was wrong, I came to a place in the depths of my heart where it was clear to me that I needed to seek God over my father. God gives us all a natural conscience of right and wrong. . . . I didn't know that there was such a thing as getting help or that the authorities would stand against what you were doing to me. I didn't know who to trust. I just knew I had to get out of there.

Here she paused, and then turned, like her brothers and sisters before her, to say good-bye.

I believe right now you are unable to admit that you have done these things wrong, because you believe that to admit to it would be to send you directly to Hell. . . . Sadly, your admitting or not admitting to the wrong is not what makes it true. God and your whole family know that you did these things. Like Romans One says, you have turned the truth of God into a lie and as a result you remain in the chains of your own deception, unless you realize that it is not your perfection that gets you to heaven, but the mercy and grace of God. . . .

Father will you please forgive me for taking part in your adulterous sin. For fearing you over God. For my selfishness in not being willing to sacrifice my own life for the sake of what I desperately knew was right, deep in my heart. . . . For my bitterness that has lived in my heart against you for so long. I pray to God to deliver me from it. For I have learned that bitterness is the only way I can allow you to destroy the beautiful work that God has done in setting me free from the horrors of the past.

Forgive me for my lack of trusting God to hear my prayers, for I have cried hard unto him, and he did answer my cry.

THE NEXT morning, Robert Hale got his chance to speak.

This time he arrived with no Bible and asked for one. The judge said he had no Bible at hand, and neither did Richard Payne. The prosecutor leaned into the gallery to consult quietly with the family, then responded that no one had an extra Bible to lend.

Hale opened anyway with a prayer—"Lord reveal the truth, untie the knot that's hidden so many things." Then in a soft, mournful drawl he started to unspool one last time the long sorrowful odyssey of Papa Pilgrim, starting with his heroic father and the accidental death of his teenage bride. Soon he was blaming Rose for problems in a nostalgic, regretful tone. "I realized at some point I was probably the only one in the family who knew God." His love for his wife had been greatly quenched, he conceded, because of all the sins she'd allowed her children to commit. He paused and wept at the memory. He'd never given anything but mild corrections, and only out of fatherly love. "I can hardly believe the lips of my children, using words like 'beat unmercifully,'" he said. No one ever complained of harsh conditions back in New Mexico. Reading and writing had been his wife's responsibility—"It's like there's this whole thing of blame everything on Papa," he said. The only brainwashing he could see had come from Buckingham, who had coveted his family from the start. He felt really sorry for Jim Buckingham, for he would reap what he had sown.

After more than two hours, Judge Hopwood interrupted to say he needed to finish up.

Hale began grabbing at ideas with the wide eyes of a drowning man. He warned his children they risked hell for the sin of bearing false witness. "My biggest concern is their salvation. They're not

going to be able to stand before my Lord Jesus." He quoted 1 Corinthians and questioned how a court of unbelievers could ever be a
proper forum for admitting sin. He sang a verse of a sorrowful family song about lost lambs coming home. He said his children's accusations of abuse would get him killed in the jail's open population—"My
family actually signed my death warrant yesterday." He said Elishaba
had committed perjury before the grand jury and lied before God
about the correction he gave her in the wanigan. He hadn't meant to
slap her, he just pushed her away because the woodstove door was
hanging open to the flame and "sometimes you hit the wrong place on
an eye and the whole face goes black." He said Scripture foretold how
Christians would be imprisoned in the last days, their very families
turning against them. "Everyone who wants to live in Christ Jesus will
suffer persecution. There's just no other way about it. That's what
carrying the cross is, and that's where I am now."

The stove door was hanging open again and we stared in at the
consuming furnace of Papa Pilgrim's mind. Hopwood said he had just
a few minutes remaining.

It was like the executioner had been summoned. Papa Pilgrim's
murmur faltered at last. In a whimper, he begged his daughter to with-
draw her testimony. "In God's eyes, we're like a sheep in a meadow.
Now and then a man goes astray, and open arms should await his return. I realized yesterday that there probably wouldn't be a response,
and I guess that breaks my heart, because they're in real danger of
eternal judgment."

And with that, he spoke faintly, as we watched him sinking for the
last time. "I don't intend to ever see them again. I know this is the last
time I'll be with them. And they know that too. Lord Jesus, thank you
for being here today. Each tear has its reward. In Jesus's name."

THE FAMILY lingered afterward in the hall outside the courtroom.
They were relieved—even elated—by Judge Hopwood's words at the

end. They had never been in the presence of an authority higher than their father. Elishaba was still at the point of tears. "Just hearing what the judge said, he saw right through to the truth of it all," she said.

Judge Hopwood had called Robert Hale a liar. He praised the courage and eloquence of the children. It was a classic case of the worst kind of domestic violence, he said—the way it starts, the way it escalates, the damage it causes. And yet, he said, this story had a strange twist. Robert Hale had grown up in a good home with a good father, and fled to a lifestyle that rejected society's values and lived off the labor of others. Whereas his children, growing up with a terrible father, were gentle, and industrious, and believed in truth and now in the rule of law. "It would not have surprised me if some of the family had opted out, like their dad did, a long time ago," the judge said.

In my notebook I had circled in red a comment along the same lines that morning from Robert Hale himself: "If my children look good, walk good, talk good, *are* good, well then how did they get to *be* good, if their father is so evil? Can a thorn bush bear oranges?" I had scribbled a big question mark next to the quote.

As I talked in the hallway with the children, Country Rose sought me out. Under her arm was an old book. It was the illustrated *Pilgrim's Progress* from the homestead, the storybook whose line drawings the children used to stare at for hours. She held the pages out to me, open to the illustration of the Man in the Iron Cage. Emaciated, straggle-bearded, eyes full of terror as he gazed through the iron bars at eternity: It was an exact drawing of Papa Pilgrim.

Epilogue: Peaceful Harbor

S OMEWHERE ALONG the way, the government dropped its
civil case against the Pilgrims.

The decision may have been made as early as 2004, when the
town of McCarthy was concluding they had a madman in their midst
and the federal courts were ruling against the Pilgrims' legal initia-
tives. More likely, no final decision was ever made—only a decision to
put off a decision until a future meeting that was never convened.

The paper trail in the Department of the Interior files peters out
after undated handwritten notes of a meeting at which the "egregious
action by Pilgrims" was weighed against the negatives of appearing to
force park inholders off their land. At that point, the Park Service had
a preliminary estimate for damages to park resources of $561,621, of
which more than half would have gone to repay the cost of sending all
those experts up the valley to do the damage assessment work. Much
of what the Pilgrims had done in McCarthy Creek—scavenging lumber from historic mine buildings in the park, scraping new switchbacks up the rockslides to the Mother Lode—could not be undone.

As for the bulldozed road that had started everything, biologists recommended restoration through natural erosion and revegetation, a process that had already commenced at no cost to the taxpayer.

IN McCARTHY these days, Rick Kenyon still preaches in church once a week and publishes the *Wrangell St. Elias News* six times a year.

The newspaper's tone seems mellower, even chastened. Its lionizing of the Pilgrims as "a caring, loving family," along with its strident advocacy for self-evident truths later rejected by the courts, had served to escalate dangerous tensions and obscure the real troubles at the Mother Lode. Rick Kenyon notes, in his defense, that he personally fell out with the quarrelsome old Calvinist a whole year before the criminal activity was revealed. He accounts for the mellower tone by saying the next crop of park administrators were more reasonable, having finally adopted a new inholder policy that lays out clear steps for securing legal access while declaring rural residents to be "part of the essential fabric" of Alaska's national parks.

The editor/pastor's chastened tone may also have to do with a painful schism at the McCarthy-Kennicott Community Church— over personalities as much as doctrines, like most such religious cataclysms—that resulted in the loss of several of his tiny congregation's most active families. Among the departing churchgoers were Laurie and Keith Rowland. McCarthy Annie's name no longer appears in the paper, but she and her handy husband remain active in the valley and helpful on many community projects, exerting dominion over the planet by building wide boulevards of crushed rock on the west side of the Kennicott River.

The falling-out over the church, and subsequent disputes between Kenyons and Rowlands over neighborhood roads, has perhaps muted the pleasure that the *Wrangell St. Elias News* might otherwise have taken in reporting Keith Rowland's success in erecting a private vehicle bridge across the river, half a mile downstream of the footbridge, which is now open to any household willing to pay three hundred dollars for an annual pass. After decades of debate, it is possible at last to drive all the way into McCarthy. As predicted, easier access has brought growth and change. But the toll bridge has proved to be an elegant and widely supported private-enterprise solution to the dilemma of getting lumber and groceries into the ghost town and keeping most tourist cars out—one that government could never have managed.

(The Rowlands, alone among the people of McCarthy, would not speak to me for this book, saying they considered my Pilgrim stories for the *Anchorage Daily News* too sympathetic toward the Park Service. I was sorry not to be able to hear McCarthy Annie's retrospective views of her neighbors, but as a McCarthy property owner I did get a warm feeling of inclusion to find myself at last on nonspeaking terms with someone in the community.)

Motorized access up the McCarthy Creek valley remains closed, but this is not the problem of the Hale-Sunstar family any longer. In 2008, the family sold the rest of their Mother Lode holdings to Alaska Land Rights Coalition founder Ray Kreig. The Park Service's most outspoken critic in Alaska now owns all the Pilgrim Family land in Wrangell–St. Elias National Park and Preserve. He says he might want to drive there someday.

"This isn't over yet," Kreig says.

THE TOWN bustles with new energy in summer these days, with more building, more visitor services, and a slow increase in travel out the McCarthy Road. What was once a rough and disorienting journey into the Alaska bush has been subtly domesticated by new national park road signs. Ben Shaine, attuned as ever to paradoxes of history and perceptions of landscape, sometimes wonders if passage of the Alaska conservation act in 1980, which protected more wilderness than any law in American history, also eliminated more true wilderness in that same single stroke, by putting it all under a watchful government eye.

Shaine is watching the evolution of park policies no less anxiously than Rick Kenyon. Working with the federal bureaucracy is like living in an old cabin in the woods, he says: You fiddle with each problem that comes along using the tools at hand, until you figure out how to jury-rig a solution.

Lately, a problem in need of jury-rigging has been how to preserve Kennicott—or "Kennecott," the official and gradually ascendant spelling. Early plans for taking over the ruins called for the national park to retain a lost-world atmosphere. Planners once spoke of a "sense of discovery" and "arrested decay." Then some park officials began pushing to restore certain buildings as brass-plaqued facsimiles of the 1938 originals and let others vanish into piles of boards. Stability was the goal; change, growth, and decline were problematic. The McCarthy Area Council has expressed fear that Park Service careerists from the lower forty-eight would rebuild the ruins and funnel visitors into tours, a concept derided locally as "Disneyland." The local council would prefer to see Kennicott preserved somehow in its abandoned, half-fallen state, as a place that reminds visitors of how tenuous great works can be—a place, in the words of an early plan, "still haunted by past residents."

TANGLED BRUSH had grown up everywhere when I finally returned to our McCarthy cabin. It was late summer and rained hard for three days. Ethan, in his teens and growing taller, came along to help with roof repairs. A heavy winter snowslide had sheared off our stovepipe. A neighbor, who wrote with the news, had temporarily patched the hole with a sheet of metal roofing and arrested the decay.

I chainsawed willows out of the clearing and reopened the footpath—making as few cuts as possible, out of respect for Sally's opinion in such matters. Except for the hole in the roof, the cabin was in remarkably good shape after twenty years. The inside walls were still plastic-sheathed pink insulation, the kitchen counter on sawhorses, everything waiting for someone to come back and finish the job.

We tried waiting out the storm while visiting friends and neighbors around McCarthy. The first night, with rain drumming on the roof, I pulled out the old guest journals and sat on the cabin's only piece of real furniture, an empty white iron bed from Sally's childhood. The place used to be busy with friends staying over, but since her death there had been few visitors. I turned to our last family entry. It was from the summer I met the Pilgrims, when Sally was in her last decline. This is what she wrote:

August 21, 2003. We leave tomorrow after five fun-filled days. Nine years since we were here—seems like a lifetime ago. In McCarthy time, seems like yesterday. People are still friendly, mostly (really completely). Controversies still brewing.

The biggest overall impression is the ever changeable landscape. Impermanence—the lesson of life. We want to hold tight to what is good and real in life, but change is inevitable. The Wrangell Mountains are a wonderful reminder of that universal lesson. The teaching continues.

On a more practical level, I've had so much exercise this week—biking and hiking. Now back to real life. Chemo on Tuesday. Love, Sally. P.S. We celebrated Ethan's *9th* birthday here with homer homemade choc. cake w/ white frosting.

The next day it was still raining and the steep metal roof was running with water. I was glad I'd brought my old climbing gear, retired now and stained ignominiously with roofing tar. Ethan held me on belay with a second rope, standing on the far side of the roof ridge, alert to my calls for tension. My son loved the McCarthy cabin: the hard work, the toasty fire when the stack was rebuilt, the kerosene light and Scrabble at night. He talked about coming out someday to live in McCarthy and go ice climbing and put up siding. His enthusiasm cheered me up.

On the last morning, the sky cleared and we saw fresh snow on the peaks. I took Ethan exploring on our land. I showed him the point above the canyon where his mom and I had sat that long-ago summer and watched the moon rise. A game trail led to the tree where we cached our food away from bears. The platform was still up there, our crude nailed-together ladder slimy wet on the ground. Somewhere nearby had been a mossy clearing where we pitched our little mountain tent. I thrashed around in the heavy brush. It all seemed so different now. Ethan asked what I was looking for but I didn't want to say.

THE SUN was threatening to break through the clouds on the afternoon Joseph Hale and Lolly Buckingham were married in a mountain meadow above the braided Matanuska River.

All the Hales and Buckinghams dressed alike that summer day—the boys in matching handmade shirts, the girls in dresses of cornflower blue gingham. They sang hymns while more than a hundred guests gathered on log benches arrayed in the Lazy Mountain field. Jim Buckingham, sporting a trim salt-and-pepper beard to mark his retirement from the military, rose to speak of the sovereign orchestration of God. He said Joseph and Lolly had purposed to be clean and pure before God and man, and had expressed this by having no physical contact during their engagement. Their younger siblings had followed them around as constant chaperones.

The children sang "Peaceful Harbor." Joseph appeared far across the hayfield and began striding toward the guests. He wore a white shirt, vest, and Stetson hat. He seemed unhurried for a young man who had waited twenty-nine years for this daydream scenario to unfold. Lolly came from the other direction, wearing white crepe and a wreath of mountain blue gentians in her long brown hair. It felt like the last chapter of a Jane Austen novel when the rolling clouds parted felicitously to bathe the couple in sunlight as they met. Joseph removed his cowboy hat and kissed a flower in his hand and gave it to Lolly, and they embraced.

Among those looking on was Lolly's sister, Sharia, who had once been teased by her father about marrying one of the Pilgrim boys. At Sharia's side was her husband, Joshua.

Four months earlier they had been the first in their families to marry. The children had been coatless that cold day at the Buckinghams', in homemade burgundy shirts, and Martha Buckingham later joked that it was a mistake to let her husband officiate outdoors in a sweater, as he warmed to the subject of God's grace and had quite a lot to say about it. He instructed the couple on their roles in a Christian marriage, telling his daughter she was only to disobey her husband if asked to do something God forbids. Joshua and Sharia rode off from the reception on horseback.

As I write this, the two young couples live in homes they have built for themselves on Lazy Mountain outside Palmer, not far from their brothers and sisters. They are contributing a new understory of children to family gatherings. Joshua, the family's horseman, has a business as a farrier, and Joseph is a building contractor who employs many family members. Because of their poor educations, the brothers rely on their wives to handle more of the businesses than might normally be comfortable in the gender roles of their tradition. But the businesses are doing well. Joseph has sent his brothers north as far as Nome on government contracts with, among other agencies, the National Park Service.

Kurina Rose Hale lives down the road from the Buckinghams. She lives alone—the younger Hale children remain under the close care of the family that rescued them. Jerusalem and Hosanna swiftly earned their high school diplomas through a correspondence program, and their siblings continue to homeschool. The older boys work in construction in the bustling Wasilla-Palmer area, sometimes alongside the Buckingham sons. David Hale also volunteered in prison ministry, and others talk of becoming missionaries. Jim and Martha Buckingham report that the children continue to struggle, but none have abandoned their faith. They still believe Jesus is coming. But there are lives to be led in the meantime.

THE THIRD Pilgrim to marry was Elishaba. She had met her husband several years earlier, when she and her sibling musicians were turned back from the Canada border with a broken windshield and sought refuge with Christians in Delta Junction. The meeting was, to them, one more example of how a providential hand had guided her way.

At first, Matthew Doerksen had strong misgivings about the Pilgrim Family. He shared his concerns with the Buckinghams when he moved to Palmer and settled in an outbuilding at their place. The Buckinghams persuaded Matthew that the children of Papa Pilgrim were sincerely trying to change their hearts. After Elishaba's escape, it took two years to move beyond stern judgment on Matthew's part and defensive anger on hers. On their wedding day, Matthew described Elishaba as a beautiful flower beaten by a terrible storm and restored by the Lord. She said his tender compassion had "opened wide the floodgates of joy in my life."

During their honeymoon, Matthew and Elishaba traveled to places that had been important in her past, including McCarthy Creek and the mountains of New Mexico. She looked up old acquaintances and asked for forgiveness. People were incredibly warm and consoling. The journey was an exorcism. At Hillbilly Heaven, Matthew found pious words of Scripture burned into the wood of the bath-house. He tore down the boards and used an old crutch of Papa Pilgrim's to break them into pieces.

ELISHABA GAVE birth to a daughter. Matthew and Elishaba named their child Esther Grace.

Later, while roller-skating with her brothers and sisters, Elishaba fell and hit her head. Her recovery was so slow that a neurologist was called in to do tests. The doctor found she was suffering from the cumulative effects of many years of undiagnosed and untreated concussions from the beatings by her father. He said Elishaba will have to be extremely careful for the rest of her life.

AS I was doing research for this book, Kurina Rose Hale joined me one afternoon to tell stories about New Mexico. As we sat and talked, I did some mental math.

You know, I said to her, if you count the four children he had before he met you, and your fifteen, plus the miscarriage of Hope, and if you count Kathleen Connally's pregnancy, Pilgrim reached his goal of twenty-one.

She looked at me, stunned. Apparently no one had ever added things up that way before. A weird smile crossed her face.

"He'll thank you for that," she said.

NOT IN this life, he wouldn't. Robert Hale had quit the mortal realm from the medical unit of the Anchorage jail on the evening of May 24, 2008, at the age of sixty-seven.

After his sentencing, six months earlier, he had gone into rapid decline. The children prayed hard in his final months. But it was not the prayer their father once coached them to utter should he lie near death before Jesus's return. They did not pray to die at his side.

Hale's oldest sons visited him in jail several times and begged him to repent. Whenever the conversation turned this way he withdrew into sulky silence.

At the last hour, Rose, Joseph, Joshua, David, Moses, and Israel arrived for a visit to find him already unconscious. Eternity! The iron cage had stayed locked shut.

"To be honest," Joseph told me, "it's a relief that he will meet his destiny and we can go on in life without the burden of worrying about praying for him and where he stands before God."

IN HIS last days, Robert Hale had written to relatives in the lower forty-eight, begging them to bring his body back to Texas. He asked to be buried next to sweet and innocent Kathleen.

When Patsy Hale heard the request, she thought: As if the Connallys are going to let you anywhere near the family ranch.

In fact, the decision was up to the wife and children he had brought north. They chose a graveyard near their new home, far from the wilderness of the Wrangell Mountains. It was the summer of 2008, a presidential election year. In just a few weeks, the town where Papa Pilgrim was buried would give the world an indelible new image of post-frontier Alaska.

Aurora Cemetery sits on a small hill in Wasilla, where birch trees screen out most of the yard lights and traffic noise. The burial was a private family ceremony of Buckinghams and Hales. Each of the children had a chance again to speak. They did not shy from talking about the meaning of their father's life.

After a while, Kurina Rose said, the driver from the funeral home walked away to wait behind the hearse. Apparently he was not used to standing at an open grave and hearing speaker after speaker consign the newly departed to hell.

Sources

With the exception of two neighbors in New Mexico, who insisted on pseudonyms if they were to be quoted, all names and dates in this book are factual and a matter of record. In addition to the sources named here, I relied on notes and interviews made at the time of my original reporting for the *Anchorage Daily News*.

1: The Road to McCarthy
The history of McCarthy and Kennecott Copper was drawn from many written sources. An excellent overview of the area, including its human and natural history, is *Community and Copper in a Wild Land* by Shawn Olson and Ben Shaine (McCarthy: Wrangell Mountains Center, 2005). A survey of the historic community for the national park is *Keeping Special Places Special* by Joseph Sax, an option paper prepared by the Wrangell Mountains Center in 1990. Among the most useful sources on the past were *Historic McCarthy: The Town That Copper Built* by M. J. Kirchhoff (Juneau: Alaska Cedar Press, 1993); *Contested Ground: An Administrative History of Wrangell–St. Elias National*

Park and Preserve by Geoffrey T. Bleakley (Anchorage: National Park Service, 2002); *The Copper Spike* by Lone Janson (Anchorage: Alaska Northwest, 1975); *Big Business in Alaska: The Kennecott Mines, 1898–1938,* by Melody Webb Grauman (Washington, D.C.: National Park Service, 1977); and *Wesley Earl Dunkle: Alaska's Flying Miner* by Charles Caldwell Hawley (Fairbanks: University of Alaska Press, 2006). An interesting take on the ghost town as a subject for environmental history is an essay by the historian William Cronon, "Kennecott Journey: The Paths Out of Town," reprinted in *Under an Open Sky: Rethinking America's Western Past* (New York: W. W. Norton, 1992).

I appreciated the work of the McCarthy-Kennicott Historical Museum and the National Park Service. In addition to Geoff Bleakley's unblinking administrative history of the park, the NPS Alaska Region has produced "The Kennecott Mines: An Investigation of the Mining and Milling Operations at Kennecott, Alaska, 1898–1938" (manuscript draft) by Logan Hovis. Hovis also shared Ocha Potter's unpublished 1939 memoir, "Sixty Years," which includes two chapters on his Alaska adventures. Useful mining background can be found in the U.S. Geological Survey bulletin 947-F of 1946, *Copper Deposits of the Nizina District, Alaska,* by Don J. Miller.

The account of the Pilgrim Family's early days in McCarthy is drawn from interviews with family members and McCarthy residents, especially Neil Darish and Walt Wigger, and from *The Road to McCarthy: Around the World in Search of Ireland* by Pete McCarthy (New York: HarperCollins, 2004). Descriptions of the Chitistone commune and the Hippie Hole were drawn from an unpublished memoir by Curtis Green, "Recollections, Chitina-McCarthy, 1963–1987," used courtesy of Sally Gibert.

2: History's Shadow

A principal source for this chapter was John Connally's autobiography, *In History's Shadow: An American Odyssey* (New York: Hyperion,

1993). I. B. Hale's biography was spelled out in a May 15, 1971, obituary in the *Fort Worth Star-Telegram*. He has also been the subject of brief biographies by the Texas Sports Hall of Fame and the American Society for Industrial Security, where he served as chairman. Additional information was obtained in interviews with surviving Hale family members, including Patsy Hale and Lucy Hale, and with Palmer Newton, a former officer with the Tallahassee, Florida, police department.

I am indebted to the writer Mark Kirby, who shared notes and newspaper clippings from the *Fort Worth Press,* the Forth Worth *Star-Telegram,* the *Dallas Morning News,* and the *Tallahassee Democrat* regarding Bobby Hale's past, and also to Jack Douglas of the *Fort Worth Star-Telegram* for information on Bobby Hale's Texas years.

3: The Bollard Wars

Information on the early contacts between the National Park Service and the Pilgrim Family, including a four-page case incident report for September 29, 2002, was obtained through a 2009 Freedom of Information Act request to the U.S. Department of the Interior. The accounts of the mail-day murders and the death of Chris Richards were drawn from my own reporting for the *Anchorage Daily News* in 1983 and 2001–2002, and a story about Richards's memorial in the *Wrangell St. Elias News.* The description of the cabin fire seen from the footbridge comes from Tom and Catie Bursch. Joseph and Joshua Hale described for me the bulldozer work in the summer of 2002, and Anne Beaulaurier told me about her backpack trip that fall, an account backed by NPS memos. The story of the Ivy Sect is taken from Curtis Green's "Recollections."

I was in McCarthy during the rebuilding of the tram in the summer of 1983. The story of the subsequent Bollard Wars was drawn from my own contemporaneous reporting in the *Anchorage Daily News* and from stories in the *Wrangell St. Elias News.* Rick and Bonnie Kenyon and Ben Shaine provided extensive autobiographical information. In addition to his writing in the *Wrangell St. Elias News,* Kenyon's views about national park policies are spelled out in his testimony before the U.S. House of Representatives Committee on Government Reform on August 14, 2006. Shaine's novel, *Alaska Dragon* (Fairbanks: Fireweed Press, 1991), provides insight into his thoughts on wilderness and human connection to place. Additional information on the college program at the Hardware Store came from *The Wrangell Mountains: Toward an Environmental Plan* (Santa Cruz: University of California Environmental Studies Program, 1973), and *One Long Summer Day in Alaska: A Documentation of Perspectives in the Wrangell Mountains* by Donald C. Defenderfer and Robert B. Walkinshaw (Santa Cruz: University of California Environmental Field Program, 1981).

4: Sunlight and Firefly

The original source for the story about John F. Kennedy, Judith Campbell Exner, and General Dynamics is *The Dark Side of Camelot* by Seymour Hersh (New York: Little, Brown, 1997). In 2003, I interviewed Hersh and several of his sources, including former FBI agent William Carter and Exner researcher Mark Allan, who shared the 1962 FBI reports from the National Archives. Patsy Hale added new details about the brothers' whereabouts in 1962 and the family's blue Corvette. Virginia Hale's contact with Lee Harvey Oswald is noted in volume 23 of the Warren Commission hearings.

Robert Hale was my original source for the story of his wanderings in the 1960s, his meeting with Kurina Rose, and his conversion experience. Kurina Rose Hale later added many details. The writer Mark Kirby made contact with several of Hale's past wives and shared his notes. Further details about these years were provided by Patsy Hale, by Rose's mother, Betty Freeman, by Mary Walker regarding life at Apple Valley, and by Ellen Sue and Ted Pilger regarding the Sunnyridge commune.

5: Motorheads

Papa Pilgrim's writings were obtained from Kelly and Natalie Bay and Neil Darish. Joseph and Joshua Hale described the slaying of "Old Slew Foot." The account of the Motorheads' visit is drawn mainly from interviews with Steve Lindbeck, Carl Bauman, Peter Dunlap-Shohl, and Darish.

6: The Rainbow Cross

An excellent source for the natural and human history of the Sangre de Cristo Mountains is *Enchantment and Exploitation: The Life and Hard Times of a New Mexico Mountain Range* by William deBuys (Albuquerque: University of New Mexico Press, 1985). Details on the history of Mora and the local Mexican land grant came from an interview with historian Malcolm Ebright of the Center for Land Grant Studies in Guadalupita, New Mexico, from *The Mora Land Grant: A New Mexican Tragedy* by Clark S. Knowlton, reprinted in *Spanish and Mexican Land Grants and the Law,* a book edited by Ebright for *Journal of the West,* 1988, and from *Lo de Mora: A History of the Mora Land Grant on the Eve of Transition* by Michael Miller (available on the website of the New Mexico Office of the State Historian). The "hippie-Chicano wars" and the arrival of Dennis Hopper and friends are detailed in *Utopian Vistas: The Mabel Dodge Luhan House and the American Counterculture* by Lois Palken Rudnick (Albuquerque: University of New Mexico Press, 1998).

Elishaba Doerksen's written account of her life was originally prepared for *Unshackled,* a Christian radio program produced by the Pacific Garden Mission in Chicago, Illinois. I quote from it with her permission. Other stories here and in chapter 8 regarding the Hale family's time in New Mexico were drawn from interviews with Kurina Rose Hale, Elishaba Doerksen, Joseph Hale, and Joshua Hale, and interviews with neighbors. Editha and John Bartley shared copies of written correspondence between Mora-area residents, the Hales, and Los Angeles agent Bob Colbert, the business manager for John J. (Jack) Nicholson. In an e-mail, Dan Keith provided details of his encounter with Bob Hale and the traveling bus, including their theological discussions and the "Last Days Map" to the Rainbow Cross Ranch.

7: Hostile Territory

A detailed narrative of the National Park Service patrol up McCarthy Creek on February 11, 2003, is found in an NPS case incident report for that date. Details were also found in a November 2003 affidavit by Chief Ranger Hunter Sharp given in the Hale/Sunstar access lawsuit against the U.S. Department of the Interior, as well as in coverage by "McCarthy Annie" in the *Wrangell St. Elias News*. The Park Service files and the FBI complaint form detailing the visit of "Robert Hale aka Pilgrim" was obtained through my 2009 FOIA request to the Department of the Interior.

Interviews with Hunter Sharp, Marshall Neeck, and former ranger Jim Hannah provided useful perspectives on the patrol that day and on the broader issues of relations between the park and local residents. An oral history by Hannah of the first years of Wrangell–St. Elias National Park is available through the University of Alaska Fairbanks Project Jukebox. Many details about early difficulties in the Wrangells have been gathered in *Locked Up! A History of Resistance to the Creation of National Parks in Alaska* by Timo C. Allan, a 2010 PhD dissertation for Washington State University, and in *Contested Ground,* Geoff Bleakley's administrative history of the park.

The story of the conservation movement and modern Alaska is told in national context in the later editions of Roderick Nash's landmark work, *Wilderness and the American Mind* (New Haven, Conn.: Yale University Press, 1982). The politics of the Alaska conservation act of 1980 are detailed in, among other places, *Do Things Right the First Time: Administrative History of the National Park Service*

and the Alaska National Interest Lands Conservation Act of 1980 by
G. Frank Williss (Washington, D.C.: National Park Service, 1985),
http://www.nps.gov/history/history/online_books/williss/adhi.htm;
Northern Landscapes: The Struggle for Wilderness Alaska by Daniel
Nelson (Washington, D.C.: Resources for the Future, 2004); and *Environmental Conflict in Alaska* by Ken Ross (Boulder: University Press
of Colorado, 2000). A less glowing interpretation of federal policy is
the collection of pieces by the Alaska Miners Association titled *d(2)
Part 2, Alaska Lands, Promises Broken,* edited by J. P. Tangen, 2000.
Three other books touching on themes in the Wrangells are *Preserving
Nature in the National Parks* by Richard West Sellars (New Haven,
Conn.: Yale University Press, 1997); *Crimes Against Nature: Squatters, Poachers, Thieves, and the Hidden History of American Conservation* by Karl Jacoby (Berkeley: University of California Press, 2001);
and *Inhabited Wilderness: Indians, Eskimos, and National Parks in
Alaska* by Theodore Catton (Albuquerque: University of New Mexico
Press, 1997).

Details of the shootout at the Silver Lake Lodge come from December 1981 stories in the *Anchorage Daily News* and *Anchorage Times.*
Jennifer Brice recounts the experiences of the Slana homesteaders in
The Last Settlers (Pittsburgh: Duquesne University Press, 1998). A
long biography of Harry Yount, written by William R. Supernaugh,
is available on the National Park Service history website, http://www
.nps.gov.

8: Holy Bob and the Wild West
This chapter was based on interviews with members of the Hale family
and with their former New Mexico neighbors, including Editha and
John Bartley, Karen Brown, Lloyd and Sue Parham, Jacob Pacheco,
Carolyn Vail, Joan Maestis, Bill Leonard, Jim Smith, Ana Martinez,
John Sanchez with the Mora County Sheriff's Office, and Michael
Francis and Tom Maserve with the New Mexico State Police.

9: God vs. the Park Service

This chapter was largely based on interviews with Hale family members and with McCarthy-area residents Stephens Harper, Tamara Egans Harper, Shawn Olson, Rick Kenyon, Bonnie Kenyon, Sally Gibert, Jim Edwards, Gary Green, Kenny Smith, Natalie Bay, Kelly Bay, Jim Miller, Ben Shaine, Gaia Marrs, Danny Rosenkrans, Arlene Rosenkrans, Rich Kirkwood, Neil Darish, and Jeremy Keller. Gary Candelaria, Ray Kreig, Carl Bauman, Marshall Neeck, and Hunter Sharp were also interviewed. I drew heavily on the extensive coverage in the May–June, July–August, and September–October 2003 issues of the *Wrangell St. Elias News.*

Martin Radovan's story is told fully in *Tunnel Vision: The Life of a Copper Prospector in the Nizina River Country* by Katherine Ringsmuth (Washington, D.C.: National Park Service, 2012).

Documents cited include a string of e-mails in late May and early June 2003 from Rick Kenyon to Ray Kreig, Chuck Cushman, and state officials; a June 4 memorandum from NPS Alaska Region director Rob Arnberger; and a June 6 e-mail from Arnberger to Interior department special assistant Cam Toohey. Details of the misdemeanor cases against Joseph and Joshua Hale were drawn from a Notice of Violations and from legal briefs and rulings in federal court.

10: The Pilgrim's Progress

The Pilgrim's Progress by John Bunyan has been the subject of many volumes of critical analysis. Helpful for my purposes were two recent collections, *The Cambridge Companion to Bunyan,* edited by Anne Dunan-Page (Cambridge: Cambridge University Press, 2010), and *Trauma and Transformation: The Political Progress of John Bunyan,* edited by Vera J. Camden (Stanford: Stanford University Press, 2008).

The stories of life at the Rainbow Cross are drawn from interviews with Kurina Rose Hale and her children, testimony given in state criminal court by the family, and name-redacted transcripts of family interviews by investigators with the Alaska State Troopers, which were obtained through a 2011 public information request to the Alaska Department of Public Safety. The quoted passages are from Elishaba Doerksen's *Unshackled* memoir.

Patsy Hale provided details of the later years of her husband, Billy. Details of the Silver City "kidnapping" case were confirmed in an interview with local New Mexico prosecutor Arnold Chavez.

11: Hillbilly Heaven

This chapter is based on my own reporting for the *Anchorage Daily News* in August 2003.

12: Flight of the Angels

This chapter is based on my reporting for the *Anchorage Daily News* in the fall of 2003 and subsequent interviews with Chuck Cushman, Ray Kreig, and Rick Kenyon. The story about the penguins was related by Natalie Bay and the story about "brainwashing" by Joseph Hale. "An Angel Falls to Heaven" appeared in the November–December 2003 issue of the *Wrangell St. Elias News*. Some of Kurt Stenehjem's comments were taken from "The Darkest Place" by Mark Kirby, which appeared in *Outside* magazine in December 2008. An edited version of the letter from Elishaba about the "feud" in Anchor Point appeared in the *Homer Tribune*.

For background on the Wise Use and property-rights movements, I drew on the "NPS and ANILCA Short Course" posted on the website of Kreig's organization, the Alaska Land Rights Association, landrights .org. A key book for critics of national land acquisition policies is *Cades Cove: The Life and Death of a Southern Appalachian Community, 1818–1937,* by the historian Durwood Dunn (Knoxville: University of Tennessee Press, 1988). A skeptical survey of the Wise Use rebellion is *The War Against the Greens* by David Helvarg (Boulder: Johnson Books, revised edition 2004). Some of these issues are examined in an Alaska context in *A Land Gone Lonesome: An Inland Voyage Along the Yukon River* by Dan O'Neill (New York: Counterpoint, 2006). Also useful on origins of the Sagebrush Rebellion and the frontier "creation myth" of white America were *The Legacy of Conquest* by Patricia Limerick (New York: W. W. Norton, 1987) and "The Current Weirdness in the West" by Richard White, *Western Historical Quarterly* 28 (Spring 1997). Other perspectives on the movement came in interviews with parks historian Richard Sellars, Jim Stratton with the National Parks Conservation Association, and Destry Jarvis.

13: The Pilgrim Family Minstrels

This chapter was drawn from my contemporaneous coverage for the *Anchorage Daily News* and later interviews with Kurina Rose Hale, Joseph and Joshua Hale, Elishaba Doerksen, Carl Bauman, Chuck Cushman, Ray Kreig, Dallas Massie, Sally Gibert, Walt Wigger, Mark Wacht, Stephen Syren, Neil Darish, Rick Kenyon, Jim Miller, Natalie Bay, Jeremy Keller, Stephens Harper, Mike Loso, and Jim Edwards. I also consulted continuing coverage in the *Wrangell St. Elias News* in 2003 and 2004.

Judge Ralph Beistline's decision was issued in federal case A03-0257 CV, *Hale and Sunstar vs. Norton et al.,* on November 18, 2003. Background information on Cushman was drawn from Helvarg's *War Against the Greens.* His 1979 trip to Alaska was recounted in "Beating the Bushes for Park Inholders," *Anchorage Daily News*, March 22, 1979. Neil Darish's piece "Let National Park Residents Thrive" ran in the *Anchorage Daily News* on May 8, 2004. Freelance correspondent Kendall Beaudry wrote about the Pilgrims' musical performances in the Pacific Northwest in "Pilgrims' Music Proves to Be Big Hit Outside," in the *Anchorage Daily News*, May 13, 2004. Lyrics quoted are from "Pilgrim's Daughter" by Butterfly Sunstar Hale on *Put My Name Down* by the Pilgrim Family Minstrels. Alaska's low rank in religious piety was measured in a January 28, 2009, Gallup Poll.

14: A Quiet Year

Information on the 2005 anniversary conference of the Alaska National Interest Lands Conservation Act (ANILCA) was mostly drawn from reporting for my article "Lands Act Still Stirs Debate" in the *Anchorage Daily News,* July 10, 2005.

15: The Wanigan

This chapter was drawn from interviews with members of the Hale and Buckingham families, especially Joseph and Lolly Hale, Joshua and Sharia Hale, Jim and Martha Buckingham, Kurina Rose Hale, Jerusalem Hale, and Elishaba and Matthew Doerksen. I also drew on testimony given in state criminal court by the family. Much of the information was cross-checked against and sometimes supplemented by transcripts of interviews that family members gave Alaska State Troopers investigators. Several scenes were also described in Elishaba's *Unshackled* memoir.

16: Exodus

The story of the daughters' escape, here and in the prologue, was drawn from interviews with Elishaba Doerksen; Jerusalem, Joseph, Joshua, Israel, and Kurina Rose Hale; Jim and Martha Buckingham; and Neil Darish. The beating of Jonathan was described in court and to investigators by many of the younger Hales. The follow-up to Israel's 911 call is detailed in Alaska State Trooper investigative reports for September 3, 2005.

17: Pilgrim's Last Stand

The criminal case against Robert Hale was partially spelled out in court files between 2005 and 2007. State trooper investigative files filled in details not in the public court record. The trooper files provided the count of six child protection cases opened against the Pilgrim Family in Alaska. Assistant district attorney Richard Payne was especially helpful in explaining the case and the evolution of his approach, as was Rachel Gernat in providing background about working with abused families. Public defender Lee de Grazia provided certain details of her work with Robert Hale. Ray and Lee Ann Kreig described to me their own parts in the manhunt.

Though I did not want to burden this chapter with a discussion of post-traumatic stress disorder and its treatment, I wanted to be sure the children's experiences and coping strategies were consistent with prevailing theories and practices. Helpful in this regard were *Trauma and Recovery* by Judith Herman (New York: Basic Books, 1992); *Faith Born of Seduction: Sexual Trauma, Body Image, and Religion* by Jennifer L. Manlowe (New York: New York University Press, 1995); *8 Keys to Safe Trauma Recovery* by Babette Rothschild (New York: W. W. Norton, 2010); and, from an explicitly Christian perspective, *Helping Victims of Sexual Abuse: A Sensitive Biblical Guide for Counselors, Victims, and Families* by Lynn Heitritter and Jeanette Vought (Minneapolis: Bethany House, 1989). Shelly Thomas of Olive Tree Counseling and Ministries in Wasilla, Alaska, offered helpful insights.

Parts of this chapter are drawn from my contemporaneous reporting of events in the *Anchorage Daily News*. Two important court hearings were covered by colleagues at the newspaper: Joe Ditzler, "Pilgrim Appears in Court," October 7, 2005; and Julia O'Malley, "Final Change of Mind Lets 'Papa Pilgrim' Avoid Trial," September 14, 2007.

18: The Man in the Iron Cage
This chapter is based on testimony given in state superior court in Anchorage on November 26 and 27, 2007, and on interviews with family members at the courthouse on those days.

Epilogue: Peaceful Harbor
Final disposition of the government's civil case against the Pilgrims is dealt with in files obtained under the federal Freedom of Information Act. The McCarthy Area Council's views on preservation plans for the

Kennecott ruins are spelled out in formal comments on the revised Interim Operations Plan for Kennecott National Historic Landmark.

The description of the aftermath for the Hale and Buckingham families is based on my own reporting and interviews with family members. I was present at the wedding of Joseph and Lolly and witnessed the felicitous beam of sunlight for myself.

Acknowledgments

The Hale and Buckingham families decided early not to participate in a book about their story. While their case was in the public eye, they had been remarkably forthcoming, both in court and in answer to my questions for the *Anchorage Daily News,* as if to make up for years of public deception. But when it was over, they were eager to leave the stain behind, and a truthful account of their lives, as one of them expressed it, was not a book that could dwell in a good Christian home. Their reluctance was probably a good thing, I decided: No writer could look forward to negotiating a median truth from the traumatized memories of sixteen family members, most of whom had never read a nonfiction book of any kind.

So I set out on my own, with notes and neighbors and public records. Over time, however, individual family members considered how their story could help others and began sharing more and more about their hidden past, profoundly enriching this unusual project. I am grateful especially to Elishaba and Matthew Doerksen, Kurina Rose Hale, Joseph and Lolly Hale, Joshua and Sharia Hale, Betty Freeman, and Jim and Martha Buckingham for the many details they ultimately provided about key moments in their lives. Thanks also to Rose for permission to quote from her husband's letters.

Among the people in and around McCarthy, I am grateful for guidance through the years from Sally Gibert, Ben Shaine, and Rick Kenyon, and appreciate the help for this book from many friends and neighbors, particularly Mark Vail, Jim Edwards, Gary Green, Kelly and Natalie Bay, Kenny Smith, Marci Thurston, Gaia Marrs, Bonnie Kenyon, Dick Mylius, Tom and Catie Bursch, John Adams, Stephens and Tamara Harper, Mike Loso, and Neil Darish. For the Texas story, I owe thanks to Karen Hale, Lucy Hale, and especially Patsy Hale, who I hope will publish her own account of the Hale family. For the New Mexico chapters, I want to thank the neighbors quoted therein, and especially Carolyn Vail for her hospitality, Editha Bartley for permission to quote from family letters, and my friend Joel Gay, for letting me drive his old pickup truck to the mountains.

Many people with the National Park Service were helpful, especially John Quinley, Logan Hovis, Katie Ringsmuth, Danny Rosenkrans, Gary Candelaria, and Hunter Sharp. For perspectives on park policies, I am grateful to Ray and Lee Ann Kreig, Chuck Cushman, Chris Allan, Jim Stratton, Destry Jarvis, Richard Sellars, Jim Rearden, Chuck Hawley, Tony Oney, Anne Beaulaurier, and Wally Cole. For help with civil and criminal legal issues, I thank Richard Payne, Rachel Gernat, Lee de Grazia, Carl Bauman, and Jeff Feldman.

At the *Anchorage Daily News,* I want to thank my horseback traveling companion, Marc Lester, for his good nature and expert photographic eye, fellow reporters Julia O'Malley, Megan Holland, and Joe Ditzler for their help keeping up with courtroom developments, and my editors, David Hulen and Pat Dougherty. Thanks also to fellow writers Mark Kirby and Jack Douglas, for sharing elements of their own research into Robert Hale's past, and to Wesley Loy for sharing his CD.

Many of the themes that make Alaska such an appealing subject were first scribed on the landscape by my teacher at Hampshire College, David Smith, who introduced the writings of Leo Marx, Henry Nash Smith, and Roderick Nash—to say nothing of *Go Down, Moses* and the "fresh, green breast of the new world" that flowered once for Dutch sailors' eyes.

This book would not have been written without the early enthusiasm and close attention of my agent, Alice Martell. At Crown Publishers/Random House, I am indebted to Miriam Chotiner-Gardner, Kevin Doughten, and to Charlie Conrad, who worked diligently to keep me from straying too far into copper country ghost stories or the arcana of ANILCA.

I am profoundly grateful to Chip Brown and Blaine Harden for helping me find and hold on to my story. Thanks also to Dan Coyle, Maurice Coyle, Tom Bodett, Nancy Lord, and Rich Chiappone for reading drafts and offering good advice, and to Howard Weaver, Barbara Hodgin, Anne Raup, Todd Stoeberl, and Fred Hirschman for help with photos. The Mesa Refuge and Ted and Frances Geballe gave me places to write portions of this manuscript. For general encouragement and sustenance through this period I want especially to thank Nancy Gordon and Steve Williams, Lisa and Tim Whip, Deb McKinney and Paul Morley, my mom, Peggy, and also my dad, Joe Kizzia, who died while this book about fathers was being born.

About the Author

Tom Kizzia has traveled widely in rural Alaska writing prizewinning stories about places, people, and politics for the *Anchorage Daily News*. His work has appeared in the *Washington Post* and has been featured on CNN. His first book, *The Wake of the Unseen Object*, was named one of the best all-time nonfiction books about Alaska by the Alaska Historical Society. He lives in Homer, Alaska.